A Creative Approach to Music Fundamentals

Music Books of Related Interest

Thomas Benjamin/Michael Horvit/Robert Nelson, *Techniques and Materials of Tonal Music with an Introduction to Twentieth-Century Techniques*, 4th Edition

Thomas Benjamin/Michael Horvit/Robert Nelson, *Music for Analysis*, 3rd Edition

Thomas Benjamin/Michael Horvit/Robert Nelson, *Music for Sight-Singing*, 2nd Edition

Phyllis Irwin, *Playing the Piano*

Carolynn Lindeman, *Pianolab*, 2nd Edition

Carolynn Lindeman/Patricia Hackett, *Music Lab: An Introduction to the Fundamentals of Music*

Charles Lindsley, *Fundamentals of Singing for Voice Classes*

Neil McKay/Marion McKay, *Fundamentals of Western Music*

Robert Nelson/Carl J. Christensen, *Foundations of Music, A Computer-Assisted Introduction* (Mac/Apple II)

Helene Robinson, *Basic Piano for Adults*

Elie Siegmeister, *Harmony and Melody*, Volumes I and II

Royal Stanton, *Steps to Singing for Voice Classes*, 3rd Edition

A Creative Approach to

Music Fundamentals

Fifth Edition

William Duckworth
Bucknell University

Wadsworth Publishing Company • Belmont, California • A Division of Wadsworth, Inc.

Music Editor: Katherine Hartlove
Editorial Assistant: Joshua King
Production Services Coordinator: Gary Mcdonald
Production: Rogue Valley Publications
Designer: Kaelin Chappell
Print Buyer: Diana Spence
Art: Mansfield Music-Graphics
Cover: Ark Stein, The Visual Group
Compositor: Thompson Type
Printer: R. R. Donnelley & Sons, Crawfordsville

This book is printed on acid-free recycled paper.

I(T)P™

International Thomson Publishing
The trademark ITP is used under license.

Printed in the United States of America
1 2 3 4 5 6 7 8 9 10 — 99 98 97 96 95

Duckworth, William.
   A creative approach to music fundamentals / William Duckworth. —
5th ed.
      p.   cm.
   Includes indexes.
   ISBN 0-534-24696-6
   1. Music — Instruction and study.   2. Music — Theory.   3. Music —
Handbooks, manuals, etc.   I. Title.   II.   Title: Music
fundamentals.
MT6.D8333C7   1995
781 — dc20
                                          94-13609
                                             CIP
                                              MN

For Will, Katherine, and Alison
who grew up with many of the songs in this book.

Contents

CHAPTER 6   **Intervals   127**

FOCUS ON SKILLS II

CHAPTER 7   **Minor Key Signatures   171**

CHAPTER 8   **Minor Scales   183**

CHAPTER 9   **Other Scales and Modes   217**

A *Creative Approach to Music Fundamentals*, fifth edition, is a college-level textbook for classes in the fundamentals of music. This fifth edition continues to emphasize basic musical skills and to stress the necessity of drill in acquiring these skills. This basic material, however, is set within a creative framework that makes music fundamentals interesting and the necessary drills musically meaningful. This approach establishes a learning environment that maintains student interest while ensuring that the basic skills of music will be practiced and eventually mastered.

The first ten chapters of this edition concentrate on the fundamental elements of music. These chapters are followed by a new chapter on tonality that unifies these musical concepts into a beginning understanding of how tonal music works. These eleven chapters are supplemented by nine appendices, covering such topics as rhythms for counting, melodies for sight-singing, acoustics, and dynamics. This material may be included or omitted as the needs of each individual class require.

This fifth edition incorporates a number of changes designed to make both the teaching and the learning of music fundamentals easier and more meaningful. These changes include the new concluding chapter on tonality that includes sections on tendency tones, the dominant/tonic relationship, cadences, and simple chord progressions; an expanded discussion of minor scales in musical situations; additional information on how to beam notes correctly; and an expanded explanation of how to write accidentals. Additionally, two new appendices have been added, one on world rhythms in two and three parts, the other on the C clef.

The book continues to stress the need for consistent practice, with written and aural *Exercises* for basic skills, and *Musical Problems* for applying these new skills to musical situations. Between chapters, four *Focus on Skills* sections test the retention and understanding of material learned over several chapters. The large number of exercises and musical problems contained in this book will ensure that each instructor will have available the materials necessary for his or her individual class.

William Duckworth

Acknowledgments

I wish to thank the following reviewers for their comments, suggestions, and assistance during the preparation of this edition: Leonard Bowie, University of North Florida; David Cannata, New York University; Daniel Goode, Rutgers University; Dan Huff, University of North Carolina, Chapel Hill; Thomas McKinley, Tulane University; J. R. Smith, Eastern Michigan University; and Mark Wilson, University of Maryland.

A Creative Approach to Music Fundamentals

Musical Talent, Musical Knowledge

The concepts of musical talent and musical knowledge can be confusing. All of us know people who play or sing extremely well but who have difficulty explaining what they do. Often, such people are able to perform music they have heard only a few times, or to write music of great charm and subtlety. Yet they cannot discuss music easily, and they often appear uncomfortable or uncertain when talking about their musical ability. On the other hand, some people seem to have little trouble putting into words what they hear taking place musically, but they do not perform nearly as well as the first group of people. Members of this second group often can discuss scales and rhythms and identify chord progressions and cadences; yet, this competence seems not to make them better performers.

What is the fundamental difference between these two types of people, both of whom are highly interested in music? Each has a particular skill that the other sometimes envies. Certainly, each wishes to know as much about music as possible. The answer is that one type relates to music primarily on the basis of musical talent, while the other utilizes a learned knowledge of music. Both kinds of musicianship are necessary to becoming a fine musician and should be developed. It is not a question of accepting one and rejecting the other.

Everyone reading this book has some musical talent, but the extent to which this talent has been developed probably varies greatly. Some of you may just be learning to play, or want to learn to play, or hope to write a song someday. Others may already play an instrument or write songs by ear. No matter what your

1

current level of competence, it is fairly safe to assume that you have not yet explored the full range of your musical talent.

This book, however, is not about developing your talent but rather about building your musical knowledge. That is, it will help you learn the facts about music. Basically, it is a book about skills. Musical skills. Skills that are shared, in varying degrees and combinations, by *all* successful musicians. For some of you, this book will help you learn concepts and terms for the things you can already play by ear. For others, working with these concepts and terms will complement the growth of your innate musical talent, thus helping you to develop faster as a performer than you otherwise might. For all of you, this book will at times be hard work.

On the other hand, this book is also designed to be more than a set of drills and exercises. When used thoughtfully, it will provide you with both the knowledge and the vocabulary necessary to enhance your understanding and enjoyment of music. It will encourage you to listen to music rather than just hear it, and enable you to discuss music objectively rather than merely describe your emotional responses.

The *Exercises* in this book are designed to develop your musical skills. Some are difficult and some are repetitive, but they are necessary. The *Musical Problems* are designed to make you *think* about music and to apply the skills you have learned to musical situations. You should read all of these problems and consider them carefully, even if your teacher is unable, because of class size or time restraints, to cover some of them. As you proceed through the book, don't assume that your musical talent will be sufficient. While talent will certainly help, it will not substitute for time spent studying and practicing the exercises.

A Theory of Music

What is a fundamental theory of music and why is it necessary? How does factual information about music make us better musicians? These questions are not easy to answer. Like the person who plays by ear, the music theorist sometimes has an understanding of the answers to these questions that cannot be completely expressed.

On one level, music theory is the *systematic* study of how music works. Basic music theory examines the various parts, or elements, of a piece of music and the ways in which these individual elements combine and interrelate to form a musical composition. Many of you will have had the experience of wanting to learn more about music but not knowing where or how to begin, or of wanting to explain something about a work you can perform but not being able to — frustrations that adequately illustrate the need for a theory and for a book such as this.

The question of how information about music makes for better musicians, however, is more difficult to answer. While theoretical knowledge will undoubtedly help you to become a "better" musician, it does not automatically mean that you will be able to write music better or play it better. It will probably happen that way; it does for most people. But don't assume that it will happen magically.

The best approach is to set musical goals for yourself. Then, as you proceed from exercise to exercise and chapter to chapter, keep these goals in mind. Try to understand how each topic relates to what you hope to accomplish. Fine musicians are a unique blend of musical talent and musical knowledge. Remember, though, that musical talent and musical knowledge are two different things. Both must be developed, and both require hard work. As you proceed, use your innate musical talent to make the work in this book less difficult and more musical.

Chapter 1

Rhythm

Students always seem less apprehensive about their skills with rhythm than about their abilities to hear and sing pitches. Often, since it is thought of as easier, the topic of rhythm is not given as much attention and drill as that of melody. Perhaps for this reason many people, even those with a great deal of musical training, have a number of misconceptions about rhythm and its contribution to a piece of music. As you begin this chapter, keep in mind that the mastery of rhythmic notation is of paramount importance to being a good musician. Keep in mind also that becoming more musical requires your active participation. You cannot do it by merely reading the text. You need to clap and play the rhythms. You need to complete the exercises, and you should go through all the musical problems as they occur in the text. It may take longer this way, but you will see the results faster.

What is musical rhythm? Almost everyone can feel it happening. Most people can even pick out the instruments of an ensemble that contribute the most rhythmically. But when asked to define rhythm, they have trouble; they give only a part of the definition. Usually, they identify and discuss *pulse, meter, note values*, or *tempo*. While each of these terms contributes, in some way, to the definition of musical rhythm, none by itself explains the concept entirely. The true explanation of musical rhythm is complex, involving the interaction of the above-mentioned, and other, rhythmic elements.

We will begin by discussing each of these rhythmic elements individually. What you will discover is that concepts such as pulse, meter, measure, note values, dotted notes, and ties are relatively simple when discussed individually. The difficulty arises in trying to combine the definitions of these terms into an accurate description of musical rhythm. Equally difficult is applying these definitions to an understanding of how a piece of music works rhythmically. As you continue with this chapter, remember that all of the individual rhythmic elements combine within a piece of music to produce its overall musical rhythm. Remember also that most of us already have an intuitive appreciation of the rhythmic qualities of a piece of music.

MUSICAL PROBLEM

Listen to a piece of music that you have listened to many times before. It may be a solo work or a piece for a small or large ensemble. It may also be something from the past such as a symphony or string quartet, or something from the present such as a popular song, rap, or dance mix. This time, however, try to concentrate on the rhythm only, shutting out the melody (and lyrics, if any), the harmony, and the sounds of the individual instruments. Are you able to direct your musical attention this selectively? If not, try again several times.

How different does the piece sound when you listen to it this way? Do you hear things in it that you have never really heard or thought much about before? Is there a steady beat? Can you hear rhythmic patterns? Do these rhythmic patterns repeat? Are there a lot of different patterns or just a few? Try to put your thoughts and feelings about the rhythmic qualities of this piece into two or three sentences. Can you?

Pulse

Most music with which you are familiar has a steady beat, or **pulse**. The pulse, which is both constant and regular, can be felt when you tap your foot to a piece of music. It can be represented visually by a line of half notes, quarter notes, or eighth notes.

Any note value, in fact, can be used to represent the pulse, including the dotted notes that we will study later.

Regardless of the note value used to represent the pulse, what is important to remember is that a steady, proportional relationship is established by the pulse, against which the combination of sounds and silences that makes up the actual music moves.

Meter

As you listen to and feel the pulse in various pieces of music, you will notice that some pulses sound stronger than others. The combination of strong and weak pulses forms a recurring pattern known as the **meter**. When musicians talk about the meter of a piece, they are referring to a particular pattern of strong and weak pulses. The most common patterns or meters are duple meter, triple meter, and quadruple meter. As the following illustration shows, in **duple meter**, the pulse is divided into a recurring pattern of one strong and one weak beat; **triple meter** divides the pulse into a recurring pattern of one strong and two weak beats; and **quadruple meter** divides the pulse into one strong and three weak beats.

duple meter

triple meter

quadruple meter

The sign > is an **accent mark**. It indicates that the note under which (or over which) it appears is to be given more stress than the surrounding notes.

MUSICAL PROBLEM

Clap each of the metrical patterns shown above twice — first slowly, then faster — giving an accent to the notes indicated. Notice that the speed you choose does not in any way alter the meter. What matters is that you keep the pulse steady and put the accents in the proper places.

Measures

As you performed the musical problem, you may have lost your place momentarily in one of the lines. At any rate, it would be hard to play a long piece of music without losing one's place. For this reason, music is divided into **measures** by means of vertical lines called **bar lines**.

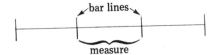

Bar lines occur immediately before an accented pulse. Thus, duple meter has two beats per measure, triple meter has three beats per measure, and quadruple meter has four beats per measure. The following example shows the common meters again, this time with the bar lines included. Notice how much easier it is to read and perform a meter when it is written in this way.

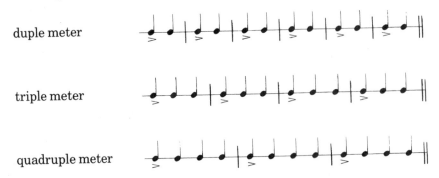

duple meter

triple meter

quadruple meter

Double bar lines have a special meaning: Their two most common uses are to signal the beginning of a new section in a large work and to mark the end of a work. You should put double bar lines at the end of any exercises or pieces you write.

MUSICAL PROBLEM

As members of the class listen, clap a steady pulse without any noticeable accents. Slowly change the pulse to duple, triple, or quadruple meter. You may want to have a contest to see how quickly members of the class can detect the shift to a measured pulse.

Note Values

Learning to read music involves mastering two musical systems: pitch notation and rhythmic notation. Pitch is indicated by the placement of a note on a five-line staff. You will learn about that in Chapter 2. Rhythm, on the other hand, is notated with the following note value symbols, which show duration:

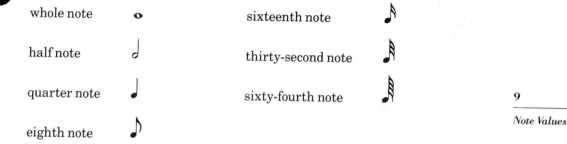

whole note	o	sixteenth note	♬
half note	♩	thirty-second note	♬
quarter note	♩	sixty-fourth note	♬
eighth note	♪		

Half notes and quarter notes consist of a notehead and a stem:

half note   quarter note

Eighth notes, sixteenth notes, thirty-second notes, and sixty-fourth notes consist of a notehead, a stem, and one or more flags:

eighth note   thirty-second note

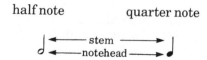

Notes that would otherwise have flags are frequently joined by beams at the top of the stems into groups of two, three, four, six, or eight that reflect pulse group-ings. This practice is used to indicate the value of the notes; it performs the same function for groups of notes as flags do for individual notes.

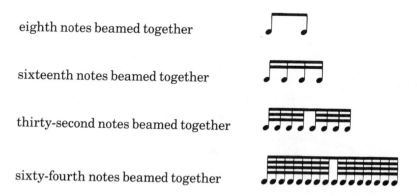

eighth notes beamed together

sixteenth notes beamed together

thirty-second notes beamed together

sixty-fourth notes beamed together

You probably noticed that the beams for the thirty-second and sixty-fourth note examples stop in the middle of the pattern and then begin again. This is done to help the eye keep its place and does not affect the value of the notes in any way. The rule is that if a stem is touched by a beam, it becomes that value, even if the beam touches only one side of the stem. Thus, in the following example, the two sixteenth-note patterns would sound identical, even though they look slightly different, because each stem is touched by two beams.

Once you begin working with rhythms of different note values you will notice that short, incomplete beams are often used.

In this example, the second and fourth notes are sixteenth notes, and the first and third are eighth notes (the function of the dot will be explained later in this chapter). Just remember that if a stem is touched by a beam, it becomes that value, and you should not have any trouble deciphering the rhythmic patterns that appear throughout the rest of this book.

EXERCISE 1·1

Before proceeding further, you should practice drawing note values. This is not difficult but does require some practice if you have not worked with them before.

Keep the following points in mind:

1. Noteheads are oval rather than round.
2. The flags on eighth, sixteenth, and thirty-second notes always point to the right, no matter which side of the note the stem is on.

Now try some on your own. Remember to draw examples of the stems both above and below the notes.

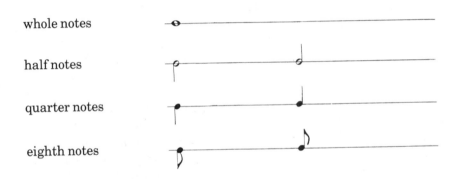

whole notes

half notes

quarter notes

eighth notes

sixteenth notes

thirty-second notes

Regardless of the speed (tempo) at which a piece of music moves, the note value symbols are proportionately related to each other. Thus, if the quarter note receives one beat, the half note will receive two beats and the whole note four beats. This proportionality can be illustrated in the following way:

One whole note is equal in duration to four quarter notes.

One half note is equal in duration to two quarter notes.

Notes of lesser value than the quarter note are proportioned in the same way:

Two eighth notes equal one quarter note in duration.

Four sixteenth notes equal one quarter note in duration.

Eight thirty-second notes equal one quarter note in duration.

If the eighth note receives one beat, the quarter note will receive two beats and the half note four beats. Similarly, if the half note receives one beat, the whole note will receive two beats, and two quarter notes will be required to complete one beat.

EXERCISE 1·2

Assuming that the quarter note receives one beat, as in the following example, how many total beats are represented by each of the combinations of note values that follow?

EXAMPLE:

𝅝 = 4 beats   𝅗𝅥 = 2   ♩ = 1   ♪ = ½   ♪ = ¼   ♪ = ⅛

𝅗𝅥 ♩ ♪ ♪ ♩ ♪ = 5½ beats

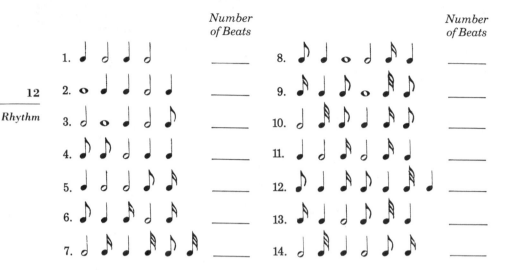

	Number of Beats		Number of Beats
1.	___	8.	___
2.	___	9.	___
3.	___	10.	___
4.	___	11.	___
5.	___	12.	___
6.	___	13.	___
7.	___	14.	___

EXERCISE 1·3

Assuming that the eighth note receives one beat, as in the following example, how many total beats are represented by each of the combinations of note values that follow?

EXAMPLE: 𝅗𝅥 = 4 beats   ♩ = 2   ♪ = 1   𝅘𝅥𝅯 = ½

♩ 𝅗𝅥 ♪ ♩   =   9 beats

Number of Beats

1. ♪ ♪ ♩ ♪   ___

2. ♩ ♪ ♪ ♩   ___

3. ♪ ♪ 𝅘𝅥𝅯 ♪   ___

4. 𝅗𝅥 ♩ ♩ ♩   ___

5. ♪ 𝅘𝅥𝅯 ♪ ♪ 𝅘𝅥𝅯   ___

6. ♪ ♪ 𝅗𝅥 𝅘𝅥𝅯   ___

EXERCISE 1·4

Assuming that the half note receives one beat, as in the following example, how many total beats are represented by each of the following combinations of note values?

EXAMPLE: 𝅝 = 2 beats   𝅗𝅥 = 1   ♩ = ½   ♪ = ¼

♩ 𝅝 ♪ 𝅗𝅥 = _3¾ beats_

Number of Beats

1. 𝅗𝅥 𝅝 𝅗𝅥 ♩ ♩ _____

2. 𝅝 𝅗𝅥 𝅗𝅥 𝅗𝅥 𝅝 _____

3. 𝅗𝅥 ♩ ♩ 𝅗𝅥 ♩ ♩ _____

4. ♩ ♩ 𝅗𝅥 ♪ ♪ ♩ 𝅝 _____

5. 𝅗𝅥 𝅗𝅥 𝅝 ♩ ♪ 𝅗𝅥 _____

6. ♩ 𝅗𝅥 ♩ 𝅝 ♩ ♩ _____

MUSICAL PROBLEM

Your instructor will select five examples from the rhythmic patterns given below and play them on the piano. In the space provided, indicate whether the examples are in duple, triple, or quadruple meter. Remember to listen for the basic, underlying pulse.

1. _____

2. _____

3. _____

4. _____

5. _____

Duple Meters

Triple Meters

Quadruple Meters

Rests

Just as the symbols for note value represent durations of sound, **rest** signs are used to indicate durations of silence. Each note value has a corresponding rest sign.

whole rest (fourth line of staff)

half rest (third line of staff)

quarter rest

eighth rest

sixteenth rest

thirty-second rest

sixty-fourth rest

The whole rest is often used to indicate one complete measure of silence. It can serve this purpose for any meter, and when used in this way it is centered within the measure.

EXERCISE 1·5

Practice drawing the following rest signs:

whole
rests

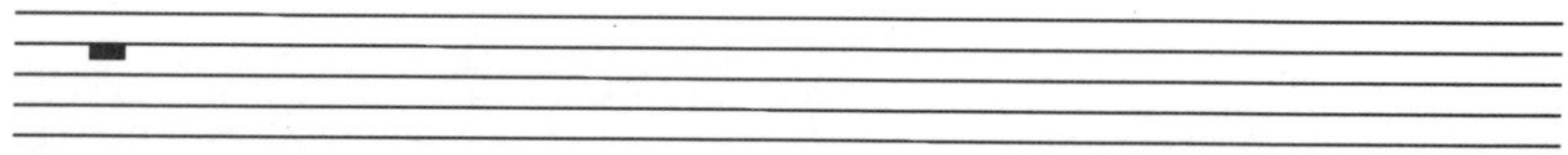

half
rests

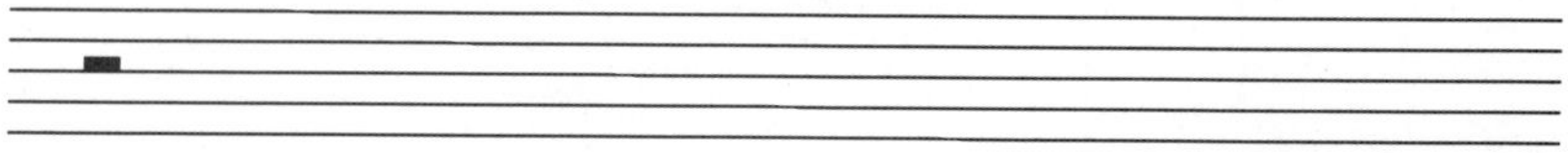

quarter
rests

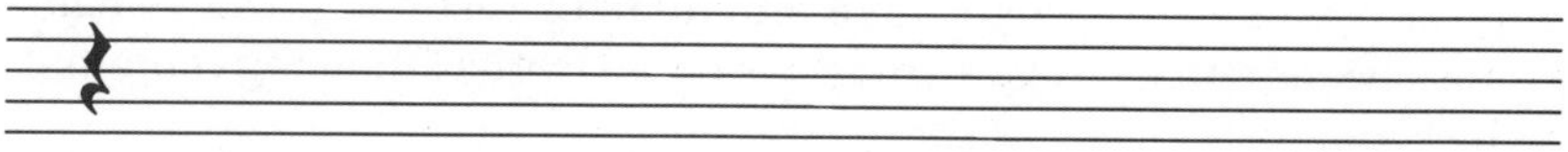

eighth
rests

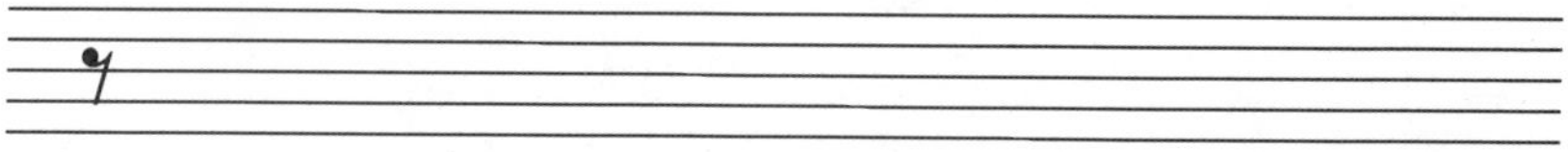

sixteenth
rests

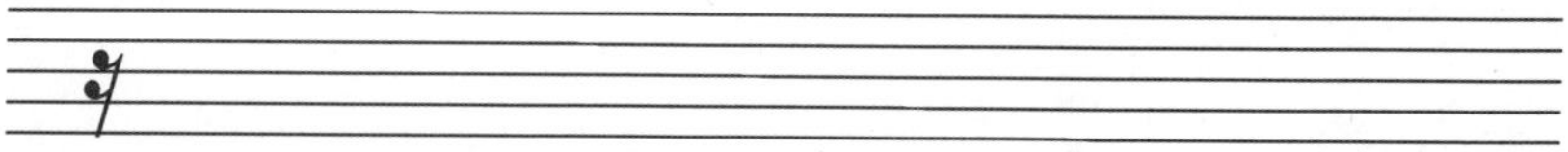

Dotted Notes

A dot placed to the right of a notehead gives the note a longer duration. In fact, the dot always increases the time value by one-half. For example, a half note is equal in value to two quarter notes.

♩ = ♩ + ♩

When a dot is placed beside a note, this new note, called a **dotted note**, becomes equal to the original value plus one-half the original value. In the case of our half note, adding a dot creates a dotted half note with a time value equal to three quarter notes.

♩. = ♩ + ♩ + ♩

Rests as well as notes can be increased in value by adding a dot, although dotted rests are used less often than dotted notes. As with notes, a dot placed to the right of a rest increases its value by one-half.

$$\bj = \eighth + \eighth$$

$$\quarterrest = \eighthrest + \eighthrest$$

$$\dottedhalf = \eighth + \eighth + \eighth$$

$$\dottedquarterrest = \eighthrest + \eighthrest + \eighthrest$$

$$\eighth = \sixteenth + \sixteenth$$

$$\eighthrest = \sixteenthrest + \sixteenthrest$$

$$\dottedeighth = \sixteenth + \sixteenth + \sixteenth$$

$$\dottedeighthrest = \sixteenthrest + \sixteenthrest + \sixteenthrest$$

EXERCISE 1·6

Assuming that the quarter note and quarter rest each receive one beat, determine how many total beats are represented by the following combinations of note values and rests.

Number of Beats

EXERCISE 1·7

Assuming that the eighth note and eighth rest each receive one beat, determine how many beats are represented by the following combinations of note values and rests.

*Number
of Beats*

1. ♪ ♪ ♩ ♪ ♩ ♩. ♩ _____

2. ♪ 𝄾 ♪ ♩ 𝄾 𝄾 ♪ ♪ _____

3. ♩ ♩. ♪ ♩ 𝄾 𝄿 ♪ _____

4. ♪ ♪ ♪ 𝄾 ♪ 𝄾 ♪ _____

5. ♩. ♩ ♪ 𝄾 ♪ 𝄿 _____

EXERCISE 1·8

Assuming that the half note and half rest each receive one beat, determine how many total beats are represented by the following combinations of note values and rests.

*Number
of Beats*

1. ♩ ♩ ♩ ♩ ♩. ♩ ♩ ♩ _____

2. ♩ ♩ ♪ ♪ 𝄿 ♩ ♩ ♪ 𝄾 ♩. _____

3. ♩ ♪ 𝄾 ♪ ♪ ♪ ♩. ♩ 𝄿 _____

4. 𝅝 ♩ ♩ ♩ ♩ 𝄿 ♩ ♩. ♩ _____

5. ♪ ♩ ♪ ♩ ▬ 𝄿 ♩ ♪ ♪ 𝄾 ♪ _____

EXERCISE 1·9

Assuming that the dotted quarter note and dotted quarter rest each receive one beat, determine how many total beats are represented by the following combinations of note values and rests.

*Number
of Beats*

1. _____

2. _____

3. _____

4. _____

Time Signatures

The **time signature** is made up of two numbers, one above the other, that appear at the beginning of a piece of music. The time signature has two functions: The top number indicates the meter of the piece; the bottom number identifies the note value that represents the pulse. For example, in the time signature $\frac{3}{4}$:

3   indicates triple meter — that is, three pulses, or beats, per measure.
4   identifies the quarter note as the pulse beat.

Although the quarter note represents the pulse for many pieces, other note values can also serve this purpose. Both the eighth note and the half note are frequently used.

Triple meter; the eighth note represents the pulse.

Triple meter; the half note represents the pulse.

Notice that the meter signature is *never* written as a fraction: $\frac{3}{4}$.

EXERCISE 1·10

Identify the meter and indicate the note value that represents the pulse for each of the meter signatures below.

EXERCISE 1·17

Give the correct terminology for each of the following meter signatures.

EXAMPLE: $\frac{3}{2}$ simple triple

1. $\frac{3}{4}$ _____

2. $\frac{4}{2}$ _____

3. $\frac{6}{8}$ _____

4. $\frac{4}{4}$ _____

5. $\frac{12}{16}$ _____

6. $\frac{6}{4}$ _____

7. $\frac{12}{4}$ _____

8. $\frac{2}{2}$ _____

9. $\frac{9}{4}$ _____

10. $\frac{2}{8}$ _____

Notational Problems

Although it is still common in vocal music to see individual eighth notes or sixteenth notes with separate flags, in instrumental music these notes rarely appear individually. Instead, two or more eighth or sixteenth notes will be grouped together, according to beats, with a connecting beam. A vocal rhythmic pattern such as

will appear in instrumental music as

Notice that eighth notes are grouped by a single beam, and sixteenth notes by a double beam.

When connecting notes with beams, it is important in all but the simplest patterns to begin each beat with a separate beam. A musician trains his or her eye to see such patterns of beats within a measure. A poorly written arrangement, such as the following, is momentarily confusing:

This pattern is confusing rhythmically because the beaming has obscured the second, third, and fourth beats of the measure. The following shows a much clearer way of constructing the same pattern:

Here, each of the four beats starts with a new beam. Remember, the purpose of beaming notes together is to make the rhythmic patterns easier to recognize, rather than more obscure.

Extra care must be taken when beaming irregular divisions of the beat, particularly dotted rhythm patterns, since these can be especially tricky. The first step is to decide whether the pattern is in simple or compound meter. Knowing this will tell you whether the basic beat is divided into subgroups of two or three. After that, try to determine where each basic beat begins. This is more or less a process of adding up the note values. Finally, combine groups of notes so that each basic beat is beamed together. Make sure, however, that you do not combine two or more beats when grouping. Each beat should be beamed separately.

The following examples may make the above explanation clearer. In a simple meter, such as $\frac{2}{4}$, the basic beat is the quarter note. This quarter note can be divided into two eighth notes or four sixteenth notes.

But the quarter note can also be divided into any combination of eighth notes and sixteenth notes that total one beat. In simple meters, for instance, there are three ways that the combination of one eighth note and two sixteenth notes can be written.

Notice that in each case the combination of notes is equal to one beat in simple meter. Notice also that the beaming (one beam for eighth notes, two for sixteenth notes) clearly indicates the beginning of each beat.

The beaming of dotted notes in simple meter is simply an extension of this same principle. Since a dotted eighth note is the equivalent of three sixteenth notes, the dotted-eighth-and-sixteenth pattern is frequently found and can be written one of two ways.

Notice that in both cases a complete beat is combined under one beam.

A similar process is employed in compound meter, with one major difference: The basic pulse is divided into three parts rather than two. In a compound meter such as $\frac{6}{8}$, the basic pulse is normally felt as two beats per measure, and the note representing this beat, the dotted quarter note, is divisible into three eighth notes or six sixteenth notes.

As in simple meter, any combination of eighth notes and sixteenth notes that adds up to a complete beat should be beamed together. The following are some of the more common combinations:

Similarly, dotted rhythms in compound meter are also grouped by beat. The most common dotted rhythm pattern in compound meter is:

The following two patterns also occur from time to time, but less frequently.

In all cases, it is important to keep the beginning of each beat clearly visible by beaming together all the notes that occur within that beat.

MUSICAL PROBLEM

Clap and count each of the rhythms given below. Then, rewrite them by beaming the eighth notes and sixteenth notes together, taking care not to place beams across beats. Next, clap the patterns you have written. Does being able to see clearly the beginning of each beat make it easier to read the patterns?

3.  **6/8** [musical notation] ‖

6/8 | | | ‖

EXERCISE 1·18

Rewrite the following rhythmic patterns by beaming the eighth notes and sixteenth notes together. Remember not to place beams across beats. Remember also that dotted eighth and sixteenth notes that occur within one beat are joined in the ways shown in the example.

EXAMPLE: [musical notation]

1.  **4/4** [musical notation] ‖

4/4 | | ‖

2. 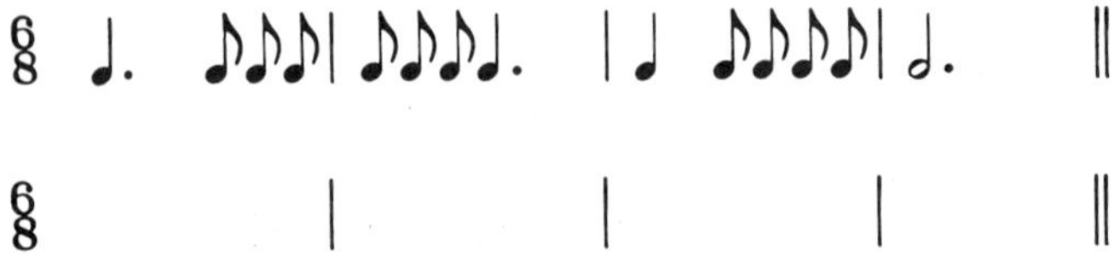 **6/8** [musical notation] ‖

6/8 | | | ‖

3. **2/4** [musical notation] ‖

2/4 | | | ‖

4. **3/4** [musical notation] ‖

3/4   | | ‖

5.  **6/8** [musical notation] ‖

6/8 | | | ‖

6.  4/4 ♪. ♪♪. ♪♪.   ♪ | ♪ ♪♪♪♪♪ 𝅗𝅥   ‖

4/4 | ‖

7.  9/8 𝅘𝅥𝅭. 𝅘𝅥𝅭. ♪♪♪♪| 𝅘𝅥 ♪♪♪♪♪♪. ♪♪| ♪♪♪♪♪ 𝅘𝅥𝅭. ‖

9/8 | | ‖

8. 2/4 ♪. ♪♪ ♪♪| ♪♪♪ ♪. ♪| ♪ ♪♪♪. ♪| 𝅗𝅥   ‖

2/4 | | | ‖

Triplets and Duplets

Sometimes, a note in simple meter is subdivided as if it were in compound meter. That is, a note normally subdivided into two equal parts is momentarily subdivided into three equal parts. This is called *borrowed division*.

♩ = ♫   normal subdivision

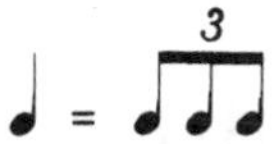

♩ = (³ ♪♪♪)   borrowed division

The *3* above the beam indicates that three even eighth notes occur within the time normally taken by two. When a borrowed division of this type occurs, it is called a **triplet**. A note of any value may be subdivided into a triplet. The three most common are:

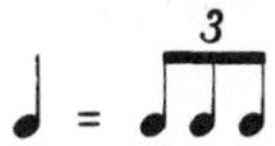

♩ = (³ ♪♪♪)   eighth-note triplet

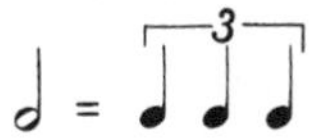

𝅗𝅥 = (³ ♩♩♩)   quarter-note triplet

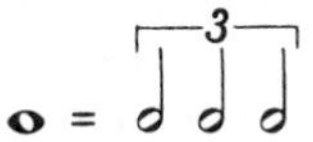

𝅝 = (³ 𝅗𝅥𝅗𝅥𝅗𝅥)   half-note triplet

Less frequently, a note in compound meter is subdivided as if it were in simple meter:

$$\text{♩.} = \text{♪♪♪} \qquad \text{normal subdivision}$$

$$\text{♩.} = \overset{2}{\text{♪♪}} \qquad \text{borrowed division}$$

When this occurs, it is called a **duplet**. The two most common duplets are:

$$\text{♩.} = \overset{2}{\text{♩♩}} \qquad \text{eighth-note duplet}$$

$$\text{♩.} = \overset{\ulcorner 2 \urcorner}{\text{♩♩}} \qquad \text{quarter-note duplet}$$

Notice that (1) in both duplets and triplets a numeral is used to alert the performer to an unusual subdivision, and (2) where no beam exists, a bracket indicates exactly which notes belong to the triplet or duplet figure.

Triplets and duplets are best employed as rhythmic exceptions, to be used sparingly in a particular piece of music. If more frequent use is necessary, it makes more sense for the entire piece to be written in the corresponding compound or simple meter.

A Counting Method

In learning to read rhythms, it is useful to learn a counting method that can be spoken aloud as you are clapping rhythms. The value of such a system is that it can be transferred to "mental" counting when you are actually performing music.

Although there are several different systems currently in use, the following one is recommended not only because it is simple and easily learned, but also because it has a different set of syllables for the subdivisions of simple and compound meter.

The Basic Beat

In this system, the basic beat is identified by the numbers "one, two, three, four," as needed. This is true for both simple and compound meter. Practice counting the following examples until you feel comfortable with them.

Simple Meters

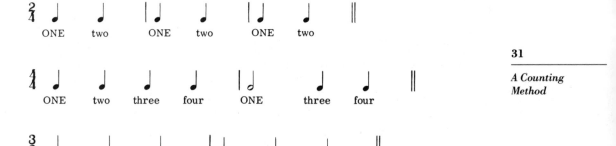

Compound Meters

Subdivisions of the Beat in Simple Meter

When dividing simple meters, *and* is used to indicate the division of the beat. Practice the following examples until they feel comfortable.

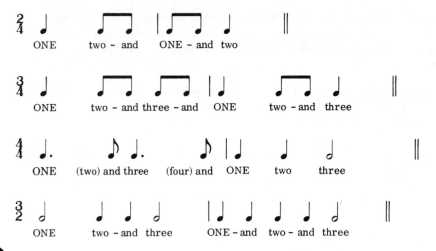

When a further subdivision is needed—that is, if you need to indicate one-quarter of the basic beat—the syllable *ta* is used. Here are some examples to practice.

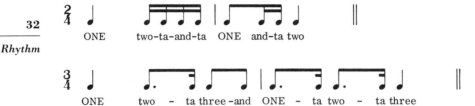

Subdivisions of the Beat in Compound Meter

Since compound meters are divided into three equal parts rather than two, a different set of syllables is used. These are *la* and *le*. Practice counting the following examples in compound meter until you feel comfortable with them. Remember that this is a different system from the one used to count simple meters. It may be confusing at first, but it will become easier with practice.

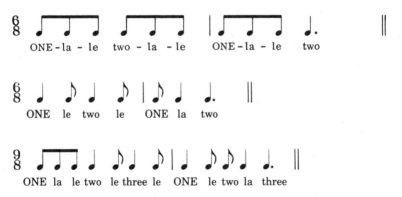

When a further subdivision of the beat in compound meter is required—that is, when you need to indicate one-sixth of the beat—the syllable *ta* is used. The following examples can be tongue twisters at first, but will grow easier as you practice them.

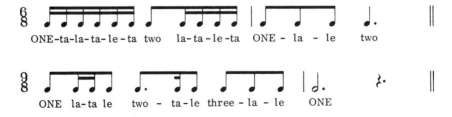

EXERCISE 1·19

Before beginning this exercise, be sure that you have studied the information and practiced the examples given until you are familiar with this system of counting. When you feel sufficiently comfortable, try writing in the counting syllables for each of the indicated rhythms.

1. ...

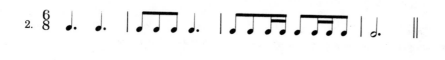

2. ...

3. ...

4. ...

5. ...

Counting Triplets and Duplets

When counting triplets or duplets, shift momentarily into compound or simple meter syllables, as needed.

ONE two - and three   ONE two - la - le three

ONE two - and   ONE - la - le   ONE

ONE - la - le two   ONE - la - le two - and   ONE

MUSICAL PROBLEM

As a class, clap and count the following rhythmic examples. Begin by saying two measures of the divided beat (1-and 2-and for simple meters; 1-la-le 2-la-le for compound meters) aloud before clapping. Experiment with a variety of speeds. When you are comfortable with this counting system, try playing the rhythms on an instrument while counting mentally.

MUSICAL PROBLEM

Your instructor will choose three of the rhythmic passages given in the preceding musical problem and play them for you several times. You will be told the meter of each example. Listen carefully to each passage, and try to notate it in the space provided below. If the passages seem too long, your instructor can divide them into shorter segments. Use the counting method to help clarify the rhythmic patterns you hear.

1. _____

_____

2. _____

_____

3. _____

_____

_____

MUSICAL PROBLEM

As a class, clap the following two-part examples, with half the class clapping the top part and half the bottom part. Then, by yourself, try tapping the examples on a desk or tabletop, one part per hand.

Ties

Often, a composer will want to hold a note beyond the end of a measure in a particular meter. Suppose, for example, we wish to have a note last four beats in $\frac{3}{4}$ meter. Obviously, four beats will not fit into a single three-beat measure. To permit the note to last four beats, we use a **tie**, which extends the note into the next measure. As shown in the following example, the tie is a curved line connecting the notehead to be prolonged with the same notehead in the next measure.

In performance, the second note will not be sounded separately. Instead, the first note will be held through the time value of the second, producing a single sound, four beats in duration.

Ties are not only useful for creating notes of longer duration than the number of beats in a measure, they are sometimes also needed at the end of a measure. In the following illustration, for example, the tie is needed because a half note cannot occur on the last beat of the first measure.

Ties are very similar in appearance to slurs, which are used to specify a smooth, connected style of playing. **Slurs** always connect different pitches, and may extend over several pitches at once, whereas ties always connect two notes of the same pitch.

EXERCISE 1·20

In the following note sequences, indicate the total number of beats each tied note
will last. Then clap and count the rhythms of each example.

EXAMPLE: $\frac{2}{4}$ ♩ ♩ ♩ ♩ | 3 quarter-note beats

$\frac{6}{8}$ ♩. ♩. ♪♪♪ ♩. | 1⅓ dotted
quarter-note beats

1. $\frac{3}{4}$ ♩ ♩ ♩ ♩ ↑ | _____

2. $\frac{2}{4}$ ♩ ♪♪ ♪♪ ♩ | _____

3. $\frac{3}{8}$ ♪ ♩ ♩. | _____

4. $\frac{4}{4}$ ♩ ♩ ♩ ♩ ♩ ♩ | _____

5. $\frac{3}{2}$ ♩ ♩ ♩ o ♩ | _____

6. $\frac{3}{2}$ o ♩♩ | ♩ o | _____

7. $\frac{3}{8}$ ♪♩. ♩. | _____

8. $\frac{4}{4}$ ♩. ♪♩ ♩ ♩. ♪♩ | _____

9. $\frac{3}{8}$ ♩ ♪ ♩ ♪♪ | _____

10. $\frac{3}{4}$ ♩ ♩ ♩ ♩. ♪♩ | _____

11. $\frac{2}{4}$ ♪♪ ♪ ♪♪ ♪♪ | _____

12. $\frac{6}{8}$ ♩. ♩ ♪♪♪♪ ♩. | _____

Another use of ties is to help make clear metric groupings, both within the bar and over the bar line. Notice in the following example that the use of ties allows the normal grouping in ⁶⁄₈ to be maintained.

EXERCISE 1·21

Rewrite each of the following rhythmic patterns in the meter indicated. To do this you will have to divide some notes (for instance, ♩ into ♪♪) and use ties.

EXAMPLE:

Syncopation

In certain styles of music, an accent is frequently placed on what would otherwise be a weak beat. When this occurs, it is called **syncopation**. Clap and count aloud the following example:

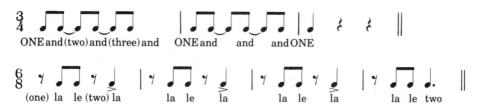

Notice that even this simple example of syncopation creates more rhythmic drive and energy. This is why some styles of music use syncopation so extensively. Here are several more examples.

An almost endless number of different syncopation figures is possible. What they all have in common is stress of the weaker beats or the weaker subdivisions of a beat in order to produce more rhythmic tension. Some music, such as jazz and rock, makes extensive use of syncopation. But syncopation is not limited to these styles. It can be found to some degree in most of the world's music.

MUSICAL PROBLEM

Select three or four interested students from the class to make a cassette tape of eight to ten short examples from popular music that illustrate the use of syncopation. The examples should be short, and the total length of the tape should be about five minutes. As a class, listen to the tape and discuss each example. What does the syncopation contribute to the overall rhythmic effect? Your teacher may wish to select one or more examples and ask you to try writing out the rhythm by ear.

Repeat Signs

Occasionally, composers want several measures in a composition to be repeated immediately. They can do this either by writing all of the measures again or by using **repeat signs**. Although it is easy enough to rewrite a few measures, for lengthier passages repeat signs are more convenient.

Repeat signs are two large dots, one above the other, that appear at the beginning and the end of the measures to be repeated. Double bar lines generally accompany the repeat signs at the beginning and the end of the repeated measures in order to call attention to the repeat signs.

This example, when performed, will sound like this:

If the repeated measures include the first measure of the composition, the repeat sign occurs only at the end of the section to be repeated and is omitted from the beginning. For example,

when performed, will sound like

MUSICAL PROBLEM

Clap and count the following rhythms, individually and as a class. Pay particular attention to the repeat signs and ties. It will also be helpful if you sing the rhythms or perform them on an instrument. Be sure to hold each note for its full value.

9. $\frac{3}{4}$ ♪♫ notation

10. $\frac{3}{8}$ ♪♫ notation

Tempo

The speed of the pulse of a composition is called the **tempo**. Whereas we might use the terms *fast* and *slow* as indications of speed, actual pieces of music use Italian terms to assign the tempo. The following is a list of the most important terms and their meanings:

Slow Tempos

largo	broad, very slow
lento	slow
adagio	slow

Moderate Tempos

andante	walking speed
moderato	moderate

Fast Tempos

allegro	fast
vivace	quick, lively
presto	very fast

In addition, the following two terms are important because they indicate gradual changes of tempo:

ritardando (*rit.*)	gradually becoming slower
accelerando (*accel.*)	gradually becoming faster

Although these terms give a general indication of how fast a piece of music should be performed, they are open to a certain amount of interpretation. A more precise method of setting tempo is to use metronome indications. The **metronome** is an instrument invented in the early 1800s that produces a specific number of clicks per minute. Each click represents one beat. The metronome indication is given at the beginning of a composition. It looks like this:

$$\text{♩} = \text{M.M.60}$$

This particular indication means that the metronome will produce sixty clicks in one minute, and that each click is to be considered the pulse of one quarter note.

Conducting Patterns

The rhythmic patterns you have been asked to clap in this chapter can be performed by the class without a conductor. To perform more complicated patterns, or patterns consisting of three or four separate parts, you would probably need a conductor to keep everyone together. Indicating the beats and keeping the group together are important functions of the conductor.

The conductor indicates the beat with movements of the right arm. The following are the basic arm movements for duple, triple, and quadruple meters.

two-beat pattern

three-beat pattern

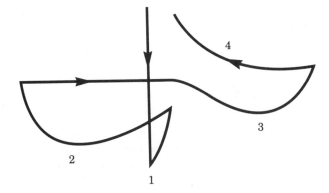

four-beat pattern

When practicing these patterns, remember the following points:

1. The beat pattern is always performed by the right arm only. This is true even if you are left-handed.
2. Always practice standing up. It is difficult to conduct correctly while sitting down.
3. The first beat of each pattern is called the **downbeat**; the last beat is called the **upbeat**.

4. Keep the beat pattern high enough for everyone to see. The center of the pattern should be level with your chest, not your waist.

5. The arm motion should always be fluid and smooth. Never let the arm come to a complete stop.

6. When beginning a pattern, always prepare for the first beat of the exercise by giving the beat that comes directly before it. Assume, for instance, that you are going to conduct an exercise that uses a three-beat pattern starting on the downbeat. To begin, you would give the previous upbeat as a preparation. This is called the *preparatory beat*.

MUSICAL PROBLEM

The following are well-known melodies in duple, triple, and quadruple meters. Practice conducting each of these melodies while your teacher or another student plays them on the piano. Then practice conducting while you yourself sing each of them on *la*. Keep practicing until you are comfortable singing and conducting simultaneously.

"Hush, Little Baby"

1.

"Scarborough Fair"

2.

"Oh Dear, What Can the Matter Be"

3.

MUSICAL PROBLEM

Clap or perform on instruments the following two- and three-part rhythmic examples with one member of the class conducting and the other members taking the parts. You may wish to practice some of the simpler exercises in Appendix A first.

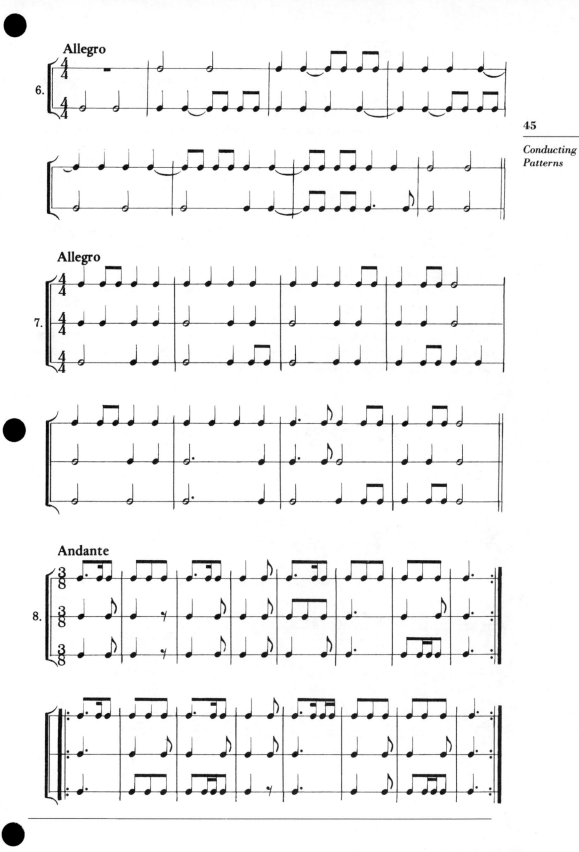

MUSICAL PROBLEM

Experiment with tapping out examples 1–6 from the preceding musical problem on a desk or tabletop, one part per hand.

If you are particularly adventurous, you might like to try tapping out the three-part examples (numbers 7 and 8). To do this, tap out the top part with your right hand, the middle part with your left hand, and the bottom part with one foot. You will probably find the three-part examples extremely difficult at first. (This kind of rhythmic coordination is what organists and trap-set drummers must use every day.)

MUSICAL PROBLEM

Below is the melody of the first part of a minuet by Bach. Probably you have heard this piece before. Clap the rhythm of the melody several times. Then, in the space provided, write a second rhythmic part that, when clapped with the rhythm of the melody, will complement it and create a two-part clapping piece. Perform the one-part and two-part clapping pieces in class and discuss the strengths and weaknesses of each piece. Then, ask someone who plays piano to play the original keyboard version, as composed by Bach.

Bach: Minuet in G Minor

Focus

This chapter began with the question, What is musical rhythm? Are we now ready to answer the question? So far, we have discussed individual rhythmic elements, but not how these elements interact within an actual composition to give it its unique rhythmic character. On one level, this interaction is relatively easy to describe: Musical rhythm is the inherent tension between the steady pulse of a particular meter and the irregular note values that occur within that meter. Unfortunately, this simplistic definition, while true, ignores the more subtle and complex aspects of the rhythm of most musical works.

In a real composition, a number of factors work together to produce its characteristic rhythm: tempo, accents, and the interaction of rhythm with melody and harmony, among others. Since the rhythmic qualities of every composition differ, musicians learn to make slight adjustments when performing a piece in order to accommodate the specific rhythmic demands.

MUSICAL PROBLEM

From memory, write out the rhythm of one or more of the following songs. If you are not familiar enough with any of these melodies you may choose a different one, but be sure to work *from memory*. Begin by singing through the entire melody to determine the meter. Does the song begin on a downbeat?

1. "America"
2. "This Land Is Your Land"
3. "Pop Goes the Weasel"
4. "Dixie"
5. "Jingle Bells"
6. "Amazing Grace"
7. "Silent Night"
8. "Greensleeves"
9. "Erie Canal"
10. "Hava Nagila"

When you have the rhythm correctly notated, write a second rhythmic part to accompany it. Perform this two-part work as a clapping piece with another member of the class.

MUSICAL PROBLEM

Listen again to the work you chose for the opening musical problem of the chapter (p. 6). This time, try to explain in more musical terms what is taking place rhythmically. Be specific when discussing the pulse, meter, and tempo. Discuss in a general way the interaction of its various rhythmic elements. In one or more paragraphs, describe your experience of the rhythm. Does this new description show that you now have a better understanding of musical rhythm in general?

Chapter 2

Melody

Music does not have to be written out on paper to exist as music. Most folk-music traditions of the world are oral, with tunes passing by rote from one performer to another and from one generation to the next. Even the classical music of some cultures, much of it of great complexity, is maintained primarily by an oral tradition. Moreover, some styles of music, such as jazz and rock in Western music, or the raga tradition in Indian music, require so much in the way of improvisational technique that any written arrangements in these styles are little more than skeletons — the "real" music appearing only at the time of performance.

Even though other musical traditions function well without a highly organized notational system, for Western music of the past 400 years there are still obvious advantages to being able to write down musical ideas. First, the ideas can be preserved exactly: They will not be forgotten or altered unconsciously. Second, complicated musical structures can be dealt with in a standard manner easily understood by most musicians. Third, the music can be efficiently transmitted to other musicians, either immediately or sometime later.

Think of the great piano and symphonic works of Western music. Could they ever have been performed in the first place, much less preserved for centuries, without an adequate notational system? Or what about the music of the Glenn Miller, Count Basie, or Stan Kenton bands of this century? Although there was a great deal of solo improvising in these bands, the arrangements themselves were tightly organized and carefully written out.

MUSICAL PROBLEM

Listen to a recording of a short orchestral work by Haydn or Mozart. As you listen, consider the fact that this music was written over a century and a half ago. It can be performed today because the notational system conveys information to the performers that allows them to re-create the music accurately. As a class, discuss the kinds of musical information the notational system contains. (You may wish to look at a score.)

In contrast, much rock music is not notated. Although the arrangements are played virtually the same way each time, they are seldom written down on paper. Listen to a popular rock piece. As a class, discuss what kind of information the notational system would have to include in order for someone who had never heard this music to play it a century and a half from now.

Written music can best be compared to a storage and retrieval system. In this system, musical information is stored by the composer in a code of shapes and symbols. A performer wishing to re-create written music must understand both the musical elements being dealt with and the manner in which they are encoded.

The key to reading and writing music is the realization that written music encodes two major musical elements: pitch (the basis of melody and harmony) and duration (from which rhythm is derived). While much additional information is given by music notation, these two elements are the primary ones. In this chapter, we will concentrate on pitch notation.

MUSICAL PROBLEM

Bring to class a piece of music borrowed from the music library or a friend. Your teacher may wish to choose several pieces to discuss as a group. Which musical symbols can you identify at this point? What do they mean? What is their purpose? Can you see that reading a piece of music is in some ways similar to reading a map?

The Staff

Music is written on a **staff**. The music staff (pl., *staves*) consists of a group of five parallel lines. In music notation, the five lines, the four spaces between the lines, and the spaces above and below the staff are all utilized. The lines and spaces are numbered from bottom to top: the lines 1 through 5, the spaces 1 through 4.

Noteheads

The lines and spaces of the staff, from the bottom to the top, indicate successively higher pitches. In technical terms, **pitch** is the frequency at which a given sound vibrates. The faster the vibration, the higher the pitch is said to be. (A more detailed explanation of the physical characteristics of sound is given in Appendix I.)

Noteheads are the small oval shapes drawn on the staff to represent particular pitches. They may appear either on a line or in a space, as in the following staff. Notice that the second notehead represents a slightly higher pitch than the first one, since the third space is above the third line.

EXERCISE 2·1

In Exercise 1-1, you were asked to practice drawing notes on a single line. Look back at that effort now. Are your noteheads clearly on the line? In order to indicate pitch, noteheads must be placed exactly on a line or in a space. Practice notehead placement once more, this time on the staff, by drawing the following noteheads. Remember to make the noteheads oval rather than round, and to draw them small enough so that they sit clearly centered either in a space or on a line.

1.

2.

3.

4.

5.

6.

MUSICAL PROBLEM

Melody   Your instructor will play, in random order, various two-note sequences from examples 1 through 16 below. Listen carefully to each of the sequences, and indicate in the numbered spaces below the examples whether the second note is higher in pitch (*H*) or lower in pitch (*L*) than the first. Remember, these examples are being played in random order.

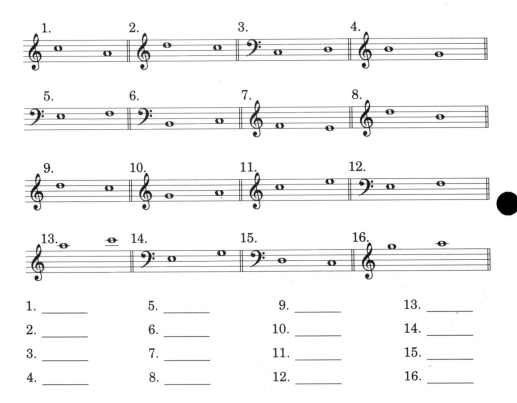

1. _____	5. _____	9. _____	13. _____
2. _____	6. _____	10. _____	14. _____
3. _____	7. _____	11. _____	15. _____
4. _____	8. _____	12. _____	16. _____

MUSICAL PROBLEM

Your instructor will randomly select and play various three- and four-note sequences from those given below. Listen carefully to each of the sequences, and in the spaces below the examples, indicate whether the last note is higher in pitch (*H*) or lower in pitch (*L*) than the first.

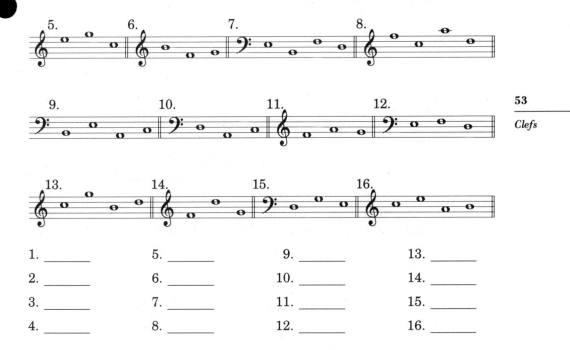

1. _____   5. _____   9. _____   13. _____

2. _____   6. _____   10. _____   14. _____

3. _____   7. _____   11. _____   15. _____

4. _____   8. _____   12. _____   16. _____

Clefs

The first seven letters of the alphabet (A through G) are used to name pitches. The staff by itself does not represent any particular set (or range) of pitches; this is the function of **clef** signs. Each clef sign locates a particular pitch on the staff. Two clef signs are in common use: treble clef and bass clef.

The Treble Clef

The **treble clef**, or **G clef**, identifies the second line of the staff as the location for the note G that is five notes above middle C (the C approximately in the middle of the piano keyboard). Notice that the lower part of the treble clef sign encircles the second line:

EXERCISE 2·2

Practice drawing the treble clef sign. It is made by first drawing a vertical line and then drawing the remainder of the clef, starting at the top of the vertical line. Remember to encircle the second line with the lower part of the clef.

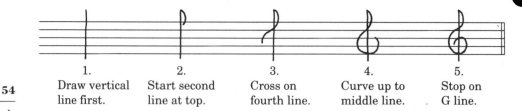

	1.	2.	3.	4.	5.
	Draw vertical line first.	Start second line at top.	Cross on fourth line.	Curve up to middle line.	Stop on G line.

Once a particular pitch is identified on the staff by a clef sign, the other pitches on that staff follow automatically in alphabetical sequence. Remember, only the first seven letters of the alphabet are used. After that, the sequence of letters repeats.

G   D   E   F   G   A   B   C   D   E   F   G

EXERCISE 2·3

Identify by letter name the following pitches in the treble clef.

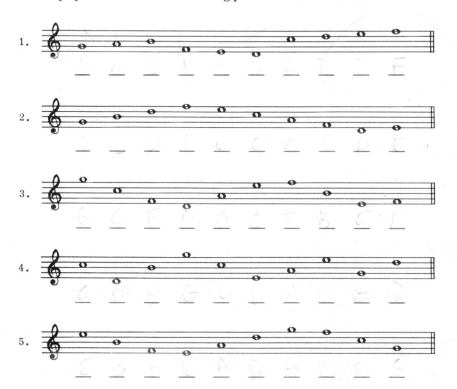

EXERCISE 2·4

Identify by letter name the pitches of the following well-known songs.

"Down in the Valley"

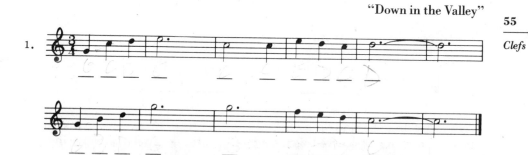

Foster: "Camptown Races"

"Wayfaring Stranger"

MUSICAL PROBLEM

Sing the songs in Exercise 2-4 using the syllable *la*. Then try singing them, in rhythm, with letter names. For each song, see whether some pitches occur more frequently than others, and identify the pitch that seems to produce the most restful feeling or clearest sense of completion.

The Bass Clef

The **bass clef**, or **F clef**, identifies the fourth line of the staff as the location for the note F that is five notes below middle C on the piano.

EXERCISE 2·5

Practice drawing the bass clef sign. It is made by first drawing a dot on the fourth line; then drawing the curved sign, beginning at the dot; and finally placing two dots to the right of the sign, one just above the fourth line and one just below.

As with the treble clef, the pitches of the bass clef are arranged in alphabetical sequence.

F   F   G   A   B   C   D   E   F   G   A   B

EXERCISE 2·6

Identify by letter name the following pitches in the bass clef.

1.

2.

3.

4.

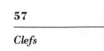

5.

EXERCISE 2·7

Identify by letter name the pitches of the following well-known songs.

"Nine Hundred Miles"

1.

"Skip to My Lou"

2.

MUSICAL PROBLEM

Sing the songs in Exercise 2-7, first with the syllable *la*, then with the letter names, in rhythm. In each song, identify the pitch that seems to produce the most restful feeling or clearest sense of completion.

MUSICAL PROBLEM

Below are two well-known melodies written with noteheads but not with the proper note values. By looking at the shape of each melody line, try to identify the melody. If this is too difficult, ask someone to play the pitches on the piano. Can you perceive a relationship between the sound of the melody and the shape of the melody on the staff?

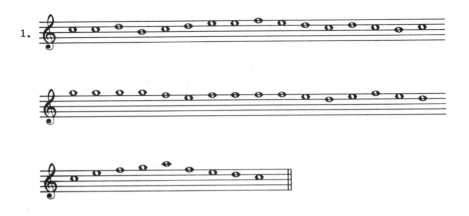

2.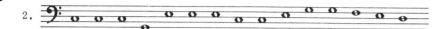

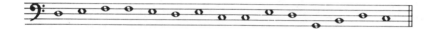

When you have identified the melodies, sing each of them using the syllable *la*. Do you perceive a relationship between the shape of the melody on the staff and the sound of the melody as you sing it?

The Great Staff

The **great staff**, also known as the grand staff, consists of a treble clef staff and a bass clef staff joined together by a vertical line and a brace.

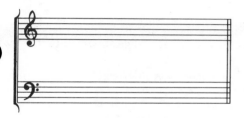

The great staff is used primarily for piano music. It is also sometimes used for choral music or any other type of music requiring a range of pitches too wide for a single staff.

In the following example, notice that one pitch, *middle C* — so-called because of its location in the middle of the piano keyboard and of the great staff — does not touch either staff. Instead, it sits on a short line, called a *ledger line*, that is not part of either staff. Ledger lines are explained in more detail on page 62.

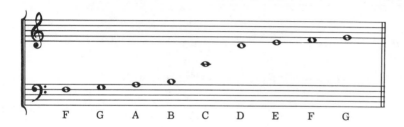

In standard music, however, middle C does not appear in the center of the great staff. Rather, it is located closer to one staff or the other.

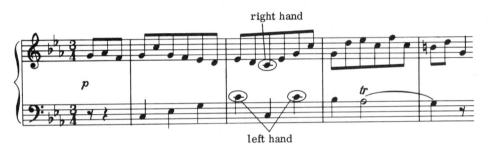

In piano music, the notes on the treble staff are usually played by the right hand, and the notes on the bass staff are played by the left hand. As shown in the following example, the position of middle C indicates which hand is to play it.

Bach: Courante from French Suite No. 2

right hand

left hand

In choral music, the location of middle C indicates which voice should sing it.

Bach: Chorale from Cantata No. 180

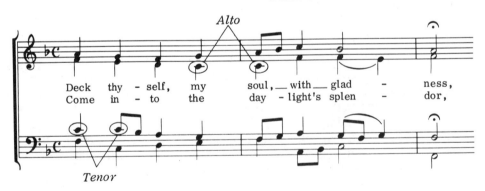

Alto

Deck thy - self, my soul, — with — glad - ness,
Come in - to the day - light's splen - dor,

Tenor

EXERCISE 2·8

Identify by letter name the following pitches on the great staff.

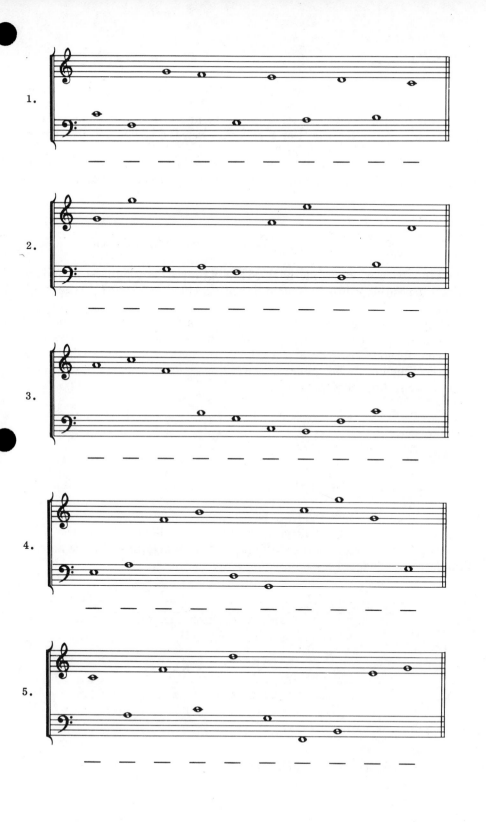

The C Clef

The G clef and the F clef, although widely used, are not the only clefs that composers have employed. Much Medieval and Renaissance music, for example, is written in a third clef, the C clef. This clef identifies a particular line of the staff as middle C. Unlike the G or F clef, however, the C clef was considered movable and was used on any of the five lines.

C clef in alto position

C clef in tenor position

Notice in the above example that the third line of the staff is designated as middle C in the alto position, while the fourth line is identified as middle C in the tenor position.

Although extensive work with the C clef is beyond the scope of this book, you should be able to recognize it and to understand the basic principles of how it is read. If your teacher wishes to explore the C clef further, or if you would like to study it on your own, more material, including some practice exercises, have been provided in Appendix F.

Ledger Lines

Often, pitches higher or lower than the range limitations of the five-line staff need to be indicated. This is done with the use of ledger lines. **Ledger lines** are short, individual lines added above or below the staff, having the effect of extending the staff. Notice (in the following example) that ledger lines are the same distance apart as the lines of the staff and that the ledger lines for one note do *not* connect to the ledger lines for another note.

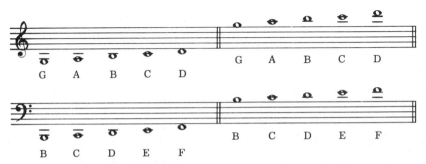

It is not necessary to enclose a pitch with ledger lines.

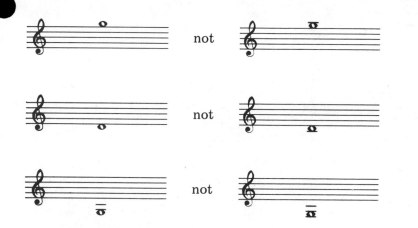

EXERCISE 2·9

Identify the following pitches by letter name.

The use of ledger lines within the great staff can be momentarily confusing. In the following example, both notes in each vertically aligned pair represent the same pitch. This notational overlap within the great staff is useful because it allows pitches to be clearly grouped with the musical line to which they belong.

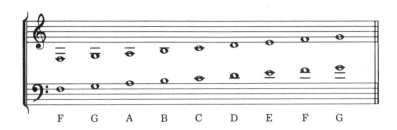

Melody   F   G   A   B   C   D   E   F   G

In the following piano music example, the left hand plays pitches located above middle C. To avoid confusion, however, these pitches are written with ledger lines in the bass clef.

Mozart: Sonata in B♭ Major, K. 570, III

Allegretto

EXERCISE 2·10

First identify the given pitch; then rewrite the same pitch, but in the other clef.

EXAMPLE:

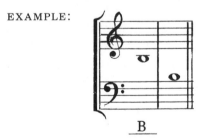

B

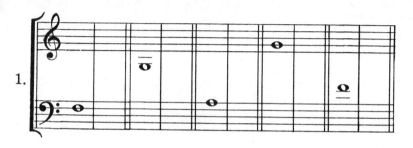

1.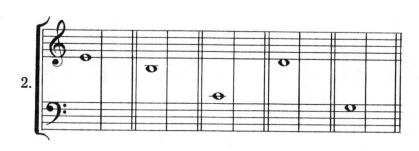

2.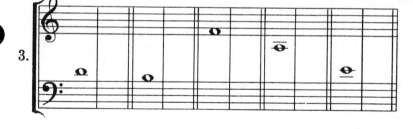

3.

4.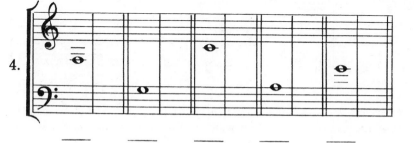

The Octave Sign

Musicians are most comfortable reading music that is written on the staff or close to it. The excessive use of ledger lines makes music difficult to read and should be avoided. The **octave sign**, *8va*⁻⁻⁻⁻⁻⌐ or *8*⁻⁻⁻⌐, is another notational device, in addition to the C clef, that helps overcome this problem.

An octave is the distance between any note and the next note of the same name, either higher or lower. The octave sign *above* a group of notes, then, indicates that the notes under the sign are to be played one octave *higher* than written.

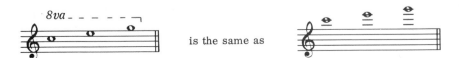

is the same as

The following example shows how the octave sign can be used to keep the ascending-scale passage on or close to the staff.

Kuhlau: Rondo from Sonatina, Op. 20, No. 1

When the octave sign appears *below* a group of notes, it indicates that those notes are to be played one octave *lower* than written. Sometimes the word *bassa* is added to the octave sign.

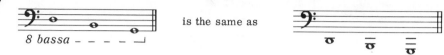

8 bassa _ _ _ _ _ ┘   is the same as

The following example, by Debussy, uses octave signs above and below pitches in order to explore the extremes of the piano range.

Debussy: "Brouillards" from Preludes, Book II

EXERCISE 2·11

Name the pitches given below. Then rewrite the passages using the octave sign to avoid the use of ledger lines.

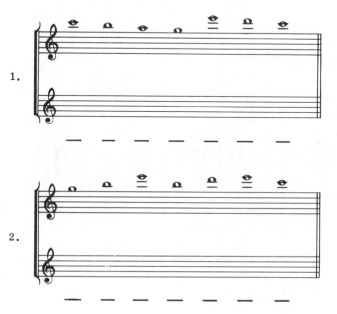

1.

2.

3.

4.

5.

Octave Identification

It is often necessary to refer to a pitch in a particular octave. To identify each octave, a special system is used.

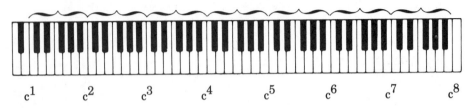

c^1 c^2 c^3 c^4 c^5 c^6 c^7 c^8

The octave beginning on middle C is labeled as follows:

c^4 b^4

Any pitch within this range can be identified by a lowercase letter with super-script numeral 4.

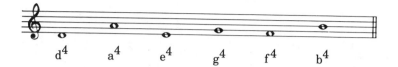

The following illustration shows how the octaves above middle C are identified.

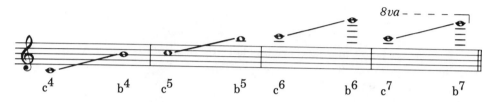

Any pitch within these ranges can be identified by a lowercase letter and the appropriate superscript.

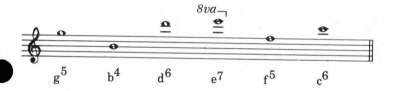

EXERCISE 2·12

Give the correct octave identification for the following pitches.

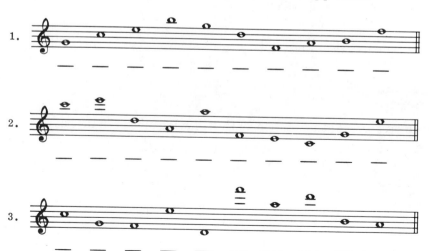

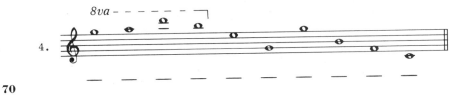

4.

5.

The octaves below middle C are labeled with descending numerals in a similar way.

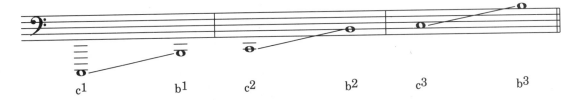

c^1 $\qquad$ b^1 $\qquad$ c^2 $\qquad$ b^2 $\qquad$ c^3 $\qquad$ b^3

The lowest three pitches on the piano, which are below c^1, are identified only by their letter name.

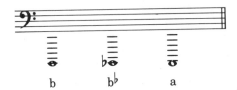

b $\qquad$ b♭ $\qquad$ a

Notice how so many ledger lines make identification of these pitches difficult.

EXERCISE 2·13

Give the correct octave identification for the following pitches in the bass clef.

1.

2.

3.

4.

8 *bassa* - - - - - - ⌐

5.

8 *bassa*

EXERCISE 2·14

Write each indicated pitch in the correct octave. The octave sign may be used
where necessary.

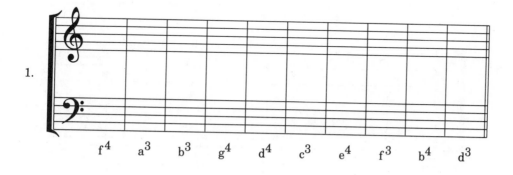

1.

f^4 a^3 b^3 g^4 d^4 c^3 e^4 f^3 b^4 d^3

MUSICAL PROBLEM

Below are two excerpts from musical compositions. Identify the circled pitches in each example with the correct name and octave identification.

Scarlatti: Sonata in C Major

Schumann: "Norse Song" from *Album for the Young*

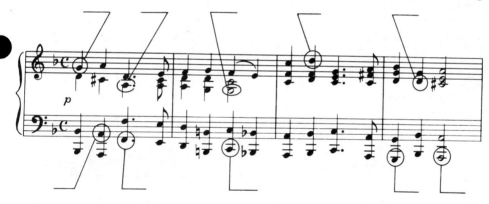

How to Read
a Musical Map

Many pieces of music are played straight through. That is, you begin at the top and play to the end, as you would read a paragraph on a page. But not all pieces are this straightforward. Some contain notational shortcuts—space-saving devices indicated by a variety of symbols and abbreviations. If you recognize the symbols and abbreviations, reading the musical map is not difficult. But if you don't, it can be hopelessly confusing.

Look for a moment at the following example, the "Sicilian" from Robert Schumann's *Album for the Young*.

Schumann: "Sicilian" from *Album for the Young*

Melody

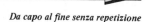

Da capo al fine senza repetizione

It may at first appear to be a piece thirty-seven measures in length, but that is definitely not the case. In fact, when performed correctly it actually contains seventy-six measures. Schumann is able to more than double the length of the printed piece through the use of several devices of repetition. Let's examine them individually.

The first one occurs in measure 8. The double bar with two dots before it is a repeat sign that should be familiar to you from your work in Chapter 1. It indicates that the first eight measures are to be repeated before continuing.

The second device, however, is new. It occurs in measures 16–17 and is called the *1st and 2nd endings*. This device is in some ways similar to the repeat sign for the first eight measures. Notice that the double bar and the two dots in measures 8 and 16 indicate that the musical material between measures 9 and 16 is to be repeated. In this case, however, there are two *different* final measures. The first time the passage is performed, the first ending is played, but on the repetition, only the second ending is used. That is, measures 9–15 are played, measure 16 is omitted, and measure 17 is played in its place.

The third device is even more complicated. Notice the Italian phrase *Da capo al fine senza repetizione* below measures 36 and 37. This phrase indicates that the performer is to return to the beginning of the piece (*Da capo* = the head, the beginning) and play to the end (*fine* = the end) without repeating either measures 1–8 or 9–16 (*senza repetizione* = without repetition). The actual end of the piece, therefore, is at measure 25, not at measure 37 as it may have appeared originally.

These devices may at first seem like extremely confusing ways to organize a score, but if you perform very much music, you will quickly grow used to them. In fact, this example contains all of the commonly used devices except one: *Dal segno al fine*. This phrase, which is similar to *Da capo al fine*, is used when the composer wishes to return to the middle of the piece rather than to the very beginning. In this case the symbol ⸙ is placed at the point where the repetition is to begin, and the performer is expected to return to the sign (*Dal segno*) and play to the end (*al fine*).

Not all pieces of music utilize devices of repetition, and even those that do can vary in slightly different ways. But if you study the following chart carefully, you should be able to find your way through almost any piece of music without too much difficulty.

Device of Repetition	Abbreviation	Meaning
Repeat signs	‖: :‖	Perform the measures located within these signs twice.
1st and 2nd endings	1. ⌐ ⌐2. :‖	Perform the indicated measures twice; the first time using the first ending, the second time using only the second ending.
Da capo al fine	D.C. al fine	Return to the beginning and play to the indicated end.
Dal segno al fine	D.S. al fine	Return to the sign and play to the indicated end.

MUSICAL PROBLEM

Ask several members of the class who perform to locate one or more scores that use various devices of repetition. As a group, discuss these pieces. Can you identify the devices and what they mean? Can you work your way through the score successfully?

Focus

Pitch identification is a major component of musical notation. This chapter has introduced and given you practical experience with pitch notation in the treble and bass clefs, as well as on the great staff. It is important that you become familiar with pitch notation as quickly as possible, since the rest of the book is based on the information contained in this chapter. One of the easiest ways of falling behind in the study of music fundamentals is by being uncertain of and too slow at pitch identification.

The system of octave identification introduced in this chapter is also important. It too will be referred to again and again throughout the book. Although the octave system of identification is basically simple, it can be momentarily confusing. Be certain that you understand it correctly and that you can quickly and accurately identify pitches using this system.

Musical sound has four characteristics — duration, pitch, timbre, and volume. While this book concentrates on developing your skills with duration and pitch, timbre and volume should not be ignored altogether. At this point, you may wish to look at Appendix G, "A Brief Discussion of Dynamics," and Appendix H, "A Brief Introduction to Timbre." Later, your teacher may ask you to study these sections in more detail. For now, keep in mind that being musical involves more than just playing the right notes in the correct rhythms.

Chapter 3

The Keyboard

The piano keyboard is an invaluable aid in the study of music theory. With it, we can visualize aural concepts such as intervals, scales, and triads. While it is also possible to do this to some extent on other instruments — for instance the fingerboard of the guitar — it can be done most easily on the piano keyboard. Future chapters will refer to the keyboard frequently in order to clarify particular points. This chapter will introduce the keyboard; explore the concepts of half steps and whole steps, accidentals, and enharmonic pitches; and provide a number of exercises to help you become familiar with the keyboard.

The piano keyboard has eighty-eight keys: fifty-two white keys and thirty-six black keys. Although synthesizers and electronic keyboards generally have fewer keys, commonly five and one-half octaves as opposed to slightly more than eight octaves for the piano, the following information still applies. The black keys are arranged in alternating groups of twos and threes. Moving from right to left on the keyboard produces successively lower pitches; moving from left to right, successively higher pitches.

The White Keys

As explained in Chapter 2, only the first seven letters of the alphabet are used to name pitches. These seven letters name the white keys of the piano, beginning at the left end of the keyboard with A and successively repeating the sequence A through G up to the other end of the keyboard. In the following illustration, the white keys are labeled according to the octave identification system introduced in Chapter 2.

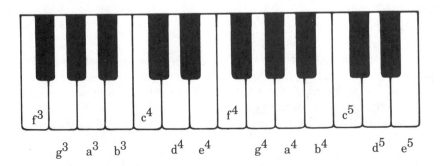

For someone just beginning to learn the keyboard, the task can be made easier by locating two landmarks. The first is the note C. In the following illustration, you will observe that the note C always occurs immediately to the left of a group of two black keys. The pitch called *middle C* (c^4) is approximately in the middle of the keyboard.

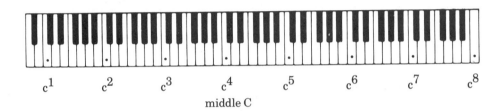

c^1 c^2 c^3 c^4 c^5 c^6 c^7 c^8

middle C

The second landmark to locate is F. This is the pitch that occurs immediately to the left of a group of three black keys.

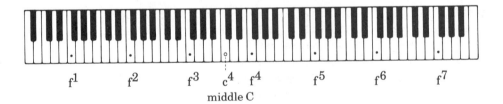

f^1 f^2 f^3 c^4 f^4 f^5 f^6 f^7

middle C

With these two landmarks you should be able to learn the rest of the keyboard more easily. Remember, too, that only the letters A through G are used, and that the alphabetical sequence runs from left to right.

You may find it helpful to memorize additional orientation keys such as G or B. Whatever means you choose to learn the keyboard, be careful not to rely too heavily on landmarks at the expense of learning all of the keys equally well. Landmarks are a convenient aid at the beginning, but you do not know the keyboard thoroughly until you can name *any* key at random.

EXERCISE 3·1

Locate the specified pitches on the following keyboards, and write each pitch on the keyboard in the correct place, using middle C (c^4) as a landmark. Then practice finding and playing the pitches on the piano.

1. f^4, c^5, f^4, d^4

2. g^4, g^3, d^5, e^4

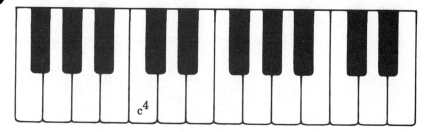

3. a^3, e^5, a^4, b^3

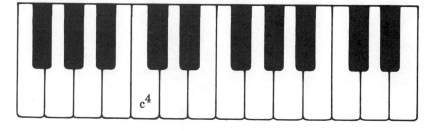

MUSICAL PROBLEM

The following pitch sequences begin well-known songs. Find and play these sequences on the piano. Write the name of the song if you recognize it.

1. c^5 a^4 f^4 a^4 c^5 f^5 a^5 g^5 f^5 a^4 b^4 c^5

   Name _____

2. g^3 g^3 c^4 d^4 e^4 c^4 b^3 a^3 f^4 f^4 f^4

   Name _____

3. c^4 g^3 c^4 g^3 c^4 d^4 e^4 c^4 f^4 f^4 c^4 d^4 e^4

   Name _____

4. c^3 e^3 g^3 e^3 g^3 a^3 g^3 e^3 g^3 a^3 g^3 e^3 g^3 g^3 e^3 f^3 e^3 d^3 c^3 d^3 e^3 d^3 c^3

   Name _____

When you have completed this problem, practice singing the four song fragments using letter names.

EXERCISE 3·2

Identify by letter name and octave designation the pitches given below. Then locate the pitches on the keyboard. Write each pitch in the correct place on the keyboard that follows. Find and play each of the pitches at the piano.

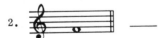

9. 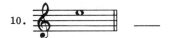 ____

10.  ____

11. 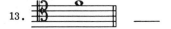 ____

12.  ____

13.  ____

14.  ____

MUSICAL PROBLEM

The following pitch sequences are the opening notes of four well-known songs. Find and play these pitches at the piano, and name each song if you can. When you have completed your work at the piano, practice singing each song fragment with letter names.

Name _____.

Name _____.

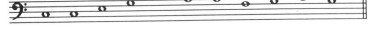

Name _____

Name _____

The Black Keys

The black keys of the piano are named in relation to the white keys that they stand between. Furthermore, each black key can be identified by two different names. For instance, the black key between F and G is called either *F sharp* (F♯) or *G flat* (G♭). F sharp identifies that black key as the pitch *above F*, while G flat tells us it's the pitch *below G*.

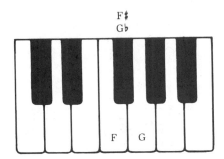

The other black keys are named in a similar way:

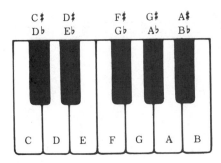

Enharmonic Pitches

The fact that F sharp and G flat, or C sharp and D flat, are the same note on the keyboard may be momentarily confusing. When two different letter names identify the same pitch on the piano, we refer to them as **enharmonic pitches**. The term means that the two pitches, while written differently, actually sound the same tone. At this point, the best way of dealing with enharmonic pitches is to remember that sharps are above the pitches they relate to, while flats are below. The reason for this duality in labeling will become clear when we discuss scales in a later chapter.

Every pitch can be raised (sharped) or lowered (flatted). Since there is no black key between E and F or B and C, however, it is necessary to have white key enharmonic sharps and flats. We identify the pitch *E sharp* as the key directly above E, which is white and also called *F*. In the same way, *C flat* is the key directly below C, which is white and also called *B*.

EXERCISE 3·3

Locate the specified pitches on the following keyboards, and write each pitch in the correct place. If the pitch is a white key, write directly on the keyboard. If it is a black key, use the answer line given above the keyboard. Then practice finding and playing each of the pitches at the piano.

1. F sharp
   D flat
   A sharp
   E flat
   F flat

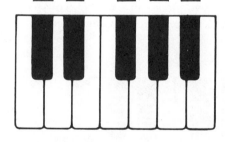

2. G flat
   B flat
   A flat
   C sharp

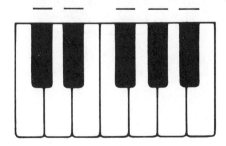

3. G sharp
    D sharp
    F sharp
    A sharp
    E sharp

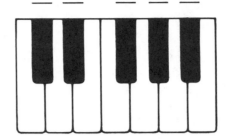

Intervals

The musical distance between two pitches, whether sounded or written on the staff, is called an **interval**.

Half Steps

The smallest interval on the piano is a **half step**. This is the distance from any key to the key immediately above or below it. The following example shows the three situations in which half steps can occur: (1) between a white key and a black key, (2) between a black key and a white key, and (3) between a white key and a white key. Notice that the third possibility, between a white key and a white key, appears in only two places in each octave — between E and F and between B and C. As you look at this example, remember than an interval is the distance *between* two notes.

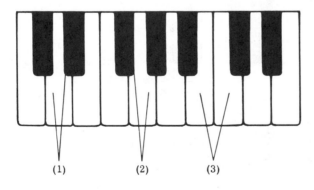

(1)   (2)   (3)

Half steps are either diatonic or chromatic. A **diatonic half step** consists of two pitches with *adjacent* letter names and staff locations. The following are all examples of diatonic half steps:

F♯ - G   B - C   D♭ - C   F - E

A **chromatic half step** employs two pitches of the *same* letter name and staff location, such as the following:

F - F♯   B - B♭   G - G♯   C - C♭

The significance of this distinction will become clear in later chapters, when we discuss major and minor scales and modes.

Whole Steps

A **whole step** consists of two half steps. On the keyboard, there will be one key between the two pitches that are a whole step apart. Whole steps can appear (1) between a white key and a white key, (2) between a black key and a black key, and (3) between a white key and a black key. In each instance, the whole step has one pitch in between.

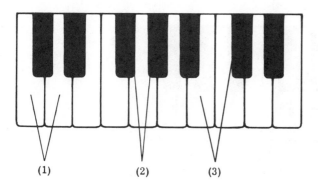

(1)   (2)   (3)

Whole steps *usually* involve pitches of adjacent letter names, as in the following cases:

F – G   B♭ – C   A♭ – G♭   F♯ – E

EXERCISE 3·4

On the following keyboards, identify each indicated interval as either a whole step or a half step. Use the letters *W* or *H* to indicate the interval and write them in the space provided.

1.

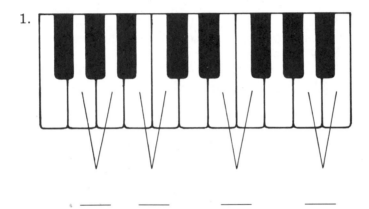

_____ _____   _____ _____

2.

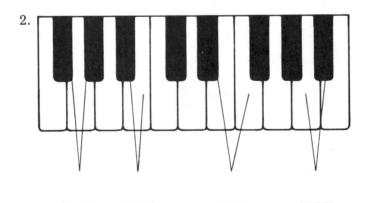

_____ _____   _____ _____

3.

_____   _____   _____   _____

MUSICAL PROBLEM

At the keyboard, play the indicated intervals. Then practice playing the given pitch and singing the other pitch.

1. d^4 to a half step above
2. a^3 to a whole step below
3. b^5 to a whole step above
4. f^4 to a whole step above
5. b^3 to a half step below
6. c^5 to a half step above
7. e^2 to a whole step below
8. g^4 to a half step above
9. f^3 to a half step below
10. c^4 to a whole step below

Accidentals

In written music, the following signs, called **accidentals**, are used to alter the pitch of a note chromatically:

♯	**sharp**	raises pitch by a half step
♭	**flat**	lowers pitch by a half step
×	**double sharp**	raises pitch by two half steps (one whole step)
♭♭	**double flat**	lowers pitch by two half steps (one whole step)
♮	**natural**	cancels a sharp, double sharp, flat, or double flat

When pitches are written as words, the accidentals follow the note (as when spoken); for example, C♯ is read C sharp. When pitches are notated on a staff, however, all accidentals are placed to the left of the pitches they affect and on the same line or space as the note.

Right   Wrong

When writing an accidental before a note on the staff it is important to remember that the placement of that accidental must be exact. If the note is centered on a space, then the accidental before it must also be centered in the *same* space. The same is true for a note located on a line — the accidental before it must be centered on the *same* line. This precision in placement is necessary because musicians read the note and the accidental as a single unit. If you are careless and place the accidental in the wrong place, you will be sending contradictory information to the performer.

Double sharps and double flats can be confusing and require some explanation at this point. As you know, the sharp sign raises a pitch by a half step. In most instances, this means that a pitch will be raised from a white key to a black key — for example, F to F♯, C to C♯. Since a double sharp raises a pitch *two* half steps, or one whole step, this means that quite often the resulting pitch is a white key. Thus, F to F× appears on the keyboard as F to G. In the same way, E to E♭♭ appears on the keyboard as E to D. (Remember, F× and G are enharmonic; so are E♭♭ and D.)

You may be wondering why we can't simply ignore double sharps and double flats. In fact, these signs seldom appear in music, but when they do they have a specific function, which we shall discuss in Chapter 8. For now, pay special attention to the double sharps and double flats in the following exercise.

EXERCISE 3·5

Locate the indicated pitches on the following keyboards by drawing a line from the written pitch to the key it represents. Then, play each of the pitches on the piano.

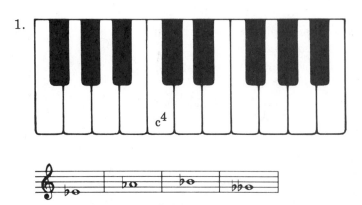

2.

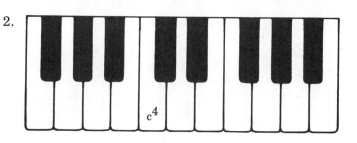

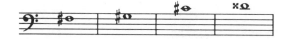

89

Accidentals

3.

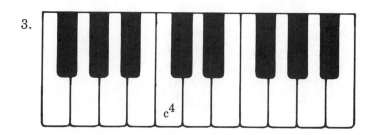

4.

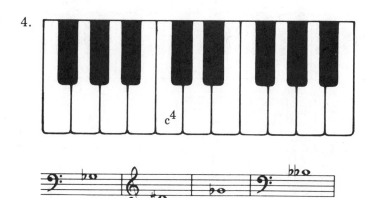

5.

c^4

EXERCISE 3·6

Locate all the Cs on the keyboard by labeling the brackets and using the octave identification system introduced in Chapter 2. Then identify by letter name and octave designation the pitches indicated on the keyboard. For the black keys, give both enharmonic possibilities.

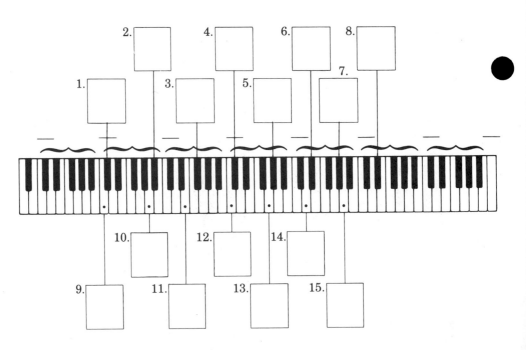

EXERCISE 3·7

Locate all the Cs on each keyboard by labeling the brackets and using the octave identification system. Then locate on the keyboards the pitches given in the great staves by placing the number of each pitch in the correct box.

1.

2.

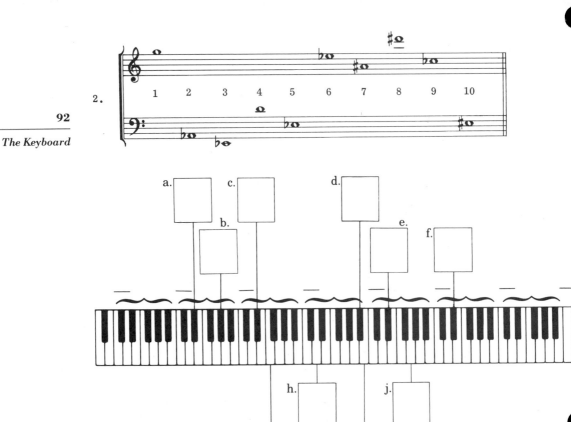

Focus

The piano keyboard is extremely useful in helping us visualize abstract musical concepts. It is also important for many other purposes, such as understanding music theory, learning voicing for arranging, and composing. Many musicians study piano as a second instrument because of its versatility; for all musicians, it is valuable as a learning tool. If you do not play piano, you should spend some time each day becoming familiar with the keyboard. The exercises in this book are useful for this purpose, as are simple song books and beginning sight-singing books. A good place to begin is Appendix D, "Melodies for Sight-Singing and Playing." Remember, becoming musical requires your participation. Remember, too, that being able to *hear* what you play *before you play it* is one sign of a good musician. Your skill at sight-singing will improve if you do it for a few minutes each time you sit down to practice piano. Try singing each exercise before you play it.

$\mathbf{A}$s you probably have discovered by now, musical knowledge is cumulative, requiring comprehension of previous information in order to grasp new concepts. For this reason it is important to check whether you fully understand the material covered so far. The following questions refer to information from the first three chapters. If you discover weaknesses in any of these basic areas, you should review the relevant sections before beginning Chapter 4.

1. Mentally identify (a) the meter and (b) the note value that represents the pulse. Then mark off measures by placing bar lines in the appropriate places in each example.

2. Rewrite the following rhythmic patterns by beaming the eighth notes and sixteenth notes.

3. Identify the following pitches by letter name and correct octave designation.

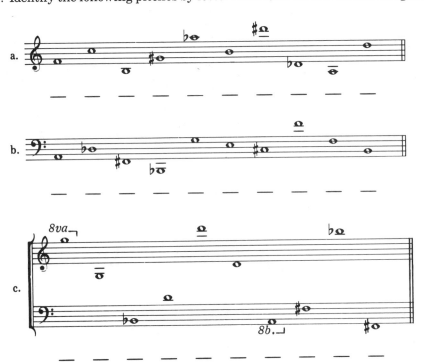

4. Write the indicated pitches in the correct octave.

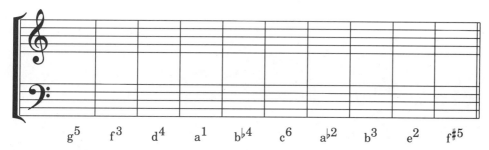

g^5 $\quad$ f^3 $\quad$ d^4 $\quad$ a^1 $\quad$ $b^\flat 4$ $\quad$ c^6 $\quad$ $a^\flat 2$ $\quad$ b^3 $\quad$ e^2 $\quad$ $f^{\sharp}5$

5. Locate the following pitches on the keyboards by writing each pitch in the correct place.

a.

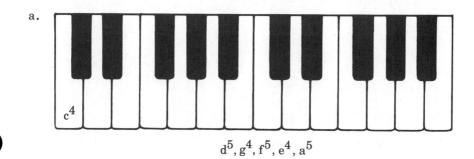

c^4

d^5, g^4, f^5, e^4, a^5

b.

c^4

g^2, e^3, c^2, d^3, f^3

Chapter 4

Major Scales

All of the world's music is built on some kind of musical scale. The **scale** is the foundation of music, much as the skeleton is the foundation of the body. Music of other cultures often sounds strange to us largely because we are unfamiliar with the scales upon which it is built. There are a multitude of different scales in use throughout the world. Some of them use intervals smaller than the half step. But the music with which we are most familiar is based almost entirely on two scale forms built on whole steps and half steps—the **major scale** and the **minor scale**. Music based on these scales is called **tonal music** and includes such widely divergent styles as the music of Bach, Beethoven, Wagner, Louis Armstrong, Charlie Parker, U2, and Madonna. It would be a great mistake, however, to assume that scales other than major and minor are unimportant. As you will see in Chapter 9, other scale forms have repeatedly appeared within the Western tradition of tonality.

Scales as Interval Patterns

Western music divides the octave into twelve equal half steps. A scale formed by dividing an octave in this way is called a **chromatic scale**.

Ascending chromatic scale (usually written with sharps):

Descending chromatic scale (usually written with flats):

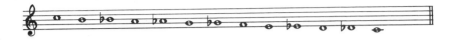

Because the chromatic scale consists entirely of half steps, it seldom functions in itself as a musical scale. Rather, it is the source material from which a huge variety of other scales can be drawn. Many scales combine whole steps and half steps, and some scales use one or more intervals larger than the whole step. This variation in interval size gives each scale, and the resultant music in that scale, a particular color, quality, or ambience. The unique interval patterns of a scale are transferred to the melody and the harmony of music written in that scale. The major scale and the natural minor scale (which will be more fully discussed later) are both seven-note scales having five whole steps and two half steps, yet they sound strikingly unlike each other because the pattern of whole steps and half steps is different. The concept of a scale as an interval pattern that controls the interval patterns of melody and harmony is fundamental to the understanding of tonal music.

EXERCISE 4·1

Write one-octave chromatic scales beginning on the pitches indicated. Remember to use sharps for the ascending scale and flats for the descending scale. Remember also to keep the notated pitch sequences B–C and E–F intact, since the interval between them is already a half step.

Ascending Scales

1. f^4

2. a^2

Descending Scales

3. d^5

4. $a^{\flat 3}$

Elements of the Major Scale

The major scale is an interval pattern of five whole steps and two diatonic half steps. The half steps always occur between the third and fourth tones and the seventh and first tones of the scale. On the keyboard, the major scale falls on all white keys when it begins on the pitch C.

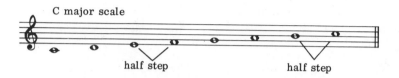

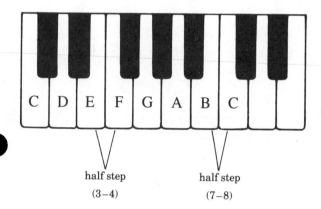

This pattern of whole steps and half steps gives the major scale its characteristic quality. The half step between the seventh and first tones creates a strong pull toward the first tone. This first tone is called a **tonic**. The tonic, sometimes also called the home note, is the pitch to which the other tones of the scale seem to be related. As you sing or play a major scale, notice how the tonic becomes the focus for a group of seemingly related pitches, similar to a center of gravity.

MUSICAL PROBLEM

Sing the following melodies and identify the tonic of each by sound. Observe how often and in which places the tonic occurs. Are these places restful or musically active? After you have sung the melody and located the tonic, sing a major scale beginning on the tonic of that melody. Do you notice a relationship between the scale and the melody?

1. "Camptown Races"
2. "Happy Birthday"
3. "Twinkle, Twinkle"

4. "Silent Night"

5. "Auld Lang Syne"

The pattern of whole steps and half steps that produces a major scale can be moved to any other beginning pitch and, if kept intact, will form a different major scale. In all, there are fifteen different major scales — seven that use flatted notes, seven that use sharped notes, and one natural scale. In the G major scale, for instance, an F♯ is needed to produce the whole step between the sixth and seventh degrees and the half step between the seventh and first degrees:

Similarly, the major scale beginning on A requires three sharps (F♯, C♯, G♯) to produce the correct pattern:

In the following example, five flats are required to produce the correct pattern of whole steps and half steps.

As you practice writing scales, remember that as long as you reproduce the pattern of whole steps and half steps exactly, the result will be a major scale, regardless of the pitch you begin on. Remember, also, that major scales are alphabetical sequences of pitches. All major and minor scales use only diatonic, not chromatic, half steps.

EXERCISE 4•2

Write ascending and descending major scales, in both treble clef and bass clef, from each starting pitch. When writing major scales, there should be only one pitch of each letter name. For example, it is incorrect to have both G♭ and G♮ in the same scale. The correct sequence is F♯–G. (The sequence of scales in this

EXAMPLE:　A　B　C♯　D　E　F♯　G♯　A

1.　A♭ ___ ___ ___ ___ ___ ___ ___

2.　C ___ ___ ___ ___ ___ ___ ___

3.　E♭ ___ ___ ___ ___ ___ ___ ___

4.　D ___ ___ ___ ___ ___ ___ ___

5.　F ___ ___ ___ ___ ___ ___ ___

6.　C♯ ___ ___ ___ ___ ___ ___ ___

7.　B ___ ___ ___ ___ ___ ___ ___

8.　C♭ ___ ___ ___ ___ ___ ___ ___

9.　B♭ ___ ___ ___ ___ ___ ___ ___

10.　G ___ ___ ___ ___ ___ ___ ___

11.　D♭ ___ ___ ___ ___ ___ ___ ___

12.　G♭ ___ ___ ___ ___ ___ ___ ___

13.　F♯ ___ ___ ___ ___ ___ ___ ___

14.　E ___ ___ ___ ___ ___ ___ ___

MUSICAL PROBLEM

Sing each of the following melodies, using a neutral syllable like *la*, the letter names of the pitches, or the scale-degree numbers. Locate the tonic by sound. Then write the sight-singing syllables below each note. Finally, notate the major scale on which each melody is built.

"Michael, Row the Boat Ashore"

do　mi　sol

Scale

"Barbara Allen"

2.

Scale

"Sur le Pont d'Avignon"

3.

Scale

4.

Scale

Naming Scale Degrees

Each scale degree has a specific name. The scale degrees, in ascending order, are: **tonic, supertonic, mediant, subdominant, dominant, submediant, leading tone**, and **tonic**. These scale-degree names always remain the same regardless of the octave in which the pitch of that name appears.

C major scale

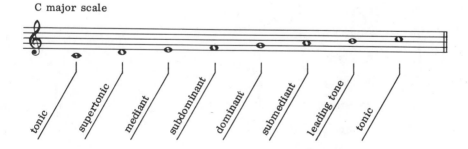

At first, these names might appear arbitrary. If, however, you consider the tonic as the tonal center of gravity, then the names logically describe the relationship between the scale degrees. Notice how the tonic becomes the central pitch when the scale degrees are arranged in the following way:

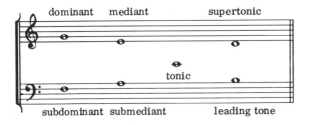

EXERCISE 4·7

Name the following scale degrees.

1. third degree _____   5. seventh degree _____

2. fifth degree _____   6. second degree _____

3. sixth degree _____   7. fourth degree _____

4. first degree _____

It may seem momentarily confusing to you that the individual pitches of a scale may be referred to in more than one way. Perhaps the following chart will be helpful in clearing up the confusion. The pitch names on the far left are an ascending C major scale; the terms to the right indicate three different ways each particular scale degree can be referred to or labeled. Although the third option (numbers) has not been previously discussed in this book (the concept is easily understood), it is used frequently in written analytical discussions of music, and all musicians should become familiar with it.

C	do	tonic	$\hat{1}$
D	re	supertonic	$\hat{2}$
E	mi	mediant	$\hat{3}$
F	fa	subdominant	$\hat{4}$
G	sol	dominant	$\hat{5}$
A	la	submediant	$\hat{6}$
B	ti	leading tone	$\hat{7}$

EXERCISE 4·8

Identify by letter name the following scale degrees.

1. mediant of the F major scale _____

2. supertonic of the D major scale _____

3. subdominant of the B♭ major scale _____

4. leading tone of the G major scale _____

5. mediant of the D♭ major scale _____

6. subdominant of the A♭ major scale _____

7. mediant of the C major scale _____

8. submediant of the D major scale _____

9. supertonic of the F major scale _____

10. subdominant of the C♯ major scale _____

11. mediant of the B major scale _____

12. submediant of the C♭ major scale _____

13. supertonic of the G♭ major scale _____

14. dominant of the E major scale _____

15. submediant of the F♯ major scale _____

16. subdominant of the D major scale _____

17. leading tone of the E♭ major scale _____

18. mediant of the A♭ major scale _____

19. leading tone of the F major scale _____

20. subdominant of the B major scale _____

21. supertonic of the C♭ major scale _____

22. dominant of the B♭ major scale _____

23. supertonic of the G major scale _____

24. submediant of the E major scale _____

25. submediant of the F major scale _____

MUSICAL PROBLEM

Instrumentalists should be able to play one- and two-octave major scales, both ascending and descending. If you cannot do this, you should begin at once to develop this facility. Improving your ability to play scales will be of immediate benefit, since many of the patterns of tonal music are directly related to the scales on which they are based. To begin, practice the easier scales slowly and evenly, concentrating on accuracy and quality of tone. After you have mastered these, move on to more difficult scales.

EXERCISE 4·9

Complete the following:

1. F♯ is the mediant of the _____ major scale.

2. C is the submediant of the _____ major scale.

3. E♭ is the subdominant of the _____ major scale.

4. D is the mediant of the _____ major scale.

5. A is the leading tone of the _____ major scale.

6. B♭ is the subdominant of the _____ major scale.

7. F♯ is the dominant of the _____ major scale.

8. E is the subdominant of the _____ major scale.

9. G is the mediant of the _____ major scale.

10. D is the submediant of the _____ major scale.

11. C is the leading tone of the _____ major scale.

12. F is the dominant of the _____ major scale.

13. A♭ is the subdominant of the _____ major scale.

14. C♯ is the mediant of the _____ major scale.

15. E is the supertonic of the _____ major scale.

MUSICAL PROBLEM

Sing in your mind each of the following melodies. Put a check mark by the ones that are based on a major scale.

1. "America" _____

2. "Erie Canal" _____

3. "Amazing Grace" _____

4. "Down in the Valley" _____

5. "Greensleeves" _____

6. "Silent Night" _____

7. "Scarborough Fair" _____

8. "Joshua Fit the Battle of Jericho" _____

Ear Training

All musicians need to *hear* music as completely as they can. This involves listening not to the emotional content but to the actual mechanics of the music. Identifying the instruments that are playing, distinguishing the number of lines or voices in a work, and accurately notating rhythms that you hear are all part of developing your ear. But most people, when they think of training themselves to hear better, think first of pitch and pitch discrimination.

Some people have excellent ears. That is, they have an astonishing ability to make extremely fine aural discriminations. Some people can even name pitches as they hear them played or sung. This ability is called **perfect pitch**, and the people who have it were born with it. Although there are degrees of ability within perfect pitch — some people can name all the pitches in a cluster of notes played on the piano, others can only name the notes when played individually — this ability cannot be learned.

A similar ability can, however, be developed with practice. This ability is called **relative pitch**. Relative pitch involves learning the sounds of the various intervals and applying this knowledge when listening and performing. People with highly developed relative pitch can also name notes that they hear, if they are given a beginning pitch. If you improvise or play jazz, rock, or pop music by ear, you may already have good relative pitch. But it can be even better with practice. If you want to play by ear, or write music, or just better understand the music you like to listen to, remember that these abilities can be developed and expanded with practice.

Ear training is the term musicians give to the process of developing their ability to hear better. We have already done some of this in the Musical Problems of this book, and we will do more from time to time. If this is a skill that you feel you need to develop, keep in mind that progress may be slow at first, and success may, as with most skills, seem to come in plateaus. Keep in mind too that everyone begins at a different level of ability. You should not be discouraged by other people's abilities. If you work consistently, you will see your abilities grow and develop.

MUSICAL PROBLEM

Your teacher or another member of the class will play a major scale. Then he or she will play one pitch that will be either the tonic or the dominant from that scale. In the spaces below, indicate which pitch is being played.

1. _____   5. _____
2. _____   6. _____
3. _____   7. _____
4. _____   8. _____

Now try the same thing using three pitches—tonic, dominant, and submediant.

1. _____   5. _____
2. _____   6. _____
3. _____   7. _____
4. _____   8. _____

Finally, see if you can identify one of four different pitches—tonic, dominant, submediant, or subdominant.

1. _____   5. _____
2. _____   6. _____
3. _____   7. _____
4. _____   8. _____

Focus

The major scale is known to all of us. Most people over the age of ten can sing a major scale, complete with the correct syllables. In fact, this very familiarity may be a problem for beginning music students. We tend to think of the major scale as quite simple—a stepping-stone to more interesting musical matters. Yes, we have learned the sound of the major scale, but not necessarily its function or structure.

You should not allow yourself to become complacent about scales, however. A thorough knowledge of scales is basic to understanding and performing music. The major scale seems familiar because so many of the melodies and so much of the harmony you have heard throughout your life are based on it. To deal *theoretically* with music based on major scales, you must both understand the major scale as an interval pattern and acquire skill and facility in writing, playing, and singing this common pattern.

Chapter 5

Major Key Signatures

The Key Signature

In the previous chapter, you were asked to use individual accidentals when writing scales. This practice is useful in learning scale construction, but it makes performing, particularly sight-reading, extremely complicated. Consider the difficulty reading a piece of music in a key in which every pitch has a sharp sign, as in the following example.

Bach: "Preludio III" from *Well-Tempered Clavier*, Book I
(key of C♯ major written without key signature)

Since every scale has the same consistent interval structure, a musical short-hand has been developed to indicate, just once for an entire composition, the pitches requiring accidentals. It is called the **key signature**. The key signature is a grouping, at the beginning of each staff, of all the accidentals found in the scale on which the piece is based. The following illustration shows how a key signature would be used with the previous example.

Bach: "Preludio III" from *Well-Tempered Clavier*, Book I
(with key signature)

An important point to remember is that an accidental appearing in the key signature applies to that note in all octaves. For instance, an F♯ in the key signature indicates that all Fs encountered in the piece are to be played or sung as F♯s. A similar rule holds for chromatic alterations *within* a measure. That is, once an accidental is introduced in a measure, it remains in force for the entire measure unless canceled by a natural sign.

Sharp Keys

The number and placement of sharps and flats in a key signature is not arbitrary; there is a definite order, an order that makes key signatures easy to read and remember. The following shows the order for the sharp major keys. Study it carefully and learn it.

Key Signatures: Sharp Major Keys

Notice the invariable pattern for sharp key signatures: If there is only one sharp, that sharp is always F♯; if two sharps, they are always F♯ and C♯, and so on. The complete order of sharps is F♯–C♯–G♯–D♯–A♯–E♯–B♯. You should learn both the order and the location of the sharps in both the treble and bass clefs.

EXERCISE 5•1

On the staves below, copy the pattern of sharps for the sharp major keys. Make sure that the sharps are clearly centered either on a line or in a space.

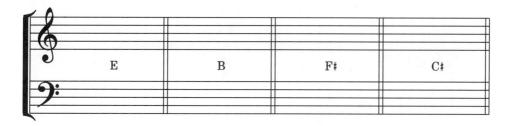

In identifying major key signatures that use sharps, the key is always the pitch a half step above the last sharp indicated in the signature. This is because the last added sharp is always the *leading tone* of that key.

This method of identifying sharp keys is useful, but you should also memorize the number of sharps associated with each major key — information that is given in the following chart. Study the chart carefully until you can identify the sharp key signatures using either method.

Major Key	Number of Sharps
C	0
G	1
D	2
A	3
E	4
B	5
F♯	6
C♯	7

EXERCISE 5·2

Identify the major key represented by each of the following sharp key signatures. Begin by drawing a circle around the sharp that represents the leading tone of that key.

1.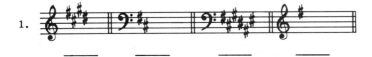

—— —— —— ——

2.

—— —— —— ——

3.

—— —— —— ——

4.

—— —— —— ——

Flat Keys

The order of flats in major key signatures is as follows:

Key Signatures: Flat Major Keys

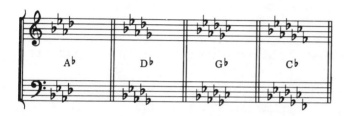

Flat key signatures, like sharp key signatures, have a consistent order and location on the staff. Notice that the last added flat is always the subdominant of that key. The complete order of flats is B♭–E♭–A♭–D♭–G♭–C♭–F♭. Both the order and the location of the flats should be learned for both the treble and bass clefs.

EXERCISE 5·3

On the staves provided, copy the pattern of flats for the flat major keys. Make certain that the flats are clearly centered on a line or in a space.

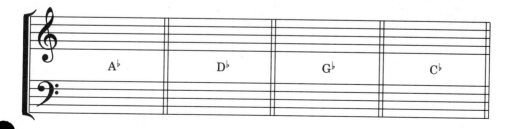

The name of the key is the same as the next to last flat. (Obviously, this does not apply to the key of F major, since F major has only one flat.) As with sharp key signatures, this method of identification should merely supplement the information contained in the following chart.

Major Key	*Number of Flats*
C	0
F	1
B♭	2
E♭	3
A♭	4
D♭	5
G♭	6
C♭	7

EXERCISE 5·4

Identify the major key represented by each of the following flat key signatures.

EXERCISE 5·5

Write out the indicated major key signatures, using either sharps or flats as required. A helpful mnemonic device for keeping all the sharps and flats in order in your mind is to remember that the order of flats — B–E–A–D–G–C–F — is the reverse of the order of sharps — F–C–G–D–A–E–B.

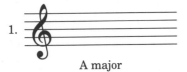

A major

E major

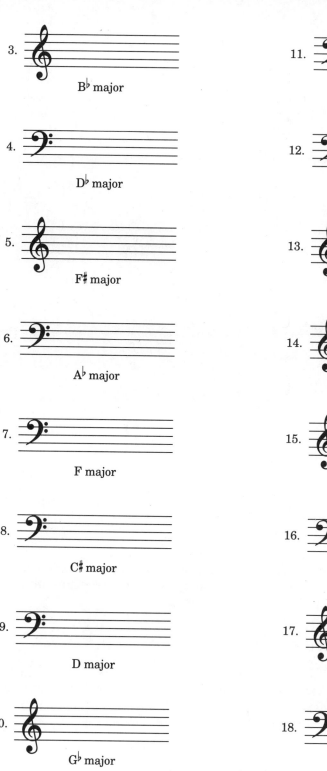

3. B♭ major

4. D♭ major

5. F♯ major

6. A♭ major

7. F major

8. C♯ major

9. D major

10. G♭ major

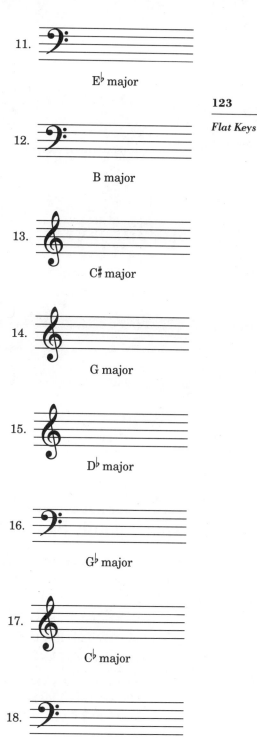

11. E♭ major

12. B major

13. C♯ major

14. G major

15. D♭ major

16. G♭ major

17. C♭ major

18. G major

19. A♭ major

20. B♭ major

21. A major

22. D major

23. F♯ major

24. C♭ major

25. B major

26. E♭ major

27. F major

28. E major

Enharmonic Keys

You may have observed that three of the sharp major scales (B, F♯, and C♯) are enharmonic with three of the flat major scales (C♭, G♭, and D♭). Thus, although they are written differently, they sound the same.

   B (5 ♯s) sounds like C♭ (7 ♭s)

   F♯ (6 ♯s) sounds like G♭ (6 ♭s)

   C♯ (7 ♯s) sounds like D♭ (5 ♭s)

In actual practice, the key of B major is found more frequently than the key of C♭ major; the keys of F♯ major and G♭ major occur with about equal frequency; and the key of D♭ major appears more often than does the key of C♯ major.

The Circle of Fifths: Major Keys

The interval of the perfect fifth turns out to be useful in understanding a special relationship among major key signatures. If the major key signatures are arranged in order of increasing number of sharps, they progress, one to the next, by a perfect fifth. Thus, C major has no sharps (or flats), G major (a perfect fifth higher) has one sharp, D major (a perfect fifth above G) has two sharps, and so on. In the flat keys, the progression by perfect fifths works in reverse order, by the number of flats. (The circle of fifths for minor keys is discussed in Chapter 7.)

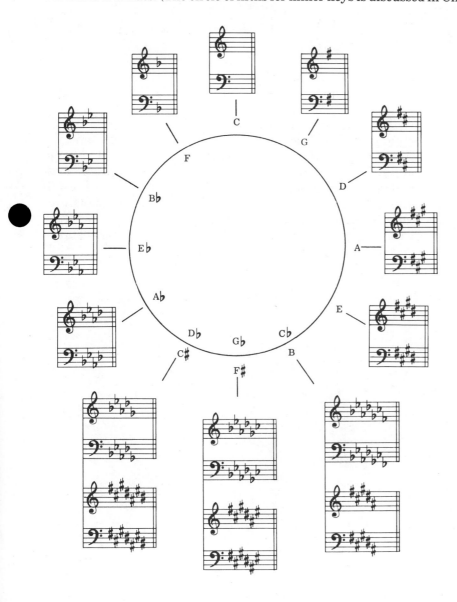

EXERCISE 5·6

Identify the correct major key, based on the number of sharps or flats indicated.

1. three sharps _____   8. two flats _____

2. six sharps _____   9. seven flats _____

3. one sharp _____   10. one flat _____

4. four sharps _____   11. five sharps _____

5. three flats _____   12. five flats _____

6. six flats _____   13. four flats _____

7. two sharps _____   14. seven sharps _____

Focus

If you play an instrument, you have undoubtedly had the experience of playing a wrong note when you momentarily forgot the key signature. At such a time, you might have felt that key signatures are a nuisance, that music would be easier to play without them. But this is *not* the case, for without key signatures most music would be sprinkled with an incredible number of accidentals. The resulting clutter would make music more difficult to read and perform. Key signatures are often perplexing at the beginning, but they are quickly mastered with the necessary drill. Once you are comfortable with the shorthand of key signatures, it will be impossible to imagine written tonal music without them.

Chapter 6

Intervals

Why is the study and understanding of intervals so necessary to an understanding of tonal music? Perhaps you or someone you know once studied piano. If so, the chances are excellent that you or they had to spend time playing scales. Too often, beginning piano students play such scale exercises mechanically, without any appreciation of their usefulness. Scale practice isn't something piano teachers inflict on their students solely to develop technique. Scales contain the patterns on which tonal music is built. By practicing these patterns in the form of scales, the performer becomes musically acquainted with material that will appear repeatedly in the music itself.

But what, exactly, are these patterns contained in scales? They are *interval patterns*. The interval patterns of scales become the interval patterns of melody and harmony. What we hear and define as music is, in actuality, combinations of interval patterns. The interval, therefore, is another basic unit of tonal music. In this chapter, we will learn a system of interval recognition and identification that will be useful in future chapters concerned with triads and harmony.

Interval Identification

As we learned in Chapter 3, an interval is the musical distance between two pitches. If these two pitches are sounded simultaneously, the interval is called a **harmonic interval**. If the two pitches are sounded in succession, like two tones of a melody, the interval is called a **melodic interval**. In either case, it is the distance between the two pitches that is identified and measured. Two elements are considered in identifying intervals: arithmetic distance and quality.

Arithmetic Distance

The first step in identifying an interval is to determine the **arithmetic distance** it covers. Sometimes this is referred to as "interval size." Determining arithmetic distance is done by counting the letter names of the two pitches whose interval we are trying to determine plus the letter names of all the pitch or pitches in between.

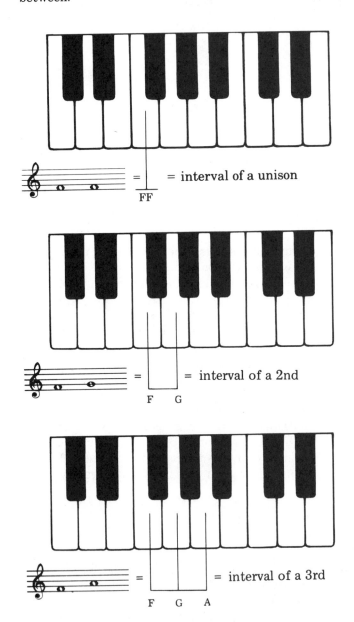

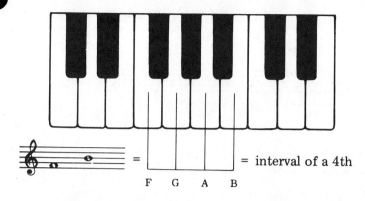

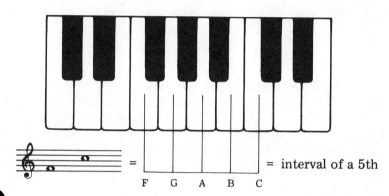 = interval of a 5th

As shown in the preceding illustration, each letter name is counted only once. Thus, in the second example, the enharmonic pitch between F and G (F♯ or G♭) was not counted in determining arithmetic distance. For this reason, it is easier to measure arithmetic distance on the staff than on the keyboard. Furthermore, the staff facilitates interval recognition because of the following rules concerning the position of intervals on the staff:

The notes of a *second* always appear on adjacent lines and spaces.

The notes of a *third* always appear on consecutive lines or spaces.

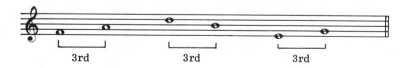

Fourths always have one pitch on a line and the other in a space, with a space and a line between.

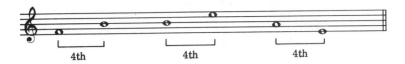

Fifths always have either (1) both pitches on lines, with one line between, or (2) both pitches in spaces, with one space between.

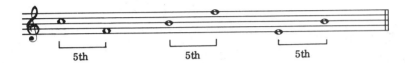

This pattern continues for sixths, sevenths, octaves (the term for the arithmetic distance of an eighth), and so on. As the pitches become farther apart, however, the pattern becomes increasingly difficult to recognize. Until you become familiar with the overall appearance of the wider intervals, it is probably wise to count the lines and spaces between the pitches of the interval.

EXERCISE 6·1

Identify the arithmetic distance of the following melodic intervals.

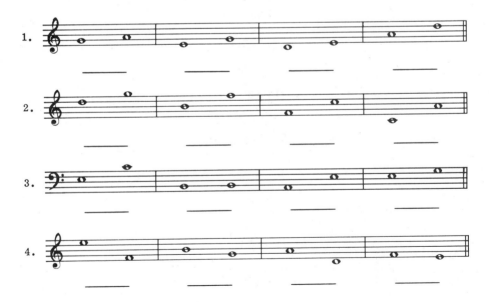

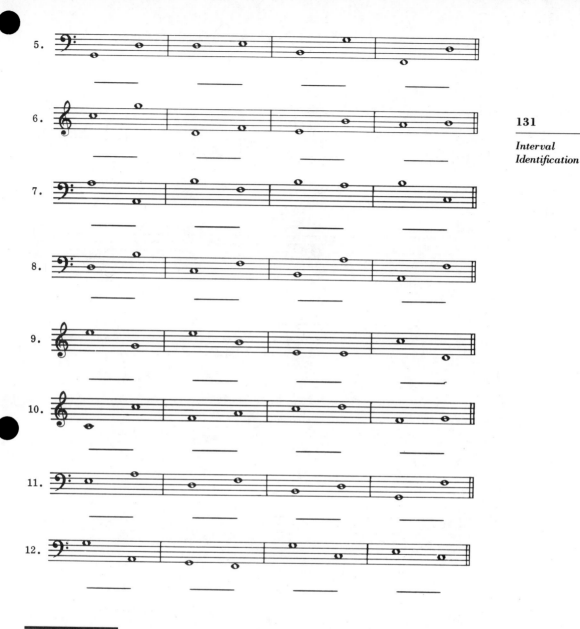

EXERCISE 6·2

Complete the following harmonic intervals by writing in the pitch that is the
correct arithmetic distance *above* the given pitch.

1.

      3rd   5th   2nd   7th

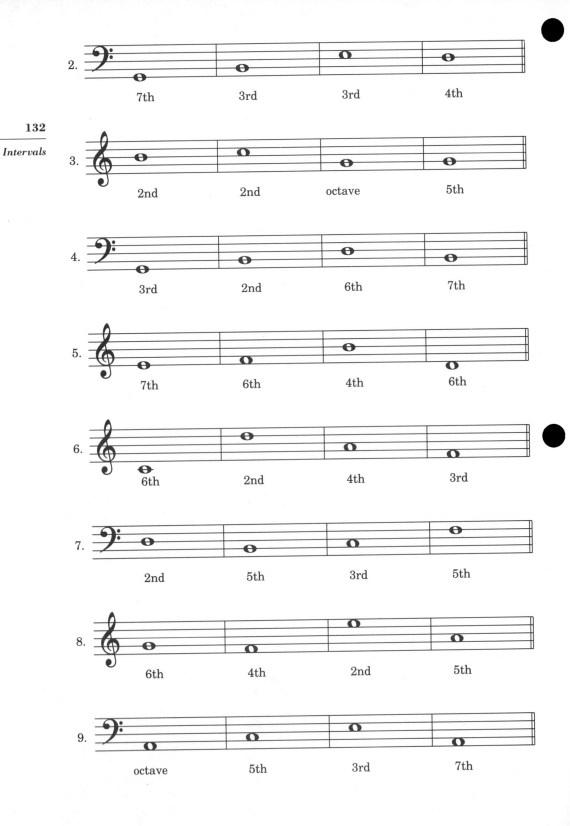

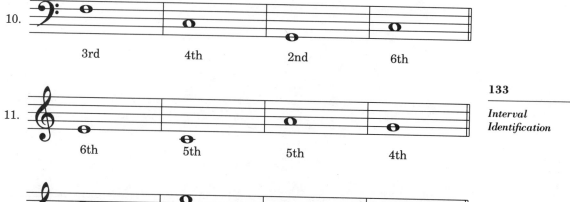

10.

3rd   4th   2nd   6th

11.

6th   5th   5th   4th

12.

4th   2nd   octave   2nd

EXERCISE 6·3

Complete the following harmonic intervals by writing in the pitch that is the correct arithmetic distance *below* the given pitch.

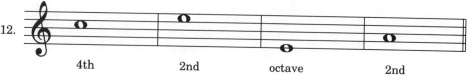

1.

5th   4th   5th   6th

2.

2nd   2nd   3rd   3rd

3.

6th   4th   6th   7th

4.

7th   2nd   4th   7th

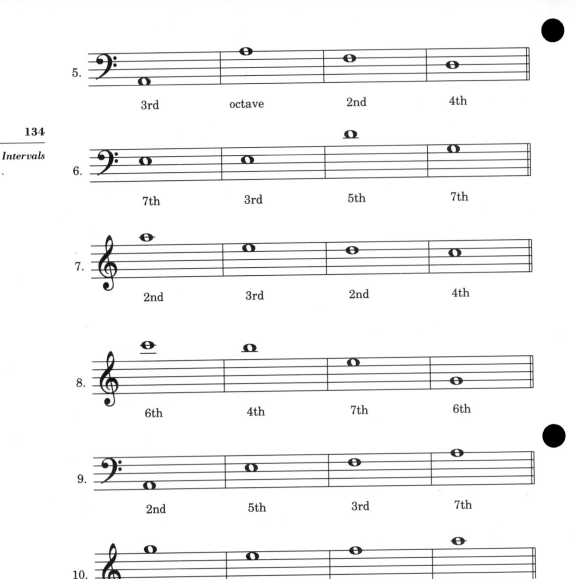

5. 3rd   octave   2nd   4th

6. 7th   3rd   5th   7th

7. 2nd   3rd   2nd   4th

8. 6th   4th   7th   6th

9. 2nd   5th   3rd   7th

10. 6th   2nd   6th   octave

EXERCISE 6·4

Identify the arithmetic distance between the pitches in each of the following sets. In the first three lines, consider the second pitch to be *above* the first pitch. In lines four, five, and six, consider the second pitch as *below* the first one.

1. E–F   D–A   G–B   F–E

    _____   _____   _____   _____

2. F–A   F–B   A–B   C–B

    _____   _____   _____   _____

3. G–E   B–E   D–F   A–D

    _____   _____   _____   _____

4. E–A   G–B   F–G   F–A

    _____   _____   _____   _____

5. G–C   G–F   A–D   A–F

    _____   _____   _____   _____

6. E–B   D–B   E–A   G–D

    _____   _____   _____   _____

Interval Quality

The second way to recognize an interval is to identify the sound *quality* or *color* of the interval, which is related to the number of half steps between the two pitches. In the following example, all four intervals are thirds. But play these combinations on the piano or sing them, and you will find that each has a distinctly different quality.

The following terms are used to describe the quality of intervals:

Interval	*Abbreviation*
Perfect	P
Major	M
Minor	m
Augmented	A or +
Diminished	d or °

Determining the quality of an interval may be done in two ways. One way is to learn the number of half steps in various kinds of intervals, and then to apply this information to new intervals. The other way is to remember the kinds of intervals that occur between the first note of a major scale and each of the other notes in the scale, and then to gauge new intervals against this information.

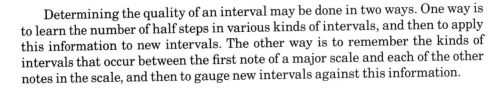

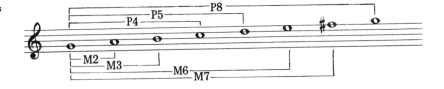

Although both ways of identifying intervals work well, the major-scale method of interval identification (when well learned) is probably the faster and more accurate. Counting half steps involves too much rote learning and is subject to error.

Perfect Intervals

Only four kinds of intervals are called *perfect intervals*: the unison, the fourth, the fifth, and the octave. They are labeled *perfect* because in Medieval and Renaissance music they were considered the only intervals suitable for momentary or permanent stopping places (called cadences) in a piece. The following illustration shows (1) the number of half steps in each type of perfect interval and (2) the standard way of identifying intervals, using letters for quality and numbers for arithmetic distance.

The arithmetic distance is still the total count of letter names included in the interval, while the quality is determined by counting half steps. For any particular interval, both the arithmetic distance and the quality must be correct. In the case of a perfect fifth, for example, the arithmetic distance must be a fifth, and the interval must contain exactly seven half steps.

In a major scale, the quality of the intervals between the tonic and the subdominant, dominant, or octave is always perfect.

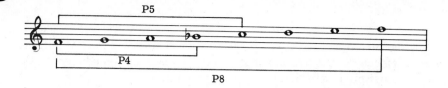

Therefore, you can quickly check the quality of any of these intervals by assuming that the lower pitch of the interval is the tonic, and asking yourself if the upper pitch is in the scale of the lower pitch. If it is, and if the arithmetic distance is a fourth, fifth, or octave, the interval is perfect in quality.

Consider the following example:

The arithmetic distance is a fourth. To determine the quality, we assume that the E♭ is the tonic of a major scale. Is A♭ in the E♭ major scale? Since the answer is yes, this is a perfect fourth. If the upper pitch were not in the scale, then the quality of the interval would be something other than perfect.

Perfect intervals can also be *augmented* or *diminished.* A perfect interval is made augmented by retaining the arithmetic distance while, at the same time, expanding the interval by a half step.

A perfect interval is made diminished by retaining the arithmetic distance and decreasing the interval by a half step.

Notice that although the augmented fourth and the diminished fifth both contain six half steps, one is identified as a fourth and the other as a fifth. This is because the arithmetic distance of the two is not the same.

EXERCISE 6·5

In the following harmonic intervals, circle the perfect unisons, fourths, fifths, and octaves. (Refer to the illustration on p. 136 if you need to.) Remember to ask yourself if the upper pitch is in the scale of the lower pitch.

10.

EXERCISE 6·6

Identify each of the following melodic intervals as either a unison, a fourth, a fifth, or an octave, and as either perfect (P), augmented (A), or diminished (d). A keyboard is provided to help you visualize the half steps. Remember that the major scale contains perfect fourths, fifths, and octaves, and that augmented intervals will be a half step larger than these, diminished intervals a half step smaller.

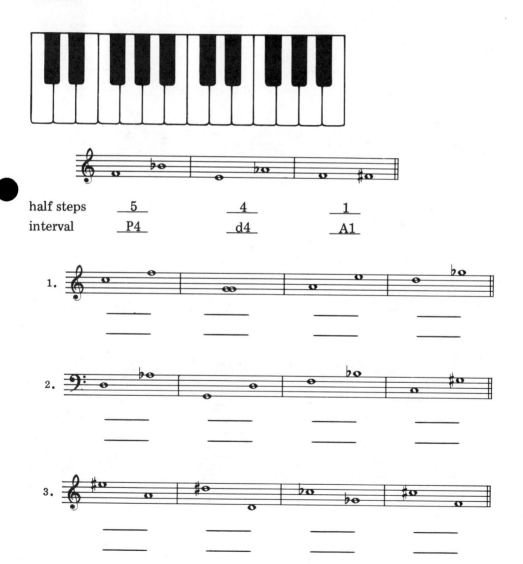

half steps	5	4	1
interval	P4	d4	A1

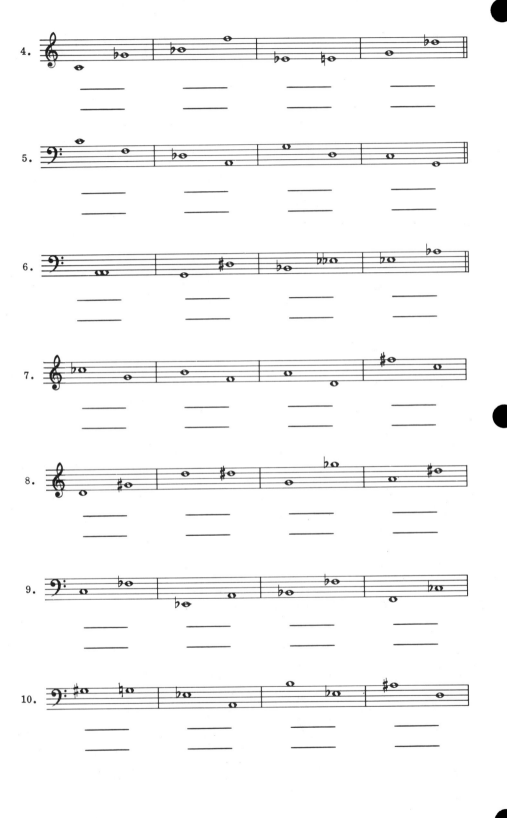

11.

12.

MUSICAL PROBLEM

When you have completed Exercise 6-6, ask someone to play some of the lines on
the piano. Try to identify the arithmetic distance and the quality of each interval. You may be able to do this all at once, or you may need to identify first the
arithmetic distance, then the quality. Note that the d5 and A4 sound the same
on the piano.

EXERCISE 6·7

Complete each of the indicated intervals by notating the correct *higher* pitch.
You may write them as either melodic or harmonic intervals. This exercise deals
with unisons, fourths, fifths, and octaves only. Use the keyboard to help you
visualize the half steps. Remember to maintain the correct arithmetic distance.
Begin by thinking of the major scale for each given pitch; this will give you the
perfect interval.

1.

     A5   P4   P5   d5

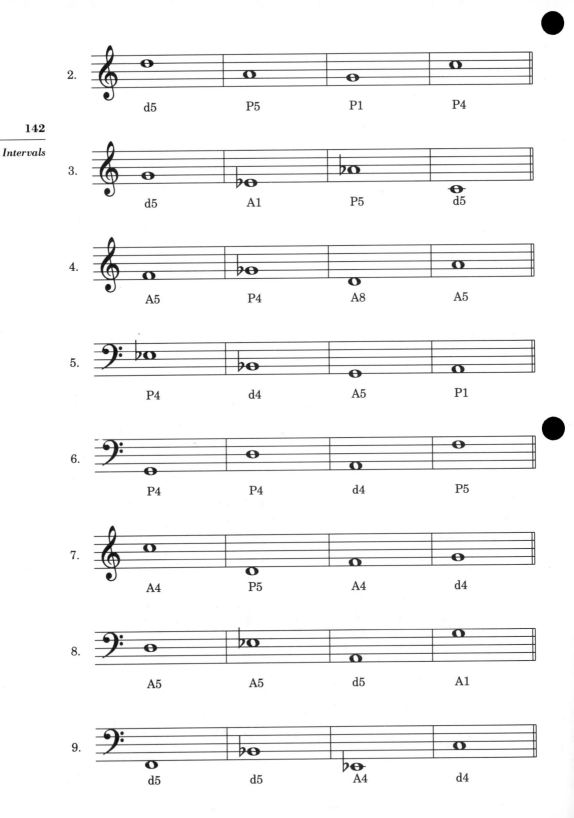

10.

P5   A4   A4   P4

EXERCISE 6·8

Complete each of the indicated intervals by notating the correct *lower* pitch. You may write them as either melodic or harmonic intervals. This exercise is somewhat more difficult than the preceding one because you cannot use the major scale as a reference. You can, however, refer to the major scale to check your answers. You may wish to start by determining the correct arithmetic distance.

This exercise deals with unisons, fourths, fifths, and octaves only. Use the keyboard to help you visualize the half steps.

1.   P4   d8   A5   P5

2.   P4   A4   P5   A4

3.   d5   d5   A4   d4

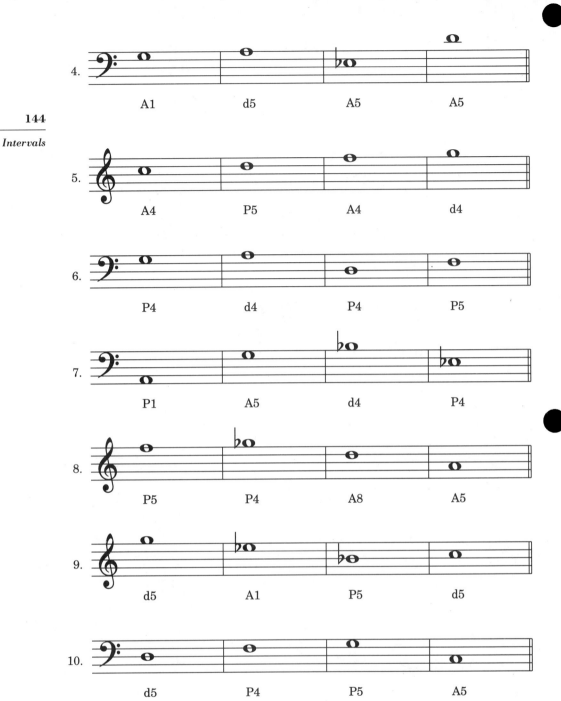

MUSICAL PROBLEM

Locate and identify all the perfect intervals in the following piece.

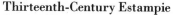
Thirteenth-Century Estampie

When you have identified the perfect intervals, play the piece, or sing it with the class. Discuss where the perfect intervals occur, and the type of sound they contribute to the piece.

Major and Minor Intervals

While any interval can be augmented or diminished in quality, perfect intervals can never be major or minor in quality. The intervals of major and minor quality are the second, the third, the sixth, and the seventh. The following illustration shows the number of half steps contained in each of the four types of major intervals.

In a major scale, the quality of the intervals between the tonic and the supertonic, mediant, submediant, and leading tone is always major.

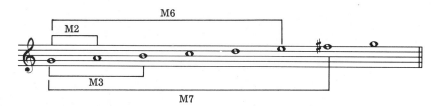

The same procedure for identifying perfect intervals can be applied to seconds, thirds, sixths, and sevenths as well. We simply assume that the lower pitch is the tonic; if the upper pitch is in the major scale of the lower pitch, the interval is major.

Another good way to learn this information is contained in the following chart. It lists the intervals found within a major scale and the number of half steps in each interval. Although you should be familiar with both ways of identifying and writing intervals, you can use whichever way seems easiest to you.

INTERVALS OF THE MAJOR SCALE

Interval	Number of Half Steps
Perfect unison	0
Major 2nd	2
Major 3rd	4
Perfect 4th	5
Perfect 5th	7
Major 6th	9
Major 7th	11
Perfect 8th	12

EXERCISE 6·9

Identify and circle the major seconds, thirds, sixths, and sevenths in the following set of harmonic intervals. Remember to ask yourself if the upper pitch is in the major scale of the lower pitch, or to use the chart of half steps.

5.

6.

7.

EXERCISE 6·10

Construct the indicated major interval, either harmonic or melodic, by writing the correct *higher* notehead. Begin by thinking of the major scale for each given pitch.

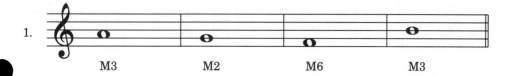

1.

      M3   M2   M6   M3

2.

      M6   M6   M7   M2

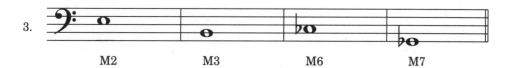

3.

      M2   M3   M6   M7

4.

      M6   M7   M2   M3

5.

      M3   M2   M7   M7

EXERCISE 6·11

Construct the indicated major interval, either harmonic or melodic, by writing the correct *lower* notehead. Check your answers by asking yourself if the given note is in the major scale of the note you have written.

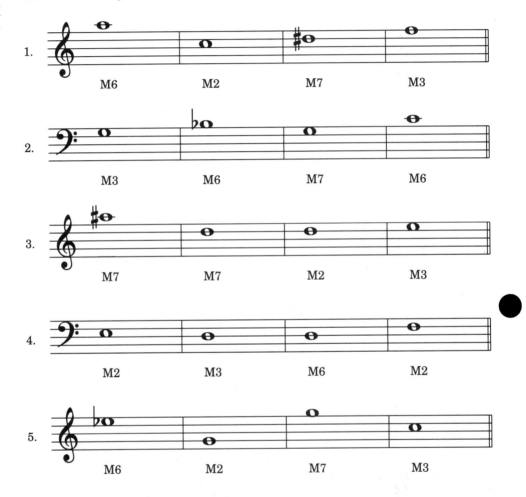

The number of half steps in each of the major intervals should be memorized. It then becomes simple to change the quality of major intervals to minor, augmented, or diminished. For example, a major interval decreased by a half step becomes minor in quality.

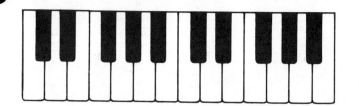

1.

| m3 | M6 | M6 | M3 |

2.

| M7 | m7 | M3 | m2 |

3.
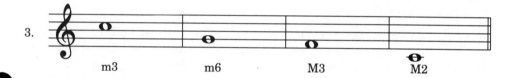

| m3 | m6 | M3 | M2 |

4.

| M2 | M6 | m2 | m3 |

5.

| d3 | m6 | m2 | m7 |

6.

| d3 | m7 | m6 | A2 |

7.

| m3 | M6 | M2 | m3 |

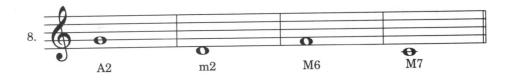

8. A2   m2   M6   M7

9. M2   m6   M2   A6

10. M6   m2   m3   A2

EXERCISE 6·14

Construct the indicated harmonic or melodic intervals by adding the correct *lower* pitch. This exercise concerns only seconds, thirds, sixths, and sevenths. Remember to keep the correct arithmetic distance. Use the keyboard to visualize the intervals. Check each answer by relating it to the major interval found in the appropriate major scale.

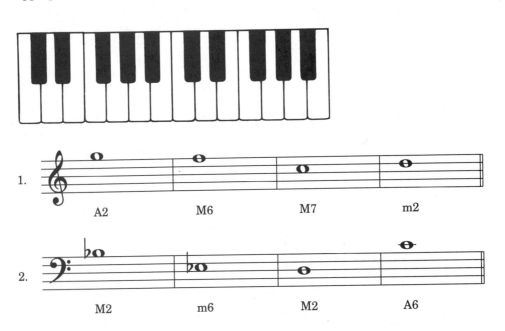

1. A2   M6   M7   m2

2. M2   m6   M2   A6

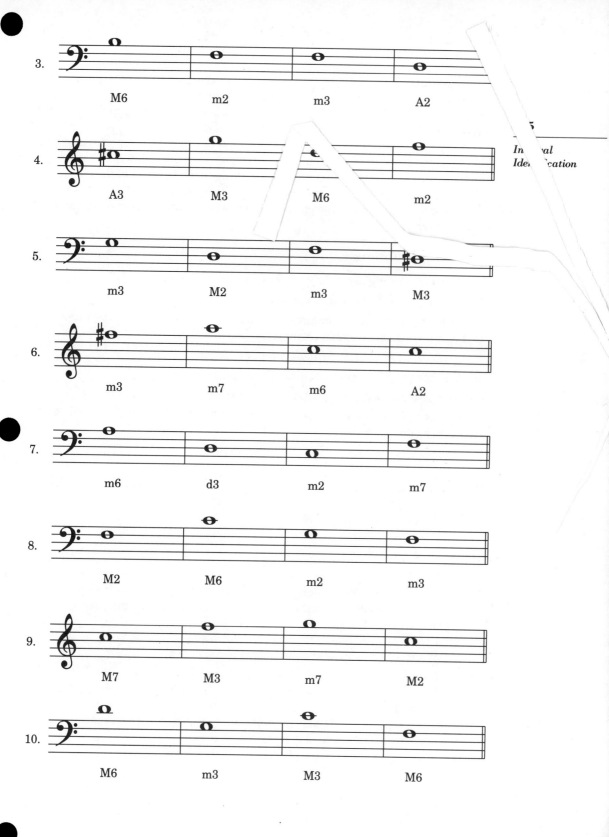

MUSICAL PROBLEM

It is important that you practice singing intervals and playing them at the keyboard. You can do both at once, using the piano to check your singing. Keep in mind that a few minutes' practice each day is far more beneficial than a lengthy practice session only once or twice a week.

You can practice interval skills any number of ways, but keep your exercises simple so that you can build on your successes. Use the following exercises as samples from which to develop your own. Perhaps each member of the class could design one singing exercise and one playing exercise for class use; these could then be shared so that every class member would have a sizable collection of practice exercises.

Sight-Singing Practice

1. Begin by singing *ascending* intervals in the major scale, as follows:

   do re, do mi, do fa, do sol, do la, do ti, do do

   When you can do this comfortably and accurately, try *descending* intervals, beginning an octave above where you began before:

   do ti, do la, do sol, do fa, do mi, do re, do do

2. Another useful ascending-interval exercise:

   do mi sol, re fa la, mi sol ti, fa la do, sol ti re, la do mi, ti re fa, mi

   This can also be done in reverse order, beginning at the top of the scale and working down:

   mi do la, re ti sol, do la fa, ti sol mi, la fa re, sol mi do, fa re ti, do

Both of the above exercises can also be sung using scale-degree numbers. Doing this will give you a slightly different perspective on the major scale and the intervals that it contains.

Keyboard Practice

1. a. Play c^4.
   b. Play a pitch a P4 higher. Name this pitch. (Remember that you must always consider the arithmetic distance as well as the number of half steps.)
   c. From the new pitch, play a pitch a m2 lower.
   d. What is the name of the pitch you have reached? _____

2. a. Play e^{b5}.
   b. Play a pitch a P5 higher. Name this pitch. (Remember to consider the arithmetic distance.)
   c. From the new pitch, play a pitch a M3 lower. Name this pitch.
   d. From this new pitch, play a pitch a P5 lower.
   e. What is the name of the pitch you are on now? _____

3. a. Play d^2.
    b. Play a pitch a M6 higher.
    c. From the new pitch, play a pitch a m3 higher.
    d. From this new pitch, play a pitch a m7 lower.
    e. What is the name of the pitch you are on now? _____

4. a. Play f♯^{4}.
    b. Play a pitch a P4 higher.
    c. From the new pitch, play a pitch a M3 higher.
    d. From this new pitch, play a pitch a P5 lower.
    e. What is the name of the pitch you are on now? _____

5. a. Play a^4.
    b. Play a pitch a M3 higher.
    c. From the new pitch, play a pitch a P4 higher.
    d. From this new pitch, play a pitch a M6 higher.
    e. What is the name of the pitch you are on now? _____

6. a. Play g^3.
    b. Play a pitch a m7 lower.
    c. From the new pitch, play a pitch a M3 lower.
    d. From this new pitch, play a pitch a P5 higher.
    e. What is the name of the pitch you are on now? _____

7. a. Play b♭^{1}.
    b. Play a pitch a M6 higher.
    c. From the new pitch, play a pitch a m2 higher.
    d. From this new pitch, play a pitch a P4 higher.
    e. What is the name of the pitch you are on now? _____

8. a. Play d♭^{4}.
    b. Play a pitch a M3 higher.
    c. From the new pitch, play a pitch a m3 higher.
    d. From this new pitch, play a pitch a A4 higher.
    e. What is the name of the pitch you are on now? _____

Compound Intervals

Intervals that are one octave or smaller in size are called **simple intervals**, while intervals larger than an octave are known as **compound intervals**. The following example illustrates a major ninth, a major tenth, and a perfect eleventh:

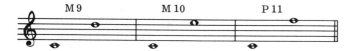

Of course, the larger the interval, the more difficult it can be to read and identify correctly. For the purposes of identification it is easier to reduce the compound interval by one octave. Thus, a major ninth becomes a compound major second; a major tenth, a compound major third; and a perfect eleventh, a compound perfect fourth.

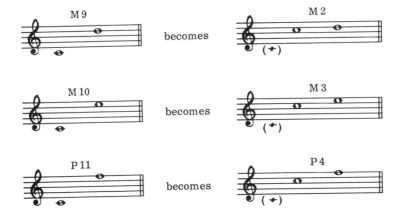

Compound intervals are major, minor, or perfect, depending on the quality of the corresponding simple interval. Remember that the quality always stays the same because all you are doing when you reduce a compound interval to a simple interval is subtracting one octave.

EXERCISE 6·15

Identify the following compound harmonic intervals by reducing them by one octave and labeling the simple interval that results:

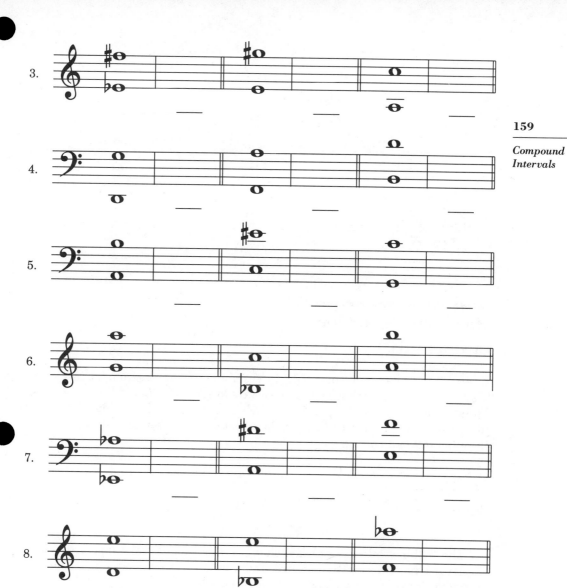

EXERCISE 6·16

Identify the following compound harmonic intervals. Even though you are not asked to reduce each interval by an octave this time, you may find it helpful to do so mentally. Remember also that the quality of the compound interval is the same as the quality of the corresponding simple interval.

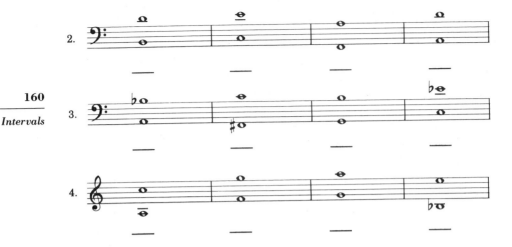

Harmonic Inversion of Intervals

Intervals are inverted harmonically by reversing the pitches from top to bottom. That is, the higher pitch is moved one octave lower so it is below the other pitch. The same interval results if the lower pitch is moved one octave higher. The point to remember when inverting intervals is that one pitch remains stationary and the other moves an octave.

inverts to

The arithmetic distance always changes when an interval is inverted. A fifth inverts to a fourth, a sixth to a third, and a seventh to a second. Notice that *the sum of the interval plus its inversion always equals nine.*

The quality of inverted intervals changes in the following ways:

Perfect intervals always invert to perfect intervals.

becomes

Major intervals always invert to minor intervals; minor intervals always invert to major intervals.

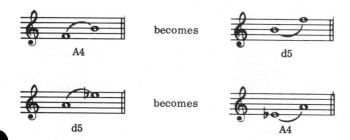

Augmented intervals always invert to diminished intervals; diminished intervals always invert to augmented intervals.

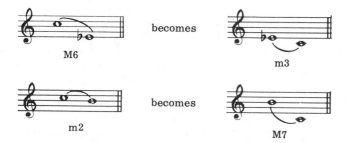

Another important point to remember is that inverted intervals can, in some ways, be considered to belong to the same interval family. That is, although the two pitches have changed location, and the interval between them has changed, the pitches themselves have not changed.

EXERCISE 6·17

First label the given melodic interval, then invert it and identify the interval that results. Remember that the sum of any interval plus its inversion always equals nine.

EXAMPLE:

1.

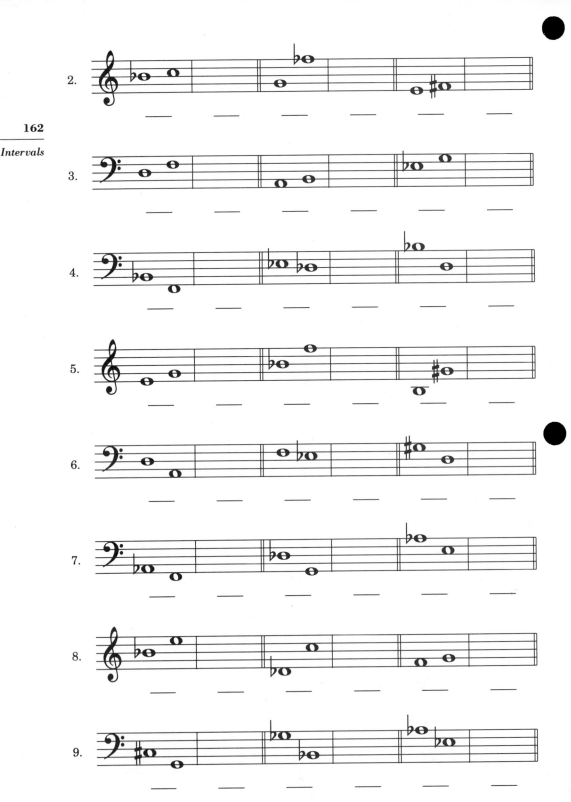

10.

11.

12.

MUSICAL PROBLEM

Your teacher or another student from the class will play various intervals, beginning on different pitches, for you to recognize by ear. These will be played as either harmonic (sounding simultaneously) or melodic (sounding in succession) intervals. The intervals have been grouped in limited combinations according to size and quality in order to make your beginning work easier. As you practice, remember that ear training is a continuous process; it grows easier as you continue. If time permits, your teacher may wish to return to this Musical Problem several times in the future. An alternative to this would be for you and a friend from the class to practice on your own.

Major 2nds and Major 3rds only

    1. _____   4. _____   7. _____

    2. _____   5. _____   8. _____

    3. _____   6. _____   9. _____

Major 3rds and Perfect 5ths

    1. _____   4. _____   7. _____

    2. _____   5. _____   8. _____

    3. _____   6. _____   9. _____

Perfect 4ths and Perfect 5ths

    1. _____   4. _____   7. _____

    2. _____   5. _____   8. _____

    3. _____   6. _____   9. _____

Major 2nds, Perfects 4ths, and Major 6ths

1. _____   4. _____   7. _____

2. _____   5. _____   8. _____

3. _____   6. _____   9. _____

All intervals from the major scale, including the Major 7th

1. _____   4. _____   7. _____

2. _____   5. _____   8. _____

3. _____   6. _____   9. _____

Focus

In this chapter, we have concentrated on identifying and notating intervals. Identifying intervals can seem mathematical and tedious if done in a purely mechanical way; it can also seem time-consuming and difficult. Nonetheless, interval patterns are the building blocks of tonal music.

Even though the mechanics of writing and recognizing intervals may at times seem like drudgery, acquiring these skills is important in advancing your understanding of tonal music. In the same way that musicians practice scales to acquaint themselves with scale patterns, they work with intervals to become familiar with interval patterns. Perhaps the following musical problem will help you appreciate that melodies, from the most harmonious to the most dissonant, are patterns of intervals.

MUSICAL PROBLEM

In your mind, sing the beginning of each of the following well-known songs. Beside the name of each, write the interval that occurs between the first and second notes of the song. This may seem difficult at first, but two hints may make it easier for you: (1) Only the intervals found in a major scale are used—P1, M2, M3, P4, P5, M6, M7, P8. (2) One of the two pitches for each song is always the tonic. If you have trouble, try singing up or down the scale from the tonic to the other note.

1. "Kum Ba Yah" _____

2. "Yesterday" _____

3. "We Wish You a Merry Christmas" _____

4. "Scarborough Fair" _____

5. "Over the Rainbow" _____

6. "Hava Nagila" _____

7. "Michael, Row the Boat Ashore" _____

8. "Joy to the World" _____

The following questions cover Chapters 4 through 6. If you have difficulty with any of them, review the relevant sections before beginning Chapter 7.

1. Write a one-octave chromatic scale, ascending and descending, starting from the following pitch.

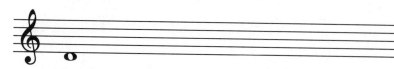

2. Write ascending major scales starting from the following pitches.

a.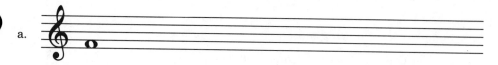

b.

c.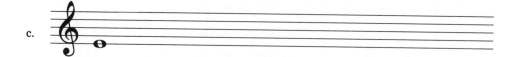

d.

e.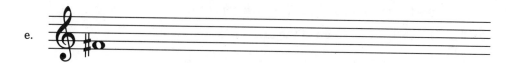

3. Write descending major scales starting from the following pitches.

a.

b.

c.

d.

e.

4. Complete the following sentences.

   a. The dominant of the B♭ major scale is _____.

   b. The submediant of the D major scale is _____.

   c. The supertonic of the G♭ major scale is _____.

   d. The mediant of the A♭ major scale is _____.

   e. The supertonic of the G major scale is _____.

   f. The submediant of the E major scale is _____.

   g. The leading tone of the F major scale is _____.

   h. The dominant of the E major scale is _____.

   i. The subdominant of the C♯ major scale is _____.

   j. The mediant of the D♭ major scale is _____.

   k. A is the mediant of the _____ major scale.

   l. D is the subdominant of the _____ major scale.

   m. E is the dominant of the _____ major scale.

   n. F♯ is the submediant of the _____ major scale.

   o. B♭ is the subdominant of the _____ major scale.

5. Write out the following major key signatures.

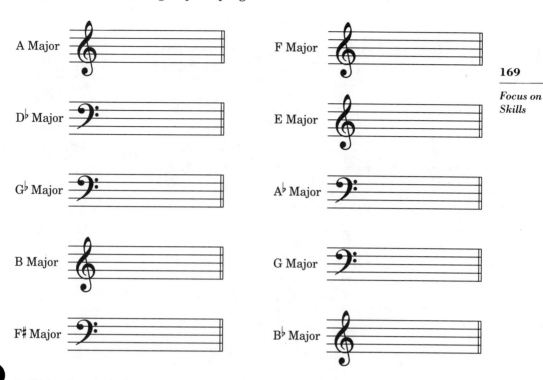

A Major

D♭ Major

G♭ Major

B Major

F♯ Major

F Major

E Major

A♭ Major

G Major

B♭ Major

6. Write the pitch that completes the indicated intervals above each given pitch.

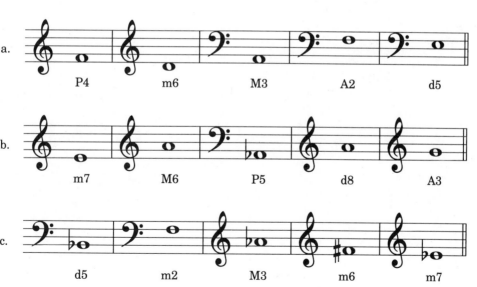

a.
P4   m6   M3   A2   d5

b.
m7   M6   P5   d8   A3

c.
d5   m2   M3   m6   m7

7. Write the pitch that completes the indicated intervals below each given pitch.

a.

  m2   M3   A4   P5   m6

b.

  M3   d4   m3   M6   d5

c.

  A2   M7   M3   d4   m7

Chapter 7

Minor Key Signatures

To learn the minor keys, you do not need to learn a whole new set of key signatures. Rather, you need only learn to recognize how minor keys are related to the major key signatures you already know. Even though there is more than one form of the minor scale (which you will learn about in the next chapter), there is only one set of minor key signatures. Once you are familiar with them, learning the minor scales will be easier.

Related Keys

There is a simple and important relationship between major and minor keys. Notice, for instance, the relationship of accidentals between the following two scales.

F major scale

D natural minor scale

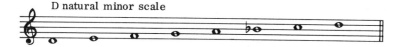

Both scales have one and the same accidental—B♭. In fact, if you begin on the sixth degree of *any* major scale and follow its note pattern for one octave, the result will always be a new, natural minor scale. Here's another example:

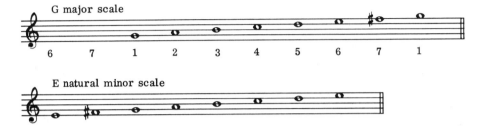

This relationship, which is constant for all of the major keys, means that there are pairs of keys—one major, one minor—related by the same pitch content, hence by the same key signature. Such keys are called **related keys**. The term *relative minor* refers to the minor key or scale that is related to a particular major scale by having the same key signature. The term *relative major* refers to the major key or scale with the same key signature as a particular minor scale.

The relative minor-major relationship may be remembered in two ways: (1) The relative minor scale always begins on the sixth degree of the major scale. (2) The relative minor scale always begins three half steps (a minor third) below its related major scale. Most students find the second way easier. Either way, remember that related scales always have the *same* key signature but *different* tonics.

EXERCISE 7·1

Identify the relative minor key for the following major keys.

1. E major _____   8. A♭ major _____

2. D major _____   9. C major _____

3. G♭ major _____   10. B major _____

4. F major _____   11. F♯ major _____

5. C♯ major _____   12. D♭ major _____

6. G major _____   13. E♭ major _____

7. A major _____   14. B♭ major _____

EXERCISE 7·2

Identify the major key and the relative minor key that have the given number of sharps or flats.

	Major	*Relative Minor*
1. two flats	———	———
2. two sharps	———	———
3. three sharps	———	———
4. four flats	———	———
5. seven sharps	———	———
6. five flats	———	———
7. six sharps	———	———
8. three flats	———	———
9. one sharp	———	———
10. six flats	———	———
11. five sharps	———	———
12. one flat	———	———
13. four sharps	———	———
14. seven flats	———	———

EXERCISE 7·3

Identify the relative major key for the following minor keys.

1. F♯ minor ———
2. D minor ———
3. A♭ minor ———
4. C♯ minor ———
5. A♯ minor ———
6. G minor ———
7. B♭ minor ———

8. E minor ———
9. D♯ minor ———
10. F minor ———
11. B minor ———
12. E♭ minor ———
13. C minor ———
14. G♯ minor ———

Parallel Keys

Parallel keys begin on the same pitch (that is, same tonic) but have different key signatures. G major and G minor, for instance, are parallel keys.

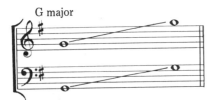

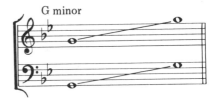

The terms *parallel major* and *parallel minor* are used frequently.

Minor Key Signatures

The minor key signatures, for sharp keys and flat keys, are given below, followed by the number of accidentals associated with each key. Notice that lowercase letters are used to indicate minor keys, which is an acceptable practice. Notice also that the last sharp added to each sharp key is the supertonic, and the last flat added to each flat key is the submediant. As you study these minor key signatures, make a mental association with the relative major for each key.

Key Signatures: Sharp Minor Keys

Minor Key	Number of Sharps
a	0
e	1
b	2
f♯	3
c♯	4
g♯	5
d♯	6
a♯	7

Key Signatures: Minor Flat Keys

Minor Keys	Number of Flats
a	0
d	1
g	2
c	3
f	4
b♭	5
e♭	6
a♭	7

As mentioned earlier, there is more than one form of the minor scale. In fact, there are three: natural minor, harmonic minor, and melodic minor. At this point it is important to remember that the key signature for minor scales supplies the accidentals for the *natural minor* scale only. A piece of music written in *harmonic minor* or *melodic minor* (as most tonal music is) will give the appropriate accidentals *within the piece*, directly before the pitches they affect. These extra accidentals never appear in the key signature. The following example is in C minor. The appearance of B natural and A natural within the excerpt is indicative of *C melodic minor*. The next chapter will explore natural minor, harmonic minor, and melodic minor scales in detail. For now, remember that the minor key signature always indicates the natural minor scale.

Scarlatti: Sonata in C Minor

Identify the minor keys represented by the following key signatures.

1.

2.

3.

4.

5.

6.

7.

8.

EXERCISE 7·5

Write out the indicated minor key signatures, using sharps or flats as required.

1.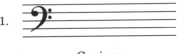

        G minor

7.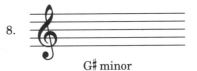

        B♭ minor

2.

        C minor

8.

        G♯ minor

3.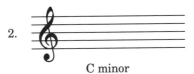

        A♭ minor

9.

        E♭ minor

4.

        C♯ minor

10.

        A minor

5.

        A minor

11.

        D minor

6.

        D♯ minor

12.

        A♯ minor

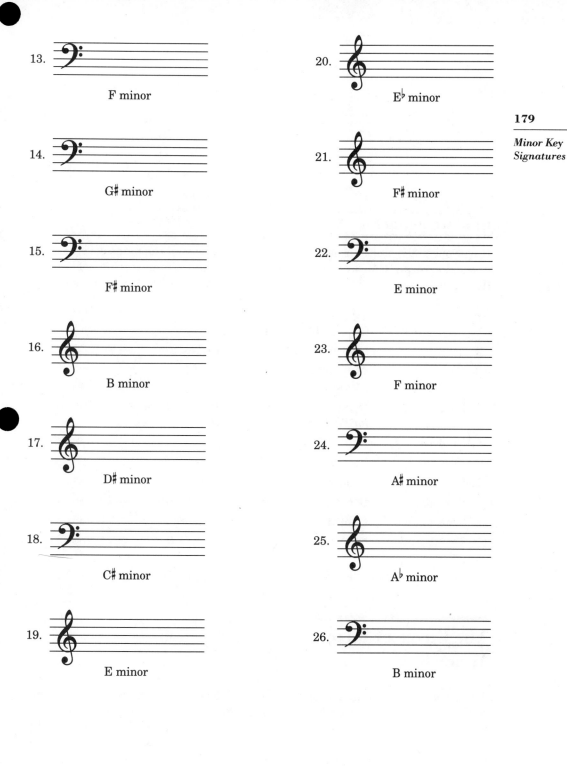

13. F minor

14. G# minor

15. F# minor

16. B minor

17. D# minor

18. C# minor

19. E minor

20. E♭ minor

21. F# minor

22. E minor

23. F minor

24. A# minor

25. A♭ minor

26. B minor

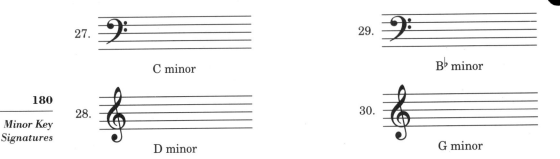

27. C minor

28. D minor

29. B♭ minor

30. G minor

MUSICAL PROBLEM

Have your teacher or another student select and play on the piano several of the musical excerpts that are listed below with their location in this book. After listening to each excerpt, decide whether it is in a major key or a minor key.

Composer	Title	Page(s)
1. Bach	Chorale from Cantata No. 180	60
2. Bach	Courante from French Suite No. 2	60
3. Bach	Minuet in G Minor	46, 185
	Minuet in G Major	184
4. Bach	"Praeludium" from *The Little Piano Book for Wilhelm Friedemann Bach*	196
5. Diabelli	Bagatelle	289–290
6. Kuhlau	Rondo from Sonatina, Op. 20, No. 1	66
7. Mozart	Sonata in B♭ Major, K. 570, III	64
8. Scarlatti	Sonata in C Minor	176
9. Schumann	Choral from *Album for the Young*	266–267
10. Traditional	"St. James Infirmary"	285–286

The Circle of Fifths: Minor Keys

For minor keys, as for major keys, a circle of fifths can be constructed. The same perfect fifth relationship between adjacent keys exists, and the enharmonic keys again appear at the bottom of the circle. Notice also that the circle of fifths for major keys can be superimposed over the one for minor keys. This works because of the parallel relationship between major and minor keys discussed earlier. At this point it might be more useful to you to combine the two in your mind so that you remember one circle of fifths for both major and minor keys.

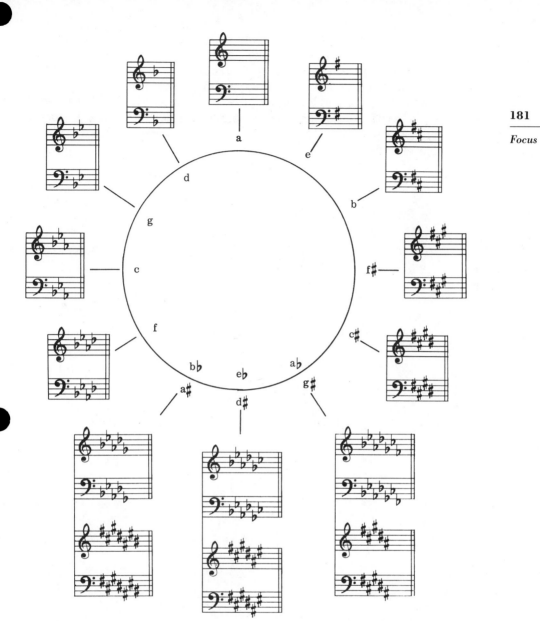

Focus

Almost all beginning musicians have favorite keys. These are usually keys with no sharps or flats, or at most one or two, which seem easier. Sometimes, people study theory or take lessons for years and still find keys with more than four or five sharps or flats too difficult to negotiate successfully. Usually, the problem feeds on itself—some keys are initially easier, therefore we *choose* to work primarily in those keys. But this is a mistake; we don't learn by avoidance.

If you are going to be a good musician, even a good amateur musician, you need to be fluent in all keys—both major and minor. This ability won't come immediately, but it will develop slowly with practice. You can make working with minor scales easier by being certain that you understand the minor key signatures and how they relate to the major keys. If you need additional practice at recognizing or writing minor key signatures, do that now, before you begin the next chapter. You will find Chapter 8 much easier to understand once you are comfortable with the minor key signatures.

Minor Scales

Just as with the major scales, fifteen tonic notes comprise the relative minor scales. But unlike the major scales, each minor scale has three different forms.

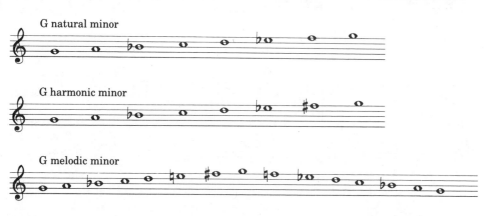

At first this may seem confusing, because of the large number of minor scales this creates. But if you keep in mind the concept of relative major/relative minor, and remember the minor key signatures you learned in the previous chapter, this confusion will quickly disappear.

Why are there so many different versions? This is a complicated question that has never been completely answered. The various forms of the minor scale evolved over a considerable amount of time. But one answer that is pertinent to our work is this: Each version has a unique harmonic advantage that makes it useful in particular musical situations. As you study this chapter, remember that each form of the minor scale has a separate pattern of whole steps and half steps that gives the resultant melody and harmony their characteristic sound.

MUSICAL PROBLEM

The following excerpts are from two minuets by Bach. The first is in the key of G major, the second is in G minor. Ask someone to perform these examples in class. Remember that the difference in sound or feeling that you hear between major keys and minor keys is a result of two different interval patterns of whole steps and half steps.

Bach: Minuet in G Major

Bach: Minuet in G Minor

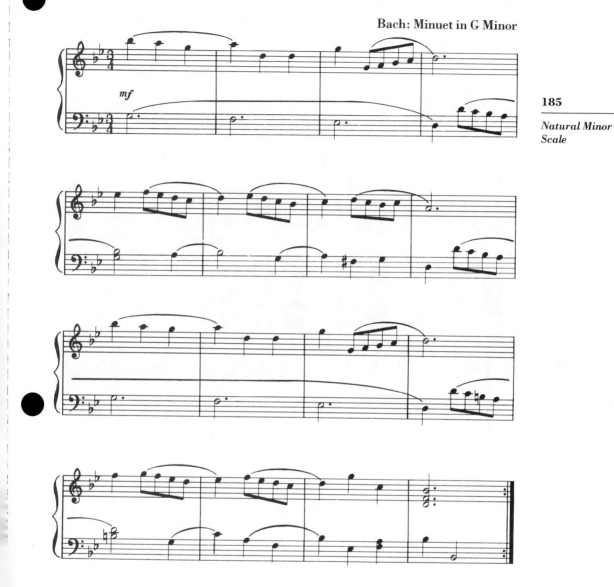

Natural Minor Scale

Like the major scale, the **natural minor scale** contains five whole steps and two half steps. The half steps, however, do not occur in the same place. This reordering of the interval pattern gives the natural minor scale its unique quality.

In the natural minor scale, the two half steps occur between the second and third degrees and the fifth and sixth degrees. The following illustration shows a natural minor scale beginning on the pitch A.

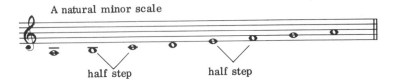

Notice that the natural minor scale beginning on A has no sharps or flats — that is, on the keyboard the pattern falls on all white keys.

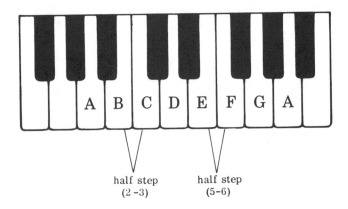

When the natural minor scale begins on any pitch other than A, one or more accidentals will be required to keep the interval pattern intact.

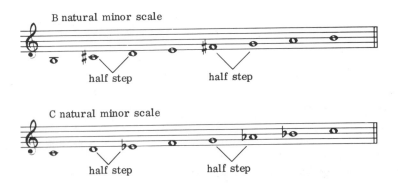

It may be useful to compare the intervals of the natural minor scale with those of the major scale. The following chart lists the intervals found within both scales and the number of half steps in each interval. In particular, compare the intervals of the third, sixth, and seventh between the two scales. It is these minor intervals above the tonic of the natural minor scale that contribute to the "minor" sound of the scale.

INTERVALS OF THE NATURAL MINOR AND MAJOR SCALES

Natural Minor		*Major*	
Interval	*Number of Half Steps*	*Interval*	*Number of Half Steps*
Perfect unison	0	Perfect unison	0
Major 2nd	2	Major 2nd	2
Minor 3rd	3	Major 3rd	4
Perfect 4th	5	Perfect 4th	5
Perfect 5th	7	Perfect 5th	7
Minor 6th	8	Major 6th	9
Minor 7th	10	Major 7th	11
Perfect 8th	12	Perfect 8th	12

EXERCISE 8·1

From each starting pitch, write ascending and descending natural minor scales in both treble clef and bass clef. The scales in this exercise are grouped in perfect fifths so that each successive scale requires one additional sharp. The new sharp is always the supertonic of that scale.

Remember that, like the major scale, the minor scale is composed of an alphabetical sequence of pitches, and thus no chromatic half steps are used. When you have written the scales, check that the half steps fall only between the second and third and the fifth and sixth degrees. Indicate the half steps in each scale.

1.

E natural minor

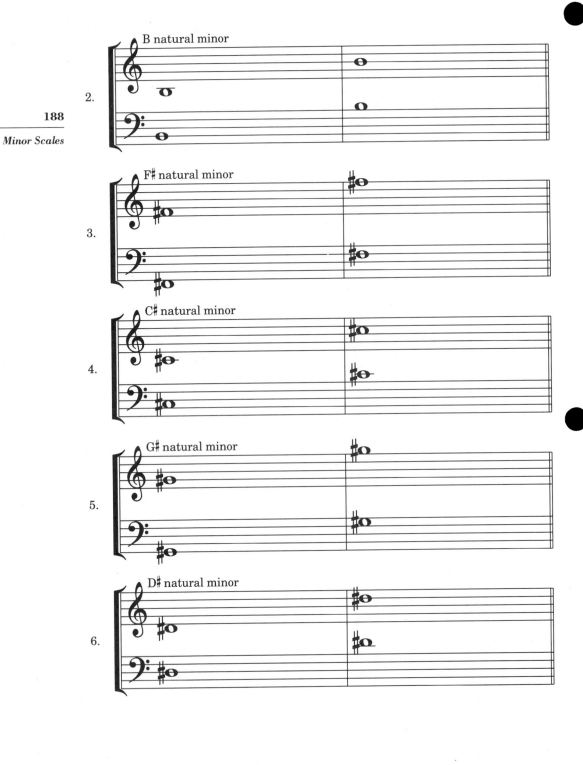

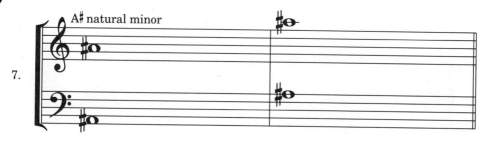

7.

EXERCISE 8·2

Write ascending and descending natural minor scales from each starting pitch.
(The scales in this exercise are grouped so that each succeeding scale requires
one additional flat—the submediant of that scale.) When you have written the
scales, check that the half steps fall only between the second and third and the
fifth and sixth degrees. Indicate the half steps in each scale.

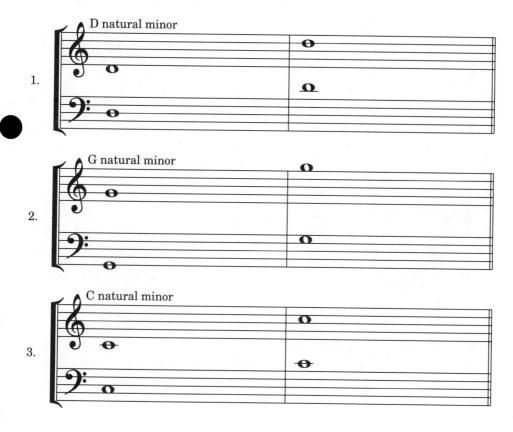

1.

2.

3.

4.

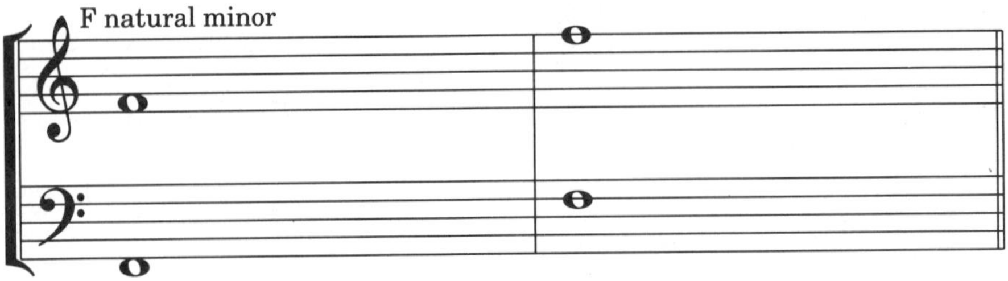

F natural minor

5.

B♭ natural minor

6.

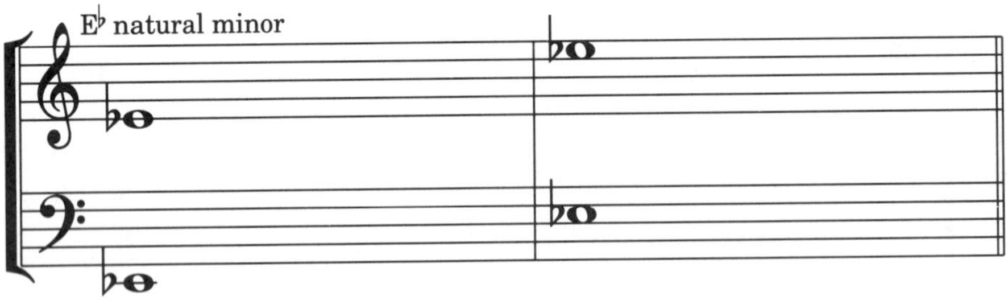

E♭ natural minor

7.

A♭ natural minor

EXERCISE 8·3

Write ascending natural minor scales beginning with the given tonic pitches. This exercise and the one following use the same scales you wrote in the previous two exercises, but now they are out of sequence.

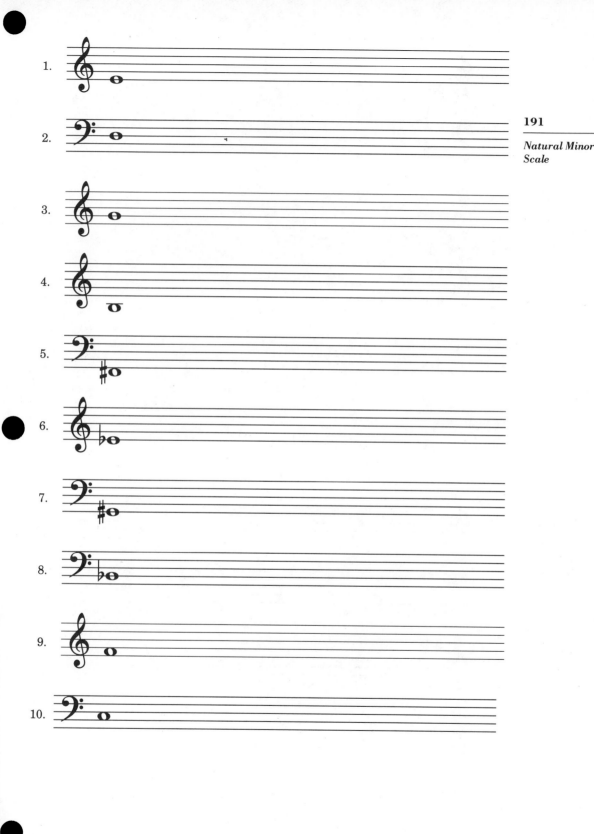

EXERCISE 8·4

Write natural minor scales in descending form, beginning with the given tonic pitches. Indicate the half steps in each scale.

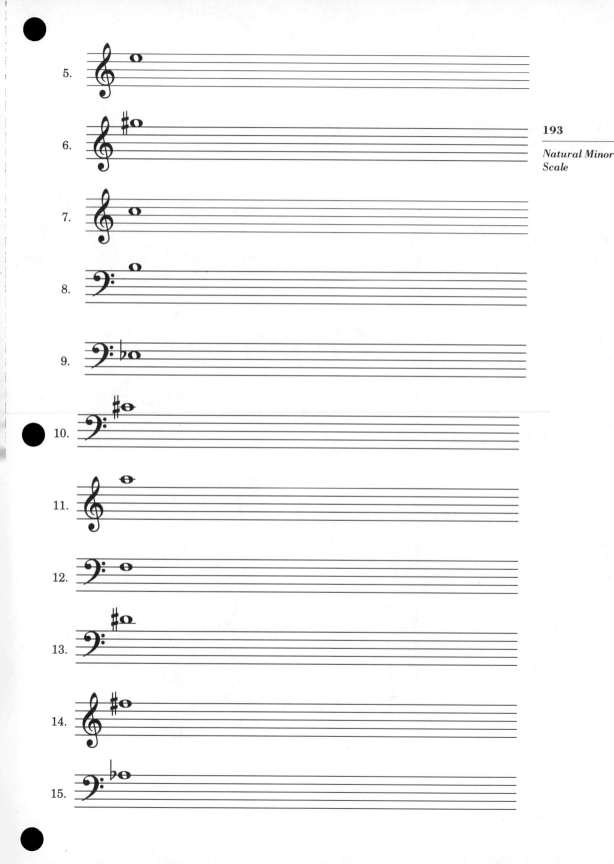

Natural Minor Scale

MUSICAL PROBLEM

The American folk song "Erie Canal" is in the key of D natural minor. In the space provided, rewrite this folk song in the key of D major. Then, sing or play both versions in class and discuss the differences between the two types of scales.

"Erie Canal"

EXERCISE 8·5

Spell the indicated natural minor scales using letter names and any necessary accidentals. Indicate where the half steps occur in each scale.

EXAMPLE:　G　A　B♭　C　D　E♭　F　G

1.　D

2.　F

3.　E

4.　C♯

5.　B♭

6.　A

7.　G♯

8.　E♭

9.　B

10.　C

11.　A♯

12.　F♯

13.　A♭

14.　D♯

Harmonic Minor Scale

Sing or play a natural minor scale. Then, sing or play a major scale. Do you notice a difference in the interval between the seventh and first degrees of the two scales? The seventh degree of the natural minor scale is not a half step below the tonic; it is a whole step away, and in this position is called a **subtonic** instead of a leading tone.

When the seventh degree of a scale is a whole step below the tonic, a somewhat ambiguous-sounding scale is created. Because of the whole step, the tonic does not seem to offer as strong a center of gravity as it does in the major scale. This weakening of the tonic's attraction is particularly striking in the harmony derived from the natural minor scale. This effect can be demonstrated by having someone in class play the following two versions of the opening measures of a "Praeludium" from *The Little Piano Book for Wilhelm Friedemann Bach* by J. S. Bach. The first version is based on the natural minor scale:

The second version is based on another form of minor scale known as the **harmonic minor scale**:

Notice how much stronger the harmonic motion feels when the chords are built from the harmonic minor scale.

The difference between the natural minor scale and the harmonic minor scale is that the subtonic of the former is raised a chromatic half step to create a leading tone.

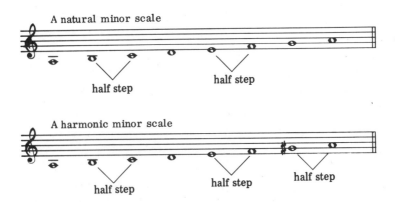

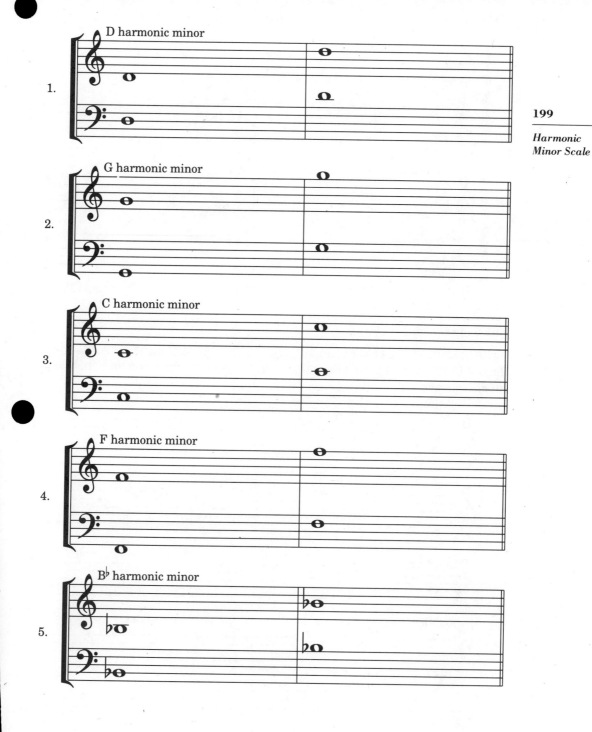

EXERCISE 8·8

Write the following harmonic minor scales in ascending form. This exercise and the one following use the same scales as in the previous two exercises, but now out of sequence.

EXERCISE 8·9

Spell the indicated harmonic minor scales using letter names and any necessary accidentals. For each scale, indicate where the half steps fall.

1. G ___ ___ ___ ___ ___ ___ ___

2. B ___ ___ ___ ___ ___ ___ ___

3. F♯ ___ ___ ___ ___ ___ ___ ___

4. E ___ ___ ___ ___ ___ ___ ___

5. F ___ ___ ___ ___ ___ ___ ___

6. C♯ ___ ___ ___ ___ ___ ___ ___

7. A♭ ___ ___ ___ ___ ___ ___ ___

8. D♯ ___ ___ ___ ___ ___ ___ ___

9. E♭ ___ ___ ___ ___ ___ ___ ___

10. A ___ ___ ___ ___ ___ ___ ___

11. G♯ ___ ___ ___ ___ ___ ___ ___

12. C ___ ___ ___ ___ ___ ___ ___

13. A♯ ___ ___ ___ ___ ___ ___ ___

14. B♭ ___ ___ ___ ___ ___ ___ ___

15. D ___ ___ ___ ___ ___ ___ ___

MUSICAL PROBLEM

Rewrite the following melody by transposing it from the original key (G major) to the key of G harmonic minor. Then, sing or play both versions in class. Discuss the differences between the major and harmonic minor versions.

"The Wabash Cannon Ball"

EXERCISE 8·10

Identify by letter name the following scale degrees.

1. supertonic of C harmonic minor _____

2. dominant of Bᵇ harmonic minor _____

3. leading tone of G harmonic minor _____

4. mediant of A harmonic minor _____

5. subdominant of B harmonic minor _____

6. tonic of Eᵇ harmonic minor _____

7. mediant of C♯ harmonic minor _____

8. submediant of D harmonic minor _____

9. supertonic of B harmonic minor _____

10. subdominant of C♯ harmonic minor _____

11. mediant of B♭ harmonic minor _____

12. submediant of C harmonic minor _____

13. supertonic of A harmonic minor _____

14. dominant of E harmonic minor _____

15. tonic of F♯ harmonic minor _____

16. subdominant of D harmonic minor _____

17. leading tone of E♭ harmonic minor _____

18. mediant of A♭ harmonic minor _____

19. submediant of F harmonic minor _____

20. leading tone of F harmonic minor _____

21. subdominant of E♭ harmonic minor _____

22. supertonic of B♭ harmonic minor _____

23. dominant of C♯ harmonic minor _____

24. supertonic of D harmonic minor _____

25. submediant of E harmonic minor _____

EXERCISE 8·11

Complete the following:

1. G is the dominant of the _____ harmonic minor scale.

2. B♭ is the mediant of the _____ harmonic minor scale.

3. F is the submediant of the _____ harmonic minor scale.

4. G♯ is the leading tone of the _____ harmonic minor scale.

5. A is the leading tone of the _____ harmonic minor scale.

6. C is the mediant of the _____ harmonic minor scale.

7. E is the leading tone of the _____ harmonic minor scale.

8. G is the subdominant of the _____ harmonic minor scale.

9. F is the dominant of the _____ harmonic minor scale.

10. C♯ is the leading tone of the _____ harmonic minor scale.

11. A is the dominant of the _____ harmonic minor scale.

12. E is the supertonic of the _____ harmonic minor scale.

13. D is the leading tone of the _____ harmonic minor scale.

14. G is the mediant of the _____ harmonic minor scale.

15. B♭ is the submediant of the _____ harmonic minor scale.

Melodic Minor Scale

While the harmonic minor scale solves the harmonic problem inherent in the natural minor scale, it creates a melodic problem. Have you been puzzled by the interval between the sixth and seventh degrees of the harmonic minor scale?

A harmonic minor scale

This interval, created by raising the seventh degree of the natural minor scale, is an augmented second (three half steps). The augmented second can be difficult to sing or play in tune. Although it appears on paper as a second, it has the same number of half steps as a minor third and thus *sounds* wider than it *looks* on the staff.

The **melodic minor scale** was developed, in part, as a means of avoiding this augmented second of the harmonic minor scale. It is the only minor scale that has one version when ascending and another when descending.

A melodic minor scale

In the ascending form of the scale, both the sixth and seventh degrees are raised. The seventh degree, as in the harmonic minor, is raised to create a half-step relationship between the seventh degree and the tonic. The sixth degree is raised to avoid the augmented second. Note, however, that these alterations create a scale in which only the third degree is different from the major scale.

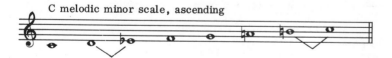

C melodic minor scale, ascending

This similarity to the major scale is so marked that it almost obscures the minor-sounding quality of the melodic minor scale. Since the leading tone is needed in ascending musical passages more than in descending ones, the descending version of the melodic minor scale lowers both the seventh and sixth degrees. This alteration, which actually produces a descending natural minor scale, balances the ascending version and helps restore a minor-sounding quality to the scale.

C melodic minor scale, descending

As in the harmonic minor, double sharp signs will occasionally be required to form the melodic minor.

D♯ melodic minor scale

EXERCISE 8·12

Write melodic minor scales, ascending and descending, in both treble clef and bass clef, beginning with the given tonic pitches. (This exercise deals with sharp scales only.) Mark the half steps in each scale.

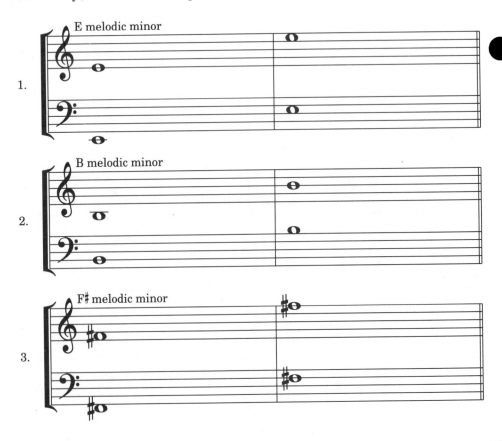

1. E melodic minor

2. B melodic minor

3. F♯ melodic minor

EXERCISE 8·13

Write melodic minor scales, ascending and descending, in both treble clef and bass clef, beginning with the given tonic pitches. Even though this exercise deals only with flat scales, you will need to use sharps occasionally to alter the seventh scale degree. Be sure to mark the half steps in each scale.

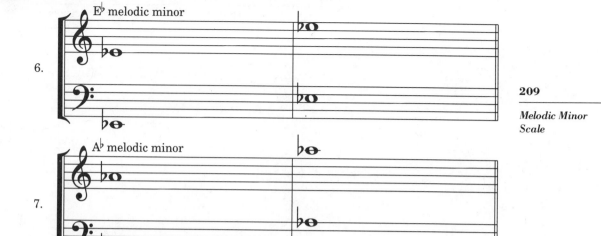

EXERCISE 8·14

Write melodic minor scales, ascending and descending, beginning with the given tonic pitches. These are the same scales as in the two previous exercises, but now out of sequence.

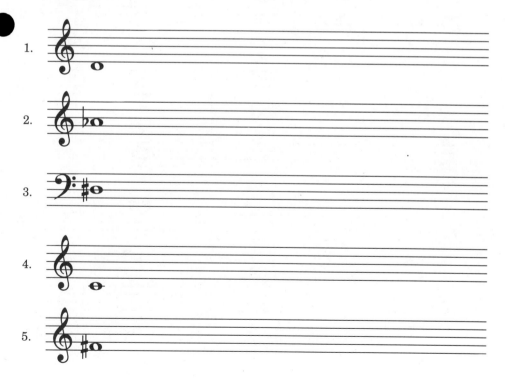

Ask someone in class who plays an instrument or the piano to prepare a well-known tune such as "The Star Spangled Banner" or "Three Blind Mice" so that he or she can play it in its original major key as well as in the three forms of the minor scale. As a class discuss the differences between (1) the major and natural minor versions and (2) the three forms of the minor versions.

Minor Scales in Musical Situations

Thus far this chapter has made it appear that there are three distinct forms of the minor scale, and that composers choose one of them, to the exclusion of the other two, when writing a piece of music in a minor key. Although it is useful to think this way when you are first learning the three forms of the minor scale, this is not what really happens in the music. In actuality, composers view the sixth and seventh degrees of the minor scale as unstable, and they sometimes use all three forms of the scale within the same composition. Thus, it is more accurate to say that the three forms of the minor scale are not really three different scales, but rather represent three different solutions, or possible approaches, to various musical problems within a composition in a minor key.

Consider for a moment the names *harmonic minor* and *melodic minor*. These names give us a clue as to why and how composers might use both scale forms within the same piece. Remember that the harmonic minor scale creates a real leading tone a half step below the tonic, and that this, in turn, creates slightly different chords and stronger harmonies. The harmonic minor scale, therefore, is used by composers primarily to create particular chords and harmonic progressions. The melodic minor scale, on the other hand, was developed partly to avoid the difficult interval of the augmented second. Thus, the melodic minor form of the scale is used to deal mainly with melodic situations.

Although this may seem confusing at first, particularly when you look at new pieces in minor keys and try to decide which forms of the scale are being used, it will become clearer with practice. Just keep in mind that the sixth and seventh degrees of the minor scale are unstable.

MUSICAL PROBLEM

If one key signature can represent two different keys, how can we tell which key a piece is in? This question can give students a great deal of unnecessary trouble. The fact is that the key signature alone does not give the answer; it gives two possibilities—the key is either major or minor. To be certain of the correct key, you must look within the music itself. The following suggestions should help.

1. Check the last note of the piece. The final note is almost certain to be the tonic.

2. Scan the piece for accidentals. Since many pieces in a minor key use the harmonic and melodic minor scale, and since the key signature can indicate only the natural minor scale, these additional accidentals within the piece indicate a minor tonality (raised sevenths mean harmonic minor, raised sixths and sevenths/lowered sixths and sevenths mean melodic minor).

Obtain a book of piano or vocal selections, and practice identifying the key of each piece by checking for the tonic and for accidentals. After practicing this method for a while, you should be able to determine the key of a new piece with little difficulty.

Sight-Singing of Minor Scales

There are conflicting opinions about the correct method of sight-singing minor scales. One school argues that the syllables of the major scale from *la* to *la* should be used to show the inherent relationship between the major scale and the minor scale. The other school argues that retaining the sound of the tonic with the syllable *do* is more important. According to this view, all scales should be started on *do* and the remaining syllables altered when necessary:

C natural minor

do   re   me   fa   sol   le   te   do

As you can see in this example for natural minor, the syllable for the third scale degree is *me*, rather than *mi*, because the third degree is lowered. Also, the syllables for pitches 6 and 7 are *le* and *te*, rather than *la* and *ti*, because the sixth and seventh scale degrees are lowered. Similar alterations in syllables are necessary for the harmonic minor and melodic minor scales.

MUSICAL PROBLEM

The two methods of sight-singing minor scales are given below for each of the three kinds of minor scales. Sing the scales both ways, and decide for yourself which system seems most advantageous. Then, practice that system until you can sing the minor scales easily and accurately.

C natural minor

1.	la	ti	do	re	mi	fa	sol	la
2.	do	re	me	fa	sol	le	te	do

C harmonic minor

1.	la	ti	do	re	mi	fa	si	la
2.	do	re	me	fa	sol	le	ti	do

C melodic minor

1.	la	ti	do	re	mi	fi	si	la	sol	fa	me	re	do	ti	la
2.	do	re	me	fa	sol	la	ti	do	te	le	sol	fa	me	re	do

EXERCISE 8•15

Spell the indicated melodic minor scales using letter names and any necessary accidentals. Indicate where the half steps occur.

1. B _ _ _ _ _ _ _; _ _ _ _ _ _ _ _
2. E _ _ _ _ _ _ _; _ _ _ _ _ _ _ _
3. C♯ _ _ _ _ _ _ _; _ _ _ _ _ _ _ _
4. D♯ _ _ _ _ _ _ _; _ _ _ _ _ _ _ _
5. A _ _ _ _ _ _ _; _ _ _ _ _ _ _ _
6. C _ _ _ _ _ _ _; _ _ _ _ _ _ _ _
7. B♭ _ _ _ _ _ _ _; _ _ _ _ _ _ _ _
8. D _ _ _ _ _ _ _; _ _ _ _ _ _ _ _
9. A♯ _ _ _ _ _ _ _; _ _ _ _ _ _ _ _
10. G♯ _ _ _ _ _ _ _; _ _ _ _ _ _ _ _
11. E♭ _ _ _ _ _ _ _; _ _ _ _ _ _ _ _
12. A♭ _ _ _ _ _ _ _; _ _ _ _ _ _ _ _
13. F _ _ _ _ _ _ _; _ _ _ _ _ _ _ _
14. F♯ _ _ _ _ _ _ _; _ _ _ _ _ _ _ _
15. G _ _ _ _ _ _ _; _ _ _ _ _ _ _ _

MUSICAL PROBLEM

Sing or play the following melodies. Locate the tonic for each melody, and identify the principal form of the minor scale on which each melody is based. Then, write the appropriate sight-singing syllables in the spaces provided, and learn to sing one or more of the melodies, using the sight-singing syllables.

"Joshua Fit the Battle of Jericho"

Tonic _____ Form of minor scale _____

"Greensleeves"

Tonic _____   Form of minor scale _____

"Johnny Has Gone for a Soldier"

3.

Tonic _____   Form of minor scale _____

"Nine Hundred Miles"

4.

Tonic _____   Form of minor scale _____

MUSICAL PROBLEM

In the previous chapter, you were asked to listen to several musical excerpts located throughout the book to determine by ear whether they were in a major or minor key. The excerpts listed below are those that were in minor keys. Listen to these excerpts once again, this time to determine if they are in natural minor, harmonic minor, melodic minor, or a combination. This is more difficult to do, and you might make mistakes at first. But keep trying—you will see improvement.

	Composer	*Title*	*Page(s)*
1.	Bach	Courante from French Suite No. 2	60
2.	Bach	Minuet in G Minor	46
3.	Bach	"Praeludium" from *The Little Piano Book for Wilhelm Friedemann Bach*	196
4.	Scarlatti	Sonata in C Minor	176
5.	Traditional	"St. James Infirmary"	285–286

Focus

The importance of scales cannot be overemphasized. All musicians, from concert pianists to jazz performers, recognize the importance of scales and practice them regularly. For the beginning music student, the first step is to learn the structure of the scales and the ways in which scales influence melody and harmony. The next step is to begin treating scales as the basic musical element they are. If you sing or play an instrument, you should devote some of your daily practice to scale work. It is only through this type of drill that you will become musically familiar with the tonal patterns of the music you wish to play. Practicing scales gives you this familiarity in a way that practicing pieces of music—no matter how difficult—does not.

MUSICAL PROBLEM

As a musician, you should begin to notice the numerous ways in which scale passages appear in tonal music. In addition, you should develop the ability to identify various kinds of scales by their sound. Ask someone who plays piano to select ten scales from Exercises 4-5, 8-3, 8-8, and 8-14 and to play them in a random order. By sound, identify each scale as major, natural minor, harmonic minor, or melodic minor. Repeat the process with different groups of scales until you are consistently successful in identifying them.

Chapter 9

Other Scales
and Modes

Not all the music we hear in our daily lives is based on major and minor scales. While it is true that the major scale and the minor scale have been the primary scales of Western music since the early 1600s, they are only two of the numerous scale forms in use before that time. Thus, much of the Medieval and Renaissance music we hear today is not based on major or minor scales. Even Chopin (1810–1849) employed scale forms other than major and minor, particularly in sections of his mazurkas. And Debussy (1862–1918), who is erroneously thought to have used the whole-tone scale almost exclusively, actually wrote in a wide variety of scales, including the major and minor scales, as well as all the scales discussed in this chapter. Twentieth-century composers have explored many other scales, including the twelve-tone scale and the microtonal scale (which uses intervals smaller than a half step), and it is impossible to listen to American folk music or the music of the Beatles without hearing pentatonic scales and modes.

Most music outside of the Western tradition has never employed major or minor scales. Because of this fact, much of the world's music may seem strange and incomprehensible to us. Some of it, however, has influenced and even infiltrated Western music in unusual ways.

In this chapter, we are going to look at three types of scales that have influenced tonal music: the pentatonic scale, which serves as the basis for most of the world's folk music; the church modes, from which the major and minor scales emerged; and the whole-tone scale, which is a synthetically derived scale used extensively in the Impressionist music of such composers as Debussy and the American Charles T. Griffes.

Although fluency in writing, singing, and playing these nontonal scales is not as essential as fluency in the major and minor scales, some familiarity is important. If because of time constraints your teacher is unable to cover this chapter in detail, you should at the least read it carefully so as to promote your understanding of these scales and their significance to the music we hear today.

Pentatonic Scales

The **pentatonic scale** is a scale with five tones per octave (Greek *penta* means *five*). It may have been one of the first scales to be used, which might explain why it is the basis for much folk music throughout the world. There is a variety of pentatonic scales, but the best-known version contains no half steps. It also has two intervals greater than a whole step:

Without any half steps, the center of gravity (the tonic) of this pentatonic scale is extremely ambiguous. It may be helpful to think of the above pentatonic scale as a simpler version of the major scale with the half steps removed (scale degrees 4 and 7). This lack of a musical center of gravity is so pronounced that any one of the five pitches of the pentatonic scale can serve as the tonic. You can demonstrate this peculiarity by playing the pentatonic scale pictured above, beginning on each of its five different pitches.

The following version of the pentatonic scale is another one in common use. Notice that in this version the half steps have been eliminated by removing scale degrees 3 and 7 from a major scale.

EXERCISE 9·1

Beginning on the indicated pitches, and using the following form as a model, write examples of the pentatonic scale. Check your solutions by singing or playing the scales you have written.

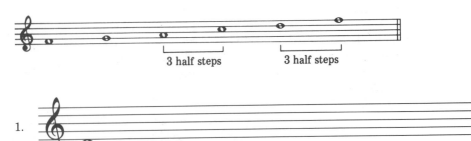

1.

12.

13.

14.

The form of the pentatonic scale in Exercise 9-1 is in wide use, including African, Chinese, Scottish, and Native American music. The following examples are drawn from Western music. Several of them could also be harmonized tonally, that is, with harmonies based on the major scale. This duality produces a most interesting musical combination: The character and ambiguity of the pentatonic scale are preserved in the pentatonic melody, while the harmony and musical center of gravity are tonal.

"Auld Lang Syne"

1.

"Ol' Texas"

2.

"Lonesome Valley"

3.

"This Train"

4.

"Tom Dooley"

5.

Rossini: *William Tell*, Overture

6.

MUSICAL PROBLEM

Sing or play the pentatonic melodies of the preceding seven examples. In each, locate and circle the tone that functions as the tonic. Beginning on the tonic, write the pentatonic scale on which each melody is based. Compare the forms of the scales you have written.

1.

2.

3.

4.

5.

6.

7.

Modes

The **modes**, also known as the *church modes* and the *diatonic modes*, are based on a system of pitch organization first used in the Medieval and Renaissance periods. These scales, from which the present-day major and natural minor scales were drawn, were the primary basis of Western music until the early 1600s and have been revived in the twentieth century by composers writing in a diverse variety of styles.

The church modes are seven-note scales based on patterns of five whole steps and two half steps. Each of the seven patterns has its own characteristic sound because the placement of the two half steps is different in each mode. The half steps are always from E to F and B to C, but their position in the scale depends on which note is the beginning pitch:

Ionian mode (present-day major scale)

Dorian mode

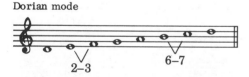

Phrygian mode

Lydian mode

Mixolydian mode

Aeolian mode (present-day natural minor scale)

Locrian mode

Of the seven modes, we are already familiar with two (Ionian mode is our present-day major scale, and Aeolian mode is our present-day natural minor scale); a third (Locrian) was historically never used until the twentieth century. Therefore, we will concentrate on only four of the modes: Dorian, Phrygian, Lydian, and Mixolydian. These four modes are easy to recognize when they occur on the white keys. But if transposed to another beginning pitch, as they often are in contemporary music, recognition becomes more difficult. Let's begin our study with the following example.

"Scarborough Fair"

A hasty glance at this piece might lead you to believe that it is in A natural minor (the key signature and last note are clues). Notice, however, that the eighth measure contains an F♯. If we begin on A (the beginning and ending pitch of the song) and construct a scale based on the pitches of the melody, we find that "Scarborough Fair" is, in fact, in Dorian mode:

2–3   6–7

One way of learning and recognizing the modes in their transpositions is to remember where the half steps are:

Mode	Half Steps
Dorian	2–3, 6–7
Phrygian	1–2, 5–6
Lydian	4–5, 7–1
Mixolydian	3–4, 6–7

If it is still difficult to distinguish the modes, it may help to relate the modes to the major and minor scales, with which you are already familiar. Thus, _Dorian mode_ is similar to the natural minor scale but with a _raised sixth degree_:

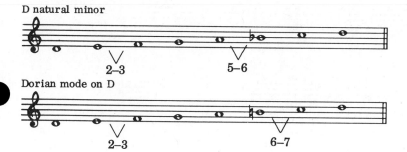

D natural minor

2–3   5–6

Dorian mode on D

2–3   6–7

To write Dorian mode on A, we write the A natural minor scale but with a raised sixth degree:

Dorian mode on A

2–3   6–7

Phrygian mode is similar to the natural minor scale but with a _lowered second degree_:

E natural minor

2–3   5–6

Phrygian mode on E

1–2   5–6

To write Phrygian mode on A, we think of the A natural minor scale, but we lower the second degree:

Phrygian mode on A

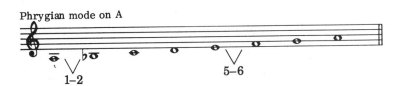

1–2   5–6

Lydian mode is similar to the major scale but with a *raised fourth degree*:

F major

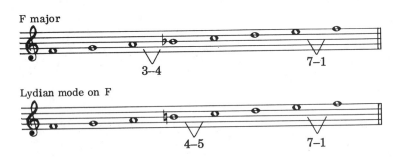

Lydian mode on F

To write Lydian mode on C, we think of the C major scale but with a raised fourth degree.

Lydian mode on C

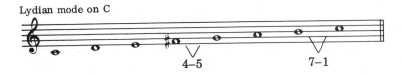

4–5   7–1

Mixolydian mode is similar to the major scale but with a *lowered seventh degree*:

G major

3–4   7–1

Mixolydian mode on G

3–4   6–7

To write Mixolydian mode on C, we think of the C major scale, but we lower the seventh degree:

Mixolydian mode on C

3–4   6–7

An alternative way to remember the modes is to relate each of them to the major scale. In this system, Dorian mode uses the pitch content of the major scale, but uses the second scale degree as the beginning pitch. Phrygian mode, likewise, can be thought of as a major scale beginning on the third scale degree; Lydian mode as a major scale beginning on the fourth scale degree; and Mixolydian mode as a major scale beginning on the fifth scale degree.

Using this system, it is relatively easy to transpose a mode to a different beginning pitch. If, for example, we wish to write Dorian mode beginning on B♭, we need only to think of B♭ as the second scale degree of a major scale, in this case the A♭ major scale, and then use the accidentals of that scale. Since the accidentals for A♭ major are A♭, B♭, D♭, and E♭, Dorian mode beginning on B♭ would be B♭–C–D♭–E♭–F–G–A♭–B♭. A similar process works for the other modes.

EXERCISE 9·2

Write the indicated modes starting from the given pitch. Before beginning, mentally note the relationship of each mode to the major or natural minor scale. Mark the half steps in each mode you write. A keyboard is provided to help you visualize each scale.

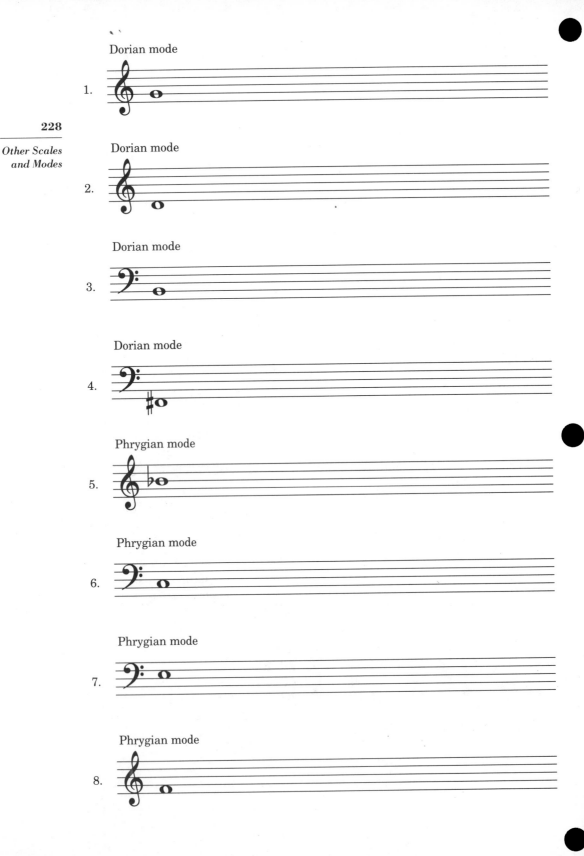

Lydian mode

9.

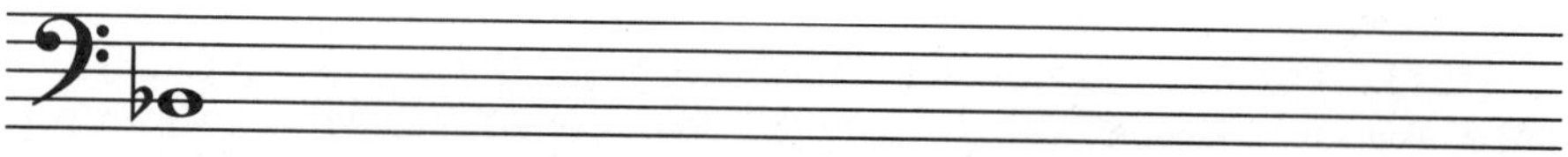

Lydian mode

10.

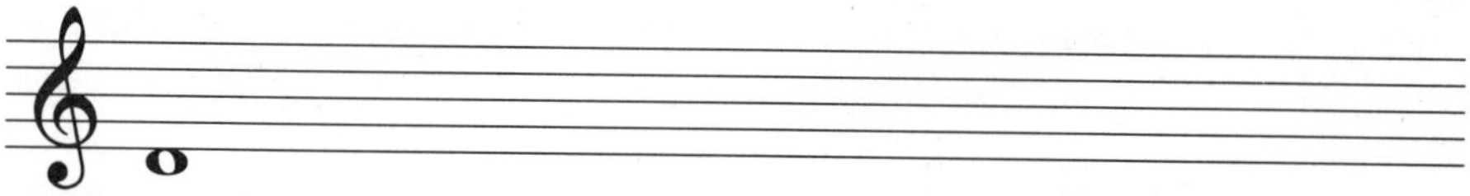

Lydian mode

11.

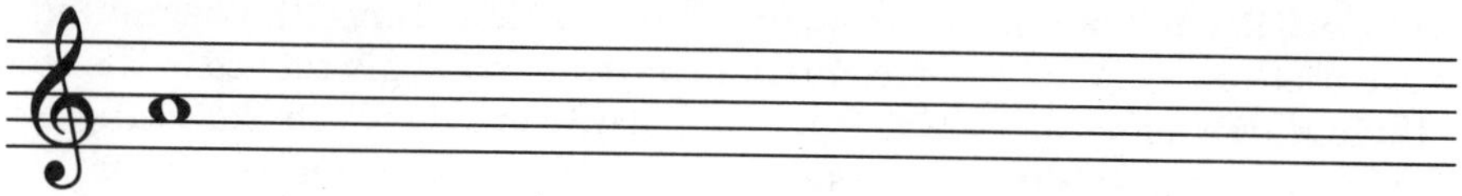

Lydian mode

12.

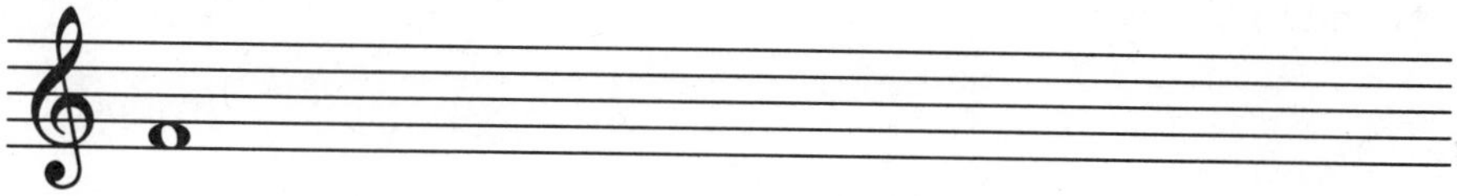

Mixolydian mode

13.

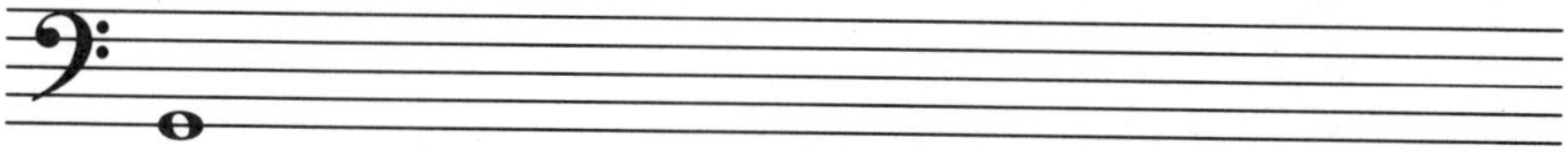

Mixolydian mode

14.

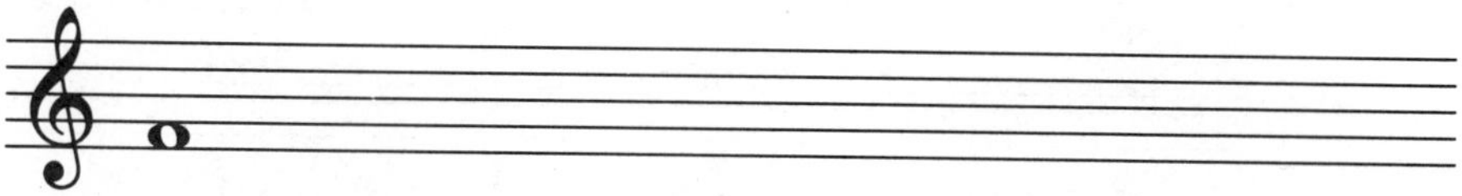

Mixolydian mode

15.

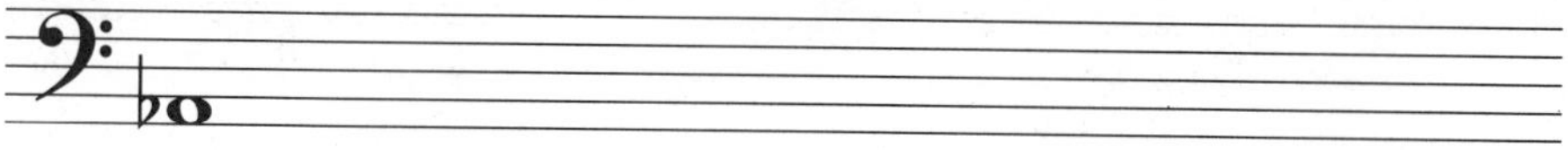

Mixolydian mode

16.

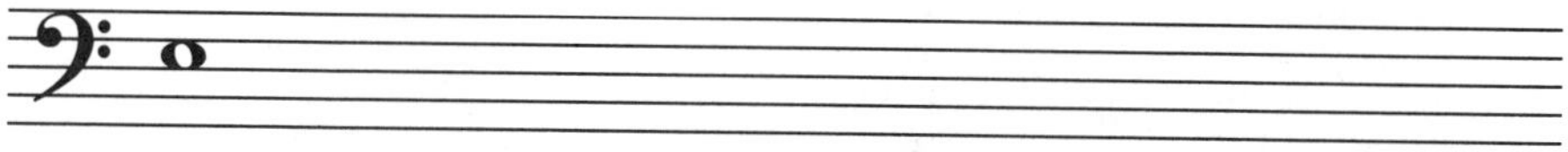

MUSICAL PROBLEM

At the keyboard, play examples of nontransposed Dorian, Phrygian, Lydian, and Mixolydian modes. Once you have the sound of each mode clearly in your ear, practice each mode on several different beginning pitches. Mentally relate the mode you are playing to the appropriate major or natural minor scale. With your ear, determine whether you have played the mode correctly. You might enjoy doing this along with another person, who can give you the beginning pitches and determine by ear whether you have played the correct notes.

As mentioned earlier, the modes were basic to Western music until the early 1600s. They fell out of use between 1600 and 1900. Since the beginning of the twentieth century, however, composers have increasingly turned to the modes in their search for new source material. This is true not only in classically inspired music but in popular music as well (for example, the Beatles' "Can't Buy Me Love," "Get Back," and "Norwegian Wood").

The following section of modal melodies spans ten centuries (the tenth to the twentieth).

Gregorian Chant

"Henry Martin"

Chopin: Mazurka in F Major, Op. 68, No. 3

Poco piu vivo

"The Drunken Sailor"

Chorus

Berlioz: *Symphonie fantastique*

232

*Other Scales
and Modes*

5.

"Old Joe Clark"

6.

Chorus

MUSICAL PROBLEM

Sing or play each of the modal melodies from the previous musical problem. For each, locate and circle the tone that acts as the modal center of gravity. Beginning on this tone, write the mode on which each melody is based. Be sure to use the actual pitches found in each piece, rather than relying solely on the key signature.

1.

2.

3.

4.

5.

6.

7.

MUSICAL PROBLEM

Modal scales are found so frequently in contemporary music that it is imperative to learn how to sing them. Singing the modes is not difficult if you remember to relate them to the major and minor scales.

Study the following modal scales and practice singing them. You may wish to test yourself at the piano as you learn. When you can sing the scales accurately, practice singing with syllables the folk songs "Scarborough Fair," "Old Joe Clark," "The Drunken Sailor," and "Henry Martin," which appear earlier in this chapter.

Dorian mode (natural minor with a raised sixth)

do   re   me   fa   sol   la   te   do

Phrygian mode (natural minor with a lowered second)

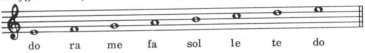

do   ra   me   fa   sol   le   te   do

Lydian mode (major with a raised fourth)

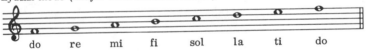

do   re   mi   fi   sol   la   ti   do

Mixolydian mode (major with a lowered seventh)

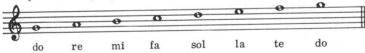

do   re   mi   fa   sol   la   te   do

The Whole-Tone Scale

The **whole-tone scale** consists of six pitches per octave, each of them a whole step apart. Since it contains only one kind of interval—the whole step—the whole-tone scale is extremely ambiguous and lacks any feeling of a center of gravity. Centers of gravity can be established in whole-tone melodies, however, by repeating certain pitches, rhythmic figures, accent patterns, and harmonic backgrounds. Another peculiarity of the whole-tone scale is that it is incapable of generating the intervals of a perfect fourth or a perfect fifth, which are considered essential to tonal music.

Whole – tone scale

Only two versions of the whole-tone scale exist, the one in the preceding example and the one following.

Whole – tone scale

Any other whole-tone scale is simply a reordering of the pitches in one of these two versions. The lack of the half-step interval allows any note within these two scale forms to function equally well as a tonic.

EXERCISE 9·3

Construct whole-tone scales on the given beginning pitches. Use the preceding examples as models. Write each scale so as to avoid double accidentals. Remember that in order to end on the octave above the beginning pitch, one of the whole steps must be notated as a diminished third.

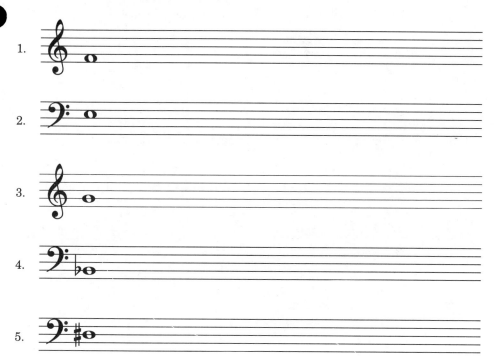

6.

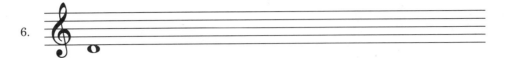

7.

8.

Although there are a few isolated examples of the whole-tone scale in the classical literature, it is found most extensively in music of the early twentieth century. Because of the whole-tone scale's ambiguity and harmonic vagueness, composers such as Debussy employed it to weaken the hold of nineteenth-century tonal practices, which they felt dominated music. Today, music based on the whole-tone scale is seldom written except as background music for movies and television.

The following examples show whole-tone music from the early twentieth century.

Debussy: *Prelude to "The Afternoon of a Faun"*

Debussy: "Voiles," Preludes, Book I

Debussy: *La Mer*

MUSICAL PROBLEM

Play the preceding examples of whole-tone music. Discuss the ways in which each example establishes its own center of gravity, and locate this center of gravity in each.

EXERCISE 9·4

Write the indicated mode, pentatonic scale, or whole-tone scale beginning on the given pitch.

Pentatonic

1.

Whole tone

2.

Lydian

3.

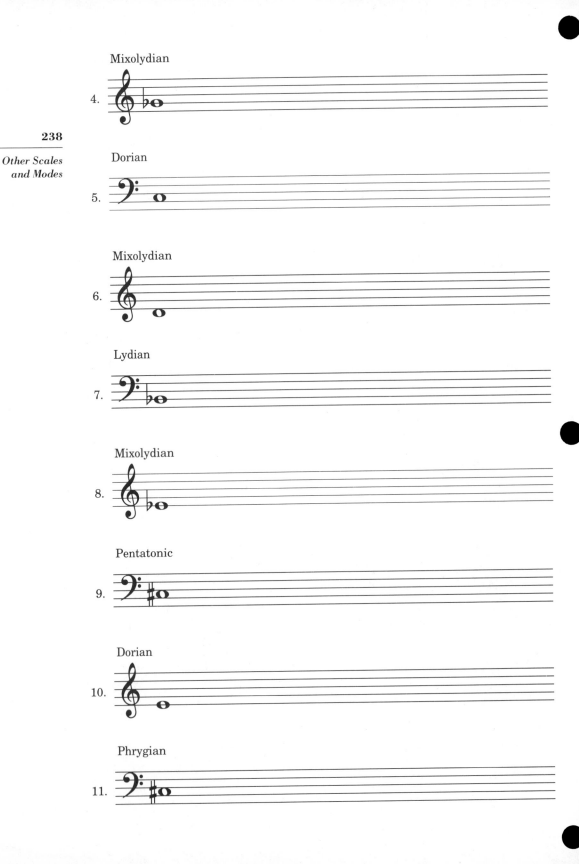

Mixolydian

4.

Dorian

5.

Mixolydian

6.

Lydian

7.

Mixolydian

8.

Pentatonic

9.

Dorian

10.

Phrygian

11.

Lydian

12. 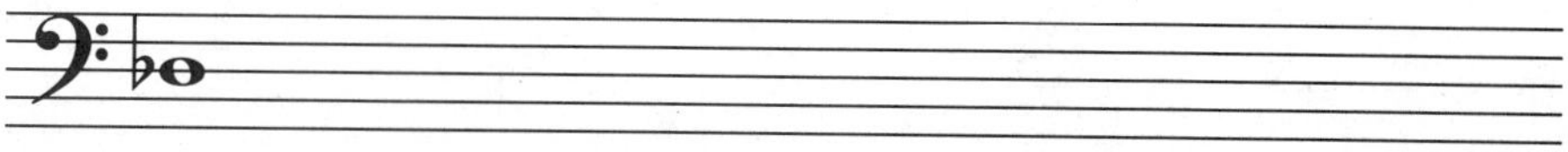 [bass clef staff with note]

*The
Whole-Tone
Scale*

Pentatonic

13. 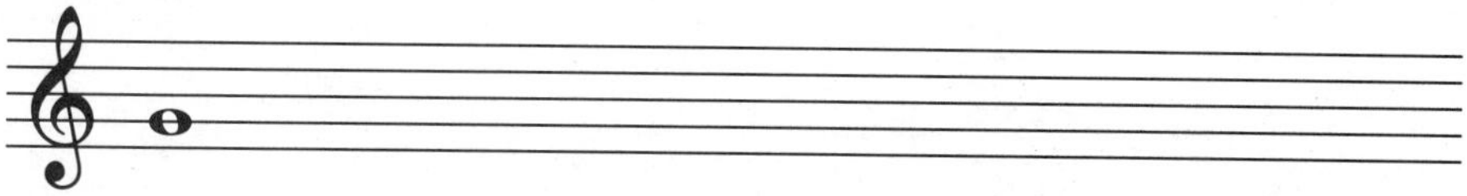 [treble clef staff with note]

Dorian

14. 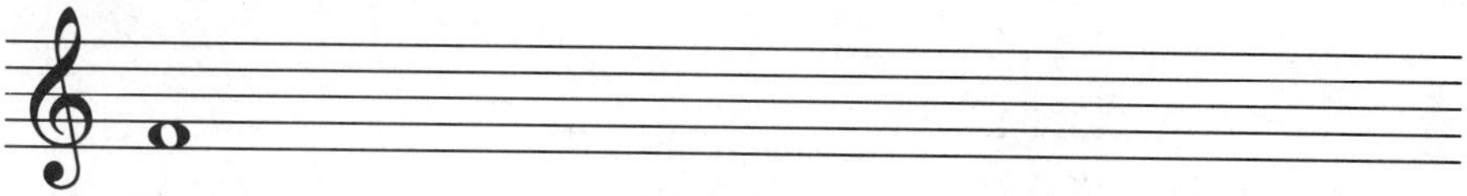 [treble clef staff with note]

Whole tone

15. 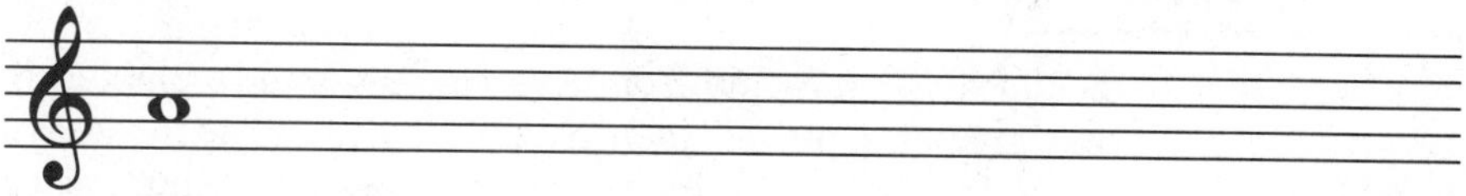 [treble clef staff with note]

Phrygian

16. 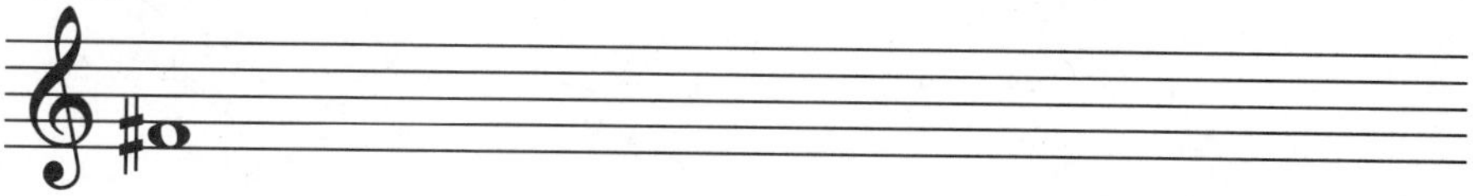 [treble clef staff with note]

Pentatonic

17. 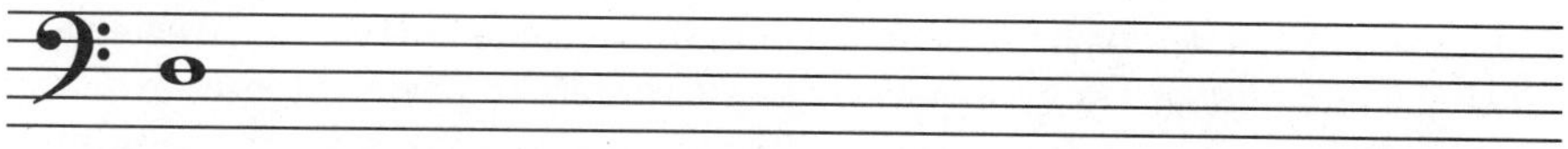 [bass clef staff with note]

Lydian

18. 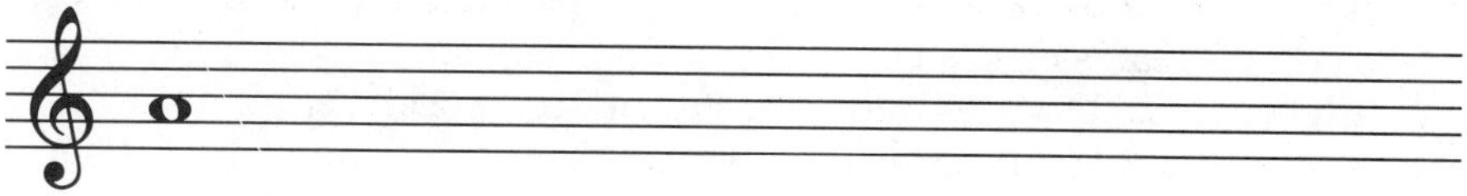 [treble clef staff with note]

Dorian

19.

Whole tone

20.

Phrygian

21.

MUSICAL PROBLEM

Ask someone to select scales randomly from Exercise 9-4 and to play each one several times. As they are being played, identify them by ear. (The modes will be less difficult to identify if you keep in mind that Dorian and Phrygian modes are similar to altered minor scales, and Lydian and Mixolydian modes resemble altered major scales.)

Focus

Major and minor scales have been the dominant scale patterns of Western music since the mid-1600s. They continue to be extremely important today, even though atonal, microtonal, and electronic techniques are strikingly obvious alternatives. Still, it is a mistake to assume that major and minor scales used to be, or are now, the only scale patterns. As this chapter has shown, a number of additional scale forms continually appear in folk, popular, and classical styles. Furthermore, the scales mentioned in this chapter are only a beginning. There are literally hundreds of scales in use throughout the world. For all musicians, and for anyone interested in how music works theoretically, an understanding of these scales is essential. This chapter is only a beginning. Now that you are aware of their existence, you will find yourself recognizing these scales—particularly modes and pentatonic scales—in a wide variety of music.

Focus on Skills

The following questions cover material presented in Chapters 7, 8, and 9. If you have difficulty with any of these questions, review the relevant sections before beginning Chapter 10.

1. Write descending natural minor scales beginning with the pitches indicated.

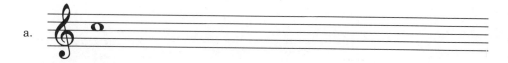

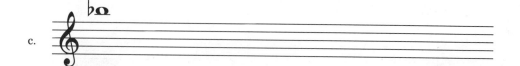

2. Write ascending harmonic minor scales beginning with the given pitches.

3. Write ascending and descending melodic minor scales beginning with the pitches indicated.

d.

e.

4. Complete the following sentences.

   a. The mediant of A natural minor is _____ .

   b. The supertonic of B melodic minor is _____ .

   c. The dominant of E harmonic minor is _____ .

   d. The submediant of F harmonic minor is _____ .

   e. The supertonic of D natural minor is _____ .

   f. The subdominant of E♭ natural minor is _____ .

   g. The leading tone of F harmonic minor is _____ .

   h. The supertonic of B♭ melodic minor is _____ .

   i. The subdominant of C♯ harmonic minor is _____ .

   j. The supertonic of C natural minor is _____ .

   k. G is the subdominant of the _____ harmonic minor scale.

   l. C♯ is the leading tone of the _____ harmonic minor scale.

   m. B♭ is the submediant of the _____ harmonic minor scale.

   n. F is the dominant of the _____ natural minor scale.

   o. A is the leading tone of the _____ harmonic minor scale.

5. Write out the following minor key signatures.

C minor

B♭ minor

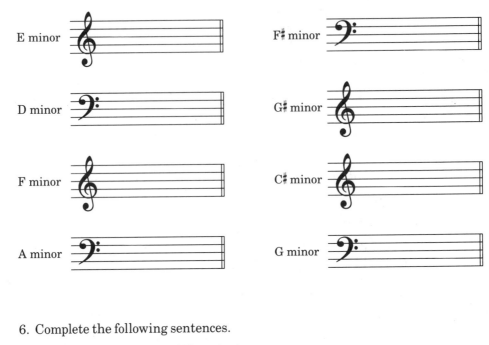

6. Complete the following sentences.

    a. The relative minor of E♭ major is _____.

    b. The relative minor of B major is _____.

    c. The parallel minor of A major is _____.

    d. The relative minor of F major is _____.

    e. The relative minor of E major is _____.

    f. The parallel major of D minor is _____.

    g. The relative major of F♯ minor is _____.

    h. The relative major of G minor is _____.

    i. The parallel major of D♭ minor is _____.

    j. The relative major of C♯ minor is _____.

7. Write two versions of the pentatonic scale beginning on the same pitch.

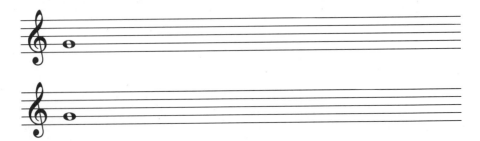

8. Write the indicated mode beginning on the given pitch.

Mixolydian

a.

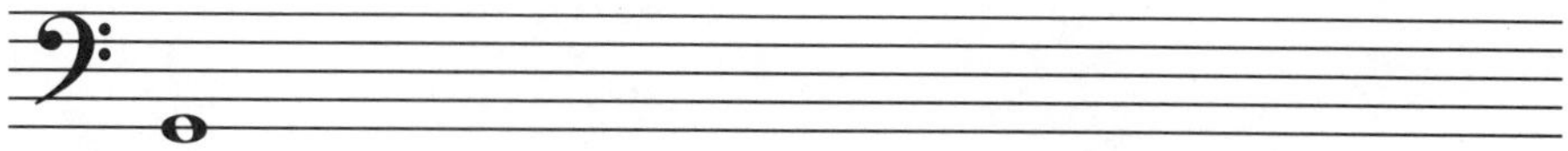

Phrygian

b.

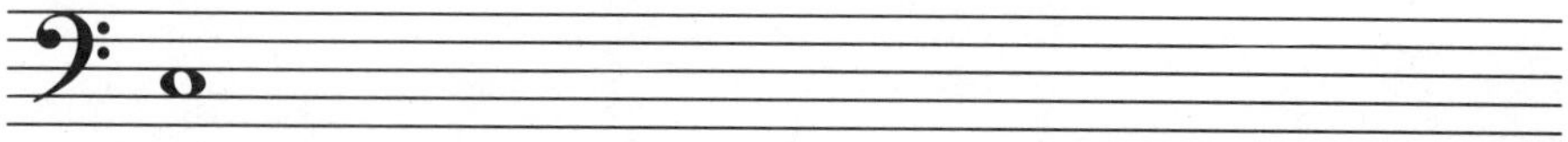

Dorian

c.

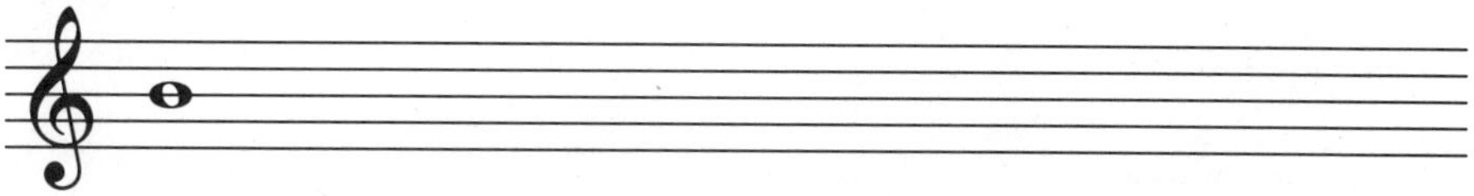

Lydian

d.

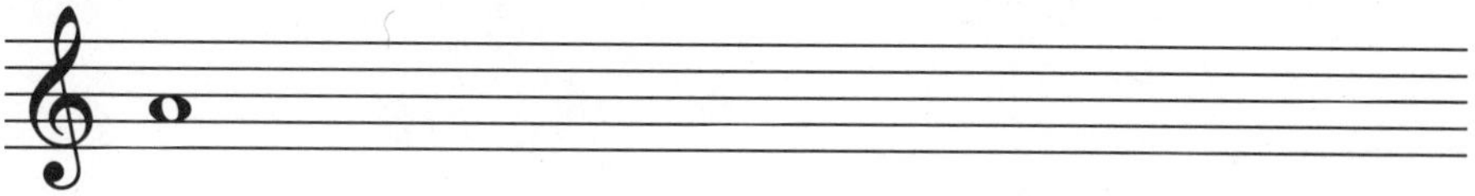

Phrygian

e.

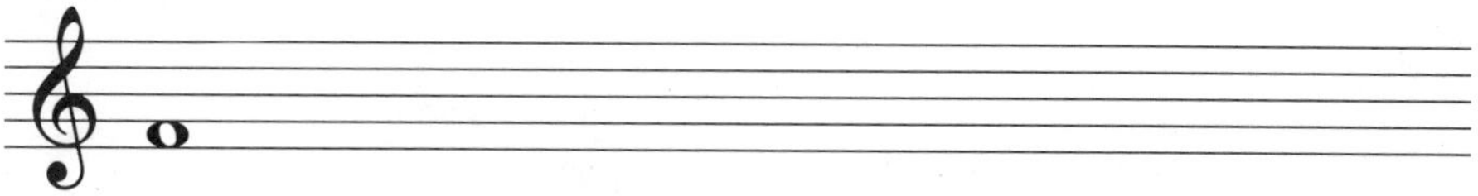

9. Write a whole-tone scale starting from the given pitch.

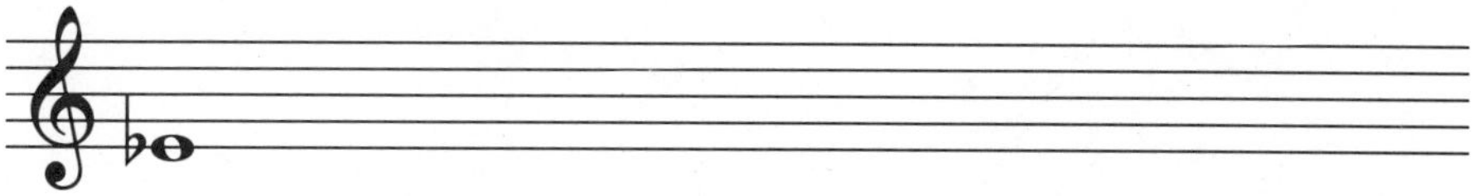

Chapter 10

Triads

The scale on which a particular piece of music is based determines the interval patterns of that music, both melodically and harmonically. Melody, as written out, is the main horizontal component of music. Harmony, when notated, is the primary vertical element of music. The major component of harmony is the **chord**, which consists of three or more pitches sounding simultaneously. Harmony itself is the horizontal movement of various chords. In this chapter, we will deal with the fundamental chord of tonal music — the **triad**.

MUSICAL PROBLEM

The following simple musical example clearly demonstrates the distinction between the horizontal character of melody and the vertical character of harmony. Play it, or listen to it played, several times. Can you, in three or four sentences, describe the ways in which the vertical (harmonic) and horizontal (melodic) components each contribute to the piece as a whole?

"Lavender's Blue"

Basic Structure of Triads

The triad is the basic chord of tonal music. Other chords—such as sevenths, ninths, and elevenths—are extensions of the triad. Four qualities of triads are possible: major, minor, augmented, and diminished. The quality of a triad is determined by the kinds of thirds it contains.

Triads are three-note chords constructed of two superimposed thirds. When the triad is written in *root position*—that is, as two superimposed thirds—we identify the three notes of the triad, from the lowest to the highest, as *the root, the third*, and *the fifth*. In the following example, notice that the third of the triad is an interval of a third above the root, and the fifth of the triad is an interval of a fifth above the root.

F Major Triad, Root Position

If the triad appears in an altered form, the terms still apply to the pitches as if they were in root position, even though the intervals are no longer a third and a fifth:

F Major Triad, Altered Forms

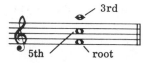

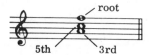

Triads take their name from the name of the root, that is, the lowest-sounding pitch when the triad is constructed as superimposed thirds.

Most beginning musicians can spell scales more easily than triads. This is because scales are based on the interval of a second while triads are based on the interval of a third. The following exercise will help you think in thirds. It deals only with the *arithmetic distance* of a third and not with the major, minor, augmented, or diminished qualities of triads.

EXERCISE 10·1

Practice reciting the following three-letter patterns until you can say them evenly.

ACE CEG EGB GBD BDF DFA FAC ACE

After you can say them evenly, work for speed. These patterns of three will help you think of triads from the root up.

Major and Minor Triads

The *major triad* (in root position) consists of two superimposed thirds, the lower of which is a major third and the upper of which is a minor third.

F Major Triad

The *minor triad* is also made up of superimposed thirds, but in reverse order: The lower third is minor and the upper third is major.

F Minor Triad

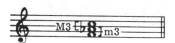

In both major and minor triads, the interval between the root and the fifth of the triad is a perfect fifth. Some students find it easier to remember major triads as a major third plus a perfect fifth above the root, and minor triads as a minor third plus a perfect fifth.

F Major Triad   F Minor Triad

EXERCISE 10·2

Write major and minor triads in root position from the same given tonic note. Remember that major triads have a major third on the bottom while minor triads have a minor third as the lower third. Remember also that the interval between the root and the fifth must always be a perfect fifth.

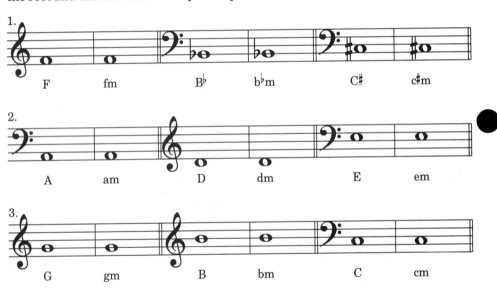

1.

F   fm   B♭   b♭m   C♯   c♯m

2.

A   am   D   dm   E   em

3.

G   gm   B   bm   C   cm

EXERCISE 10·3

Identify the root of each of the following triads, and label each as major (M) or minor (m) in quality.

EXAMPLE:

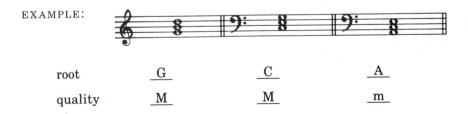

root   G   C   A

quality   M   M   m

*Major and
Minor Triads*

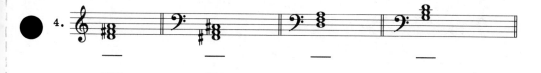

Practice playing on the piano each of the triads you identified in Exercise 10-3. Play them with each hand separately, and then both hands together using the thumbs and third and fifth fingers. As you play, listen to the difference in sound between the major and the minor triads. Then ask someone to play the triads, and see if you can identify their quality by ear.

Close and
Open Positions

When triads appear as two superimposed thirds, they are said to be in *close position*. When the notes of the triad are spaced farther apart than in close position, we call it *open position*.

D Minor Triad

Close Position   *Open Position*

Notice how open position skips one chord tone between each note.

D Minor Triad

Composers frequently employ open position to provide a change of musical color, and for reasons of voice leading. The following exercise will help you to recognize root-position triads in open position.

EXERCISE 10·4

The following are root-position triads in open position. The lowest note is the root of the triad. In each case, label the triad as major (M) or minor (m) in quality and, in the space provided, rewrite it in close position.

EXAMPLE:

m

254

Triads

1.

2.

3.

4.

5.

6.

EXERCISE 10·5

Complete the indicated major or minor triad in close position, beginning on the root given. Remember: The interval between the root and the fifth of the triad should be a perfect fifth; the interval between the root and the third of the triad will be a major third for major triads, and a minor third for minor triads.

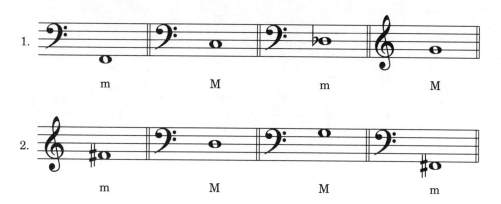

Triads

10.

m   m   m   m

11.

M   M   m   M

12.

m   m   M   M

MUSICAL PROBLEM

When you have completed Exercise 10-5, ask someone to play various lines of it on the piano, repeating each triad three times. As you listen, identify the triad as major or minor in quality.

EXERCISE 10·6

Complete the indicated close-position major or minor triads. In each case, the note given is the *third* of the triad.

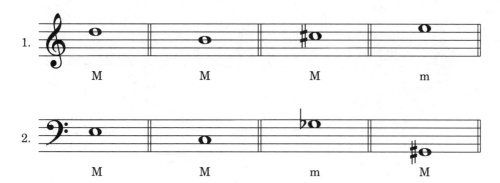

1.

M   M   M   m

2.

M   M   m   M

3.
m   m   m   M

4.
m   m   M   m

5.
m   M   M   m

6.
M   m   m   M

EXERCISE 10·7

Complete the indicated close-position major or minor triads. In each case, the note given is the *fifth* of the triad.

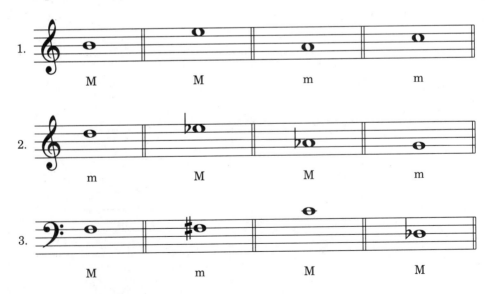

1.
M   M   m   m

2.
m   M   M   m

3.
M   m   M   M

4.

    M   M   m   m

5.

    m   M   M   M

6.

    M   m   m   m

Augmented and Diminished Triads

The *augmented triad* consists of two superimposed major thirds. Notice that the resultant interval between the root and the fifth of the triad is an augmented fifth.

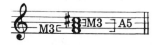

The *diminished triad* consists of two superimposed minor thirds, an arrangement that creates the interval of a diminished fifth between the root and the fifth of the triad.

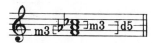

While augmented and diminished triads are found less often in tonal music than are major and minor triads, they can contribute a unique color and tension. Overuse, however, can weaken the tonal center of a piece.

EXERCISE 10·8

Identify the root of each of the following triads, and label the triads as augmented (A) or diminished (d) in quality.

EXAMPLE:

root	B	F
quality	d	A

1.

— — — —

2.

— — — —

3.
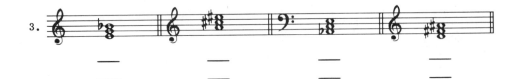

— — — —

4.
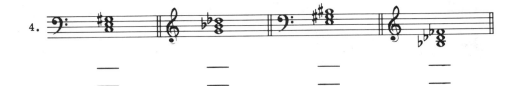

— — — —

5.

— — — —

6.

7.

8.

9.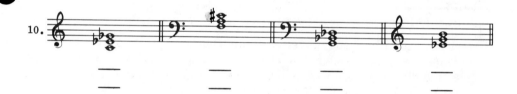

10.

MUSICAL PROBLEM

Practice playing on the piano each of the augmented and diminished triads you identified in Exercise 10-8. Play them with each hand separately, and then both hands together. Pay particular attention to the sound of each kind of triad. Then, ask someone to play the triads, and see if you can identify their quality by ear.

EXERCISE 10·9

The following are root-position triads in open position. In the space provided, label each as augmented (A) or diminished (d) in quality.

EXERCISE 10·10

Complete the indicated augmented or diminished triad starting from the given root. Remember that the augmented triad is a major third above the root plus an augmented fifth above the root, and that the diminished triad is a minor third above the root plus a diminished fifth above the root.

10.

d   d   d   d

MUSICAL PROBLEM

When you have completed Exercise 10-10, ask someone to play various lines of it on the piano, repeating each triad three times. As you listen, identify each triad as augmented or diminished in quality.

EXERCISE 10·11

Complete the indicated close-position augmented or diminished triads. In each case, the note given is the *third* of the triad.

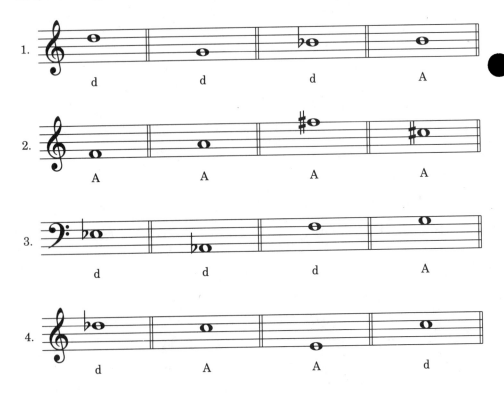

1.   d   d   d   A

2.   A   A   A   A

3.   d   d   d   A

4.   d   A   A   d

5.

A   d   A   d

6.

A   d   d   d

EXERCISE 10·12

Complete the indicated close-position augmented or diminished triads. In each case, the note given is the *fifth* of the triad.

MUSICAL PROBLEM

The following example is the Choral from Robert Schumann's *Album for the Young*, a set of forty-three piano pieces written in 1848. Listen to it as your teacher or a fellow student plays it several times. As you listen, try to identify the quality of each chord by its sound (major, minor, augmented, or diminished). Some chords will be more difficult to identify than others because they are *inverted* (the lowest note is not the root—see p. 268) or because they contain an extra pitch (a *seventh chord*—see p. 286). Still, you should be able to identify most of them after several hearings.

Then, as a class, discuss the strong harmonic character of this piece. Which line has the melody? Is the melody more important, equally important, or less important than the harmony? Does the piece sound predominantly vertical (harmonic) or horizontal (melodic)?

Schumann: Choral from *Album for the Young*

Triads and Scales

Triads can be built on any note of the major and minor scales. Musicians often identify triads built on scale degrees by the same terms as the pitches of the scale:

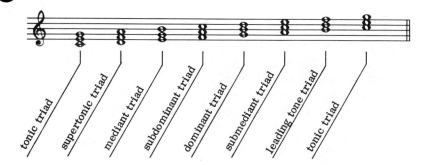

When triads are constructed on scale degrees, they must conform to the pitches of the scale. That is, if a scale has a B♭, all triads with a B will use a B♭.

Triads in F Major

Quality
of triad: M   m   m   M   M   m   d   M

Notice that the major scale produces three major triads, three minor triads, and one diminished triad.

When first beginning to work with harmony, the best version of the minor scale to use is the harmonic minor. This is because (1) unlike the natural minor scale, harmonic minor contains a true leading tone rather than a subtonic, thus creating a major V chord to resolve to the minor i, and (2) unlike the melodic minor scale, harmonic minor does not produce a confusing array of triads whose quality shifts because of the constantly changing sixth and seventh scale degrees. In actual music, however, there is often a complicated interaction between harmonic minor and melodic minor and the resulting chords. Sometimes, for example, composers will need to use chords from melodic minor because chords from harmonic minor might conflict with a melody using melodic minor.

Triads in D Harmonic Minor

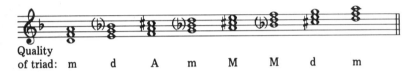

Quality of triad:	m	d	A	m	M	M	d	m

The harmonic minor scale produces two major triads, two minor triads, two diminished triads, and one augmented triad.

Inversions of Triads

Triads do not always appear in root position. Quite often the third or the fifth of the triad is the lowest-sounding pitch. Nevertheless, the triad itself does not change; the root remains the root, and the quality remains the same.

Triads can appear in two positions other than root position: first inversion and second inversion. Triads in first and second inversions add variety to the harmony of a piece, and they also serve for voice leading.

In first inversion, the triad has the *third* of the root-position triad as the lowest-sounding pitch.

D Minor Triad

Root Position   *First Inversion*

Remember that a triad in root position appears on the staff as two superimposed thirds. In first inversion, the triad consists of the same three pitches, but now there is the arithmetic interval of a fourth between the *upper* two pitches.

The triad in second inversion has the *fifth* as the lowest-sounding pitch.

D Minor Triad, Second Inversion

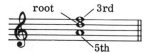
root   3rd

5th

In second inversion, the triad has the arithmetic interval of a fourth between the *lower* two pitches.

As you begin the next exercise, keep in mind that the triad does not change simply because its notes change position. This is because we hear the identifying interval of the triad in root position (the perfect fifth) differently from the way we hear the identifying interval of the triad in first or second inversion (the perfect fourth). The perfect fifth directs our ear to hear the lower pitch as the root, while the perfect fourth directs our ear to the upper pitch. Therefore, the pitch we hear as the root of the triad doesn't change with inversion.

In the study of harmony, it is essential that you be able to identify triads correctly in an inversion. This means that you must first recognize the *kind* of inversion (first or second); otherwise you will identify the wrong pitch as the root.

EXERCISE 10·13

The following triads are in either first inversion or second inversion. Identify the inversion, the root of the triad, and the quality of the triad.

EXAMPLE:

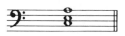

inversion   1st

root   A

quality   m

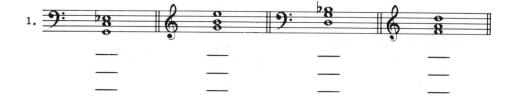

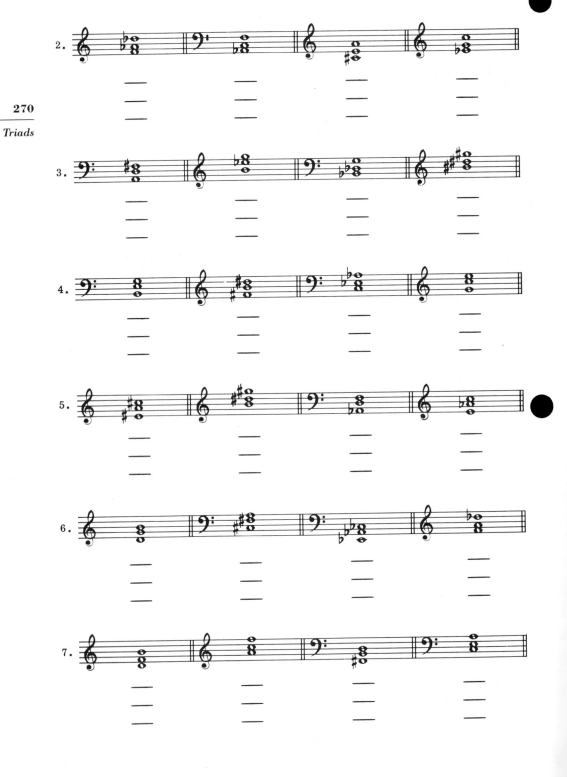

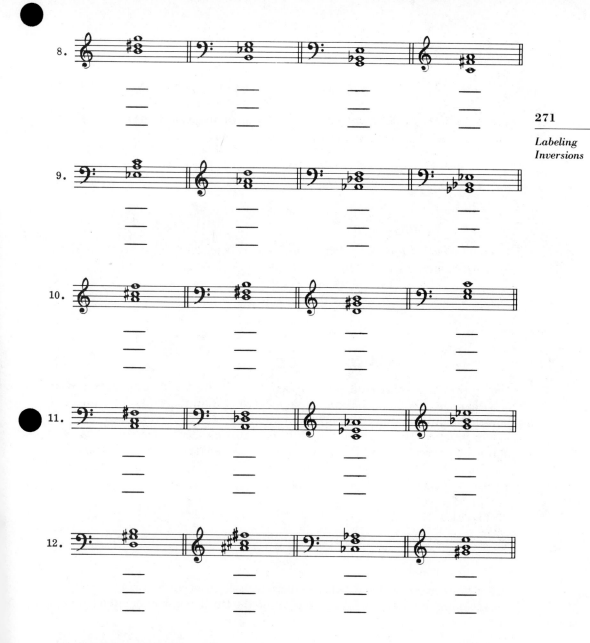

Labeling Inversions

In order to indicate whether a triad is in root position or in an inversion, a set of shorthand symbols has been developed. This shorthand system refers to the *arithmetic intervals above* the lowest-sounding pitch. Thus, a triad in *root position*, with intervals of a third and a fifth above the lowest-sounding pitch, could be shown as follows:

1
3

272

Triads

A triad in *first inversion*, with intervals of a third and a sixth above the lowest-sounding pitch, can be indicated by the following notation:

6
3

A triad in *second inversion*, containing intervals of a fourth and a sixth above the lowest-sounding note, can be shown as:

6
4

Notice that this shorthand system does *not* indicate the quality of the triad. Whether the triad is major, minor, augmented, or diminished is determined by how that triad functions in a particular key.

In practice, the shorthand system for labeling triad inversions has been abbreviated even further. For a triad in root position (the most common chord in tonal music), the numerals are omitted and the intervals of a fifth and a third are simply understood to be present.

Root Position

For a first-inversion triad, whose characteristic interval is a sixth above the lowest-sounding note, a 6 is indicated while the third, being understood as present, is not marked.

First Inversion

6

For a second-inversion triad, both of the numerals 6 and 4 are used so as to distinguish it from first inversion.

Second Inversion

Today, this system of labeling functions primarily in harmonic analysis. During the Baroque period (1600–1750), however, it was common for composers to write the keyboard part of an orchestral piece with only the bass line, plus subscript numerals to indicate inversions. This part was called *figured bass*. The keyboard musician was expected to play the written bass line, along with another instrument like cello or bassoon, and to fill in the harmonies according to the shorthand symbols. This practice, which persisted for almost 200 years, is similar to the technique of today's jazz pianists when they weave an appropriate musical fabric from a melody line and a set of mere chord symbols.

The following is an example of figured bass from the Baroque period. The top stave is the solo flute part. The bottom stave contains the figured bass part from which the keyboard performer was expected to create a suitable accompaniment.

Handel: "Siciliana" from Flute Sonata in F Major

EXERCISE 10·14

Write the indicated triad for each figured bass symbol. Each given note is the lowest-sounding pitch of a major triad. The subscript numerals indicate whether the triad is in root position or in an inversion.

1.

     6       $\frac{6}{4}$ 6   6

2.

     6   6   6   6

3.

     $\frac{6}{4}$ $\frac{6}{4}$ $\frac{6}{4}$

4.

      $\frac{6}{4}$ 6 $\frac{6}{4}$

5.

     6       $\frac{6}{4}$ $\frac{6}{4}$

MUSICAL PROBLEM

Return to the Choral from Schumann's *Album for the Young* (p. 266). Locate and circle the inverted triads. Identify the inversion and the root of each triad you have circled. You will see that all of the triads in this work have one of the three pitches doubled; that is, the same letter name appears twice. This does not in any way change the nature of the basic triad. Ignore any chords that have four *different* pitches, because they are not triads.

    After you have located the inverted triads, listen to the work again, paying particular attention to the triads. Remember that triads in inversion serve for both harmonic color and better voice leading.

Two Systems for Labeling Triads

There are two distinct methods of labeling triads in tonal music. Since each way gives important information about the harmony, musicians need to be familiar with both possibilities. *Roman numeral analysis* is the preferred method in theoretical discussions of music, when an understanding of the relationship between the triads is significant; if you continue the study of music theory, you will employ this system of labeling extensively. The other system, *pitch name identification*, appears most frequently as a performing system in popular music, jazz, and rock. If you expect to develop your performing skills, from singing folk songs to playing with a jazz or rock group, you will need to understand this type of labeling.

Roman Numeral Analysis

In roman numeral analysis, uppercase and lowercase roman numerals identify both the scale degree on which a triad is built as well as the quality of each particular triad. The uppercase roman numerals (I, IV, and V) identify the major triads; the lowercase roman numerals (ii, iii, and vi) identify the minor triads; and the symbol ° added to a lowercase numeral (vii°) identifies the diminished triad. A subscript 7 following the roman numeral means that the interval of a seventh has been added above the root. The key is indicated at the beginning of the analysis: an uppercase letter for a major key, a lowercase letter for a minor key.

C: I   ii   iii   IV   V   vi   vii°   I

EXERCISE 10·15

Use roman numerals to label the triads in the following major keys.

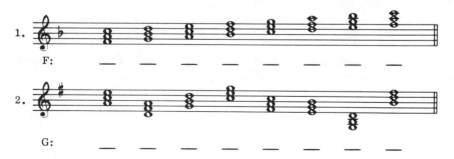

3. D: ____ ____ ____ ____ ____ ____ ____

4. B♭: ____ ____ ____ ____ ____ ____ ____

5. E: ____ ____ ____ ____ ____ ____ ____

6. D♭: ____ ____ ____ ____ ____ ____ ____

7. B: ____ ____ ____ ____ ____ ____ ____

8. A♭: ____ ____ ____ ____ ____ ____ ____

9. A: ____ ____ ____ ____ ____ ____ ____

Triads built on the harmonic minor scale are labeled as follows:

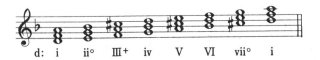

d: i   ii°   III⁺   iv   V   VI   vii°   i

The symbol + beside an uppercase roman numeral (III +) indicates an augmented triad. Study this example before undertaking the next exercise.

EXERCISE 10·16

Use roman numerals to label the triads in the following harmonic minor keys.

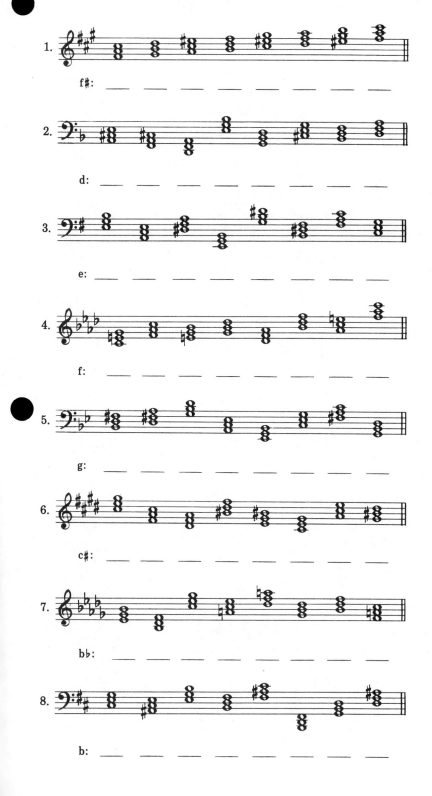

1. f#: ___ ___ ___ ___ ___ ___ ___ ___

2. d: ___ ___ ___ ___ ___ ___ ___ ___

3. e: ___ ___ ___ ___ ___ ___ ___ ___

4. f: ___ ___ ___ ___ ___ ___ ___ ___

5. g: ___ ___ ___ ___ ___ ___ ___ ___

6. c#: ___ ___ ___ ___ ___ ___ ___ ___

7. bb: ___ ___ ___ ___ ___ ___ ___ ___

8. b: ___ ___ ___ ___ ___ ___ ___ ___

9.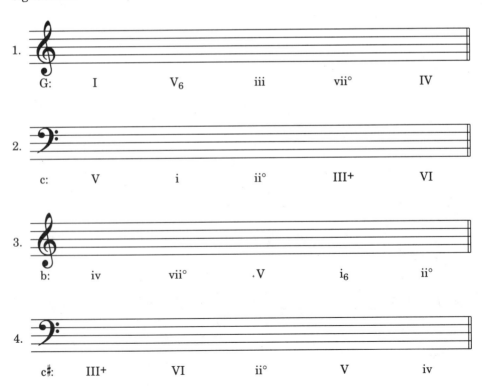

c: ___ ___ ___ ___ ___ ___ ___ ___

Every major scale and every harmonic minor scale produces the same patterns of triads; that is, the quality of each triad remains constant no matter what the key. The information given in the following chart will prove extremely useful in writing triads. Study it carefully before completing the next exercise.

Major Keys	Quality of Triads	Minor Keys
I, IV, V	major	V, VI
ii, iii, vi	minor	i, iv
vii°	diminished	ii°, vii°
none	augmented	III+

EXERCISE 10·17

Write the indicated triads for each given key. Use accidentals rather than key signatures.

1.

G: I   V₆   iii   vii°   IV

2.

c: V   i   ii°   III+   VI

3.

b: iv   vii°   .V   i₆   ii°

4.

c♯:   III+   VI   ii°   V   iv

5. D♭:   ii   vi   I$_6^4$ V   iii

6. g♯:   III+   VI   ii°   V   iv

7. A: vii°   IV$_6$ ii   vi   I

8. f: III+   i   vii°   VI   ii°

9. E♭:   V   vi   IV   iii   I$_6^4$

10. b♭:   VI   vii°   i   III+   iv

11. D: ii$_6$ vii°   V   vi   IV

12. d♯:   V   ii°   VI   III+   iv

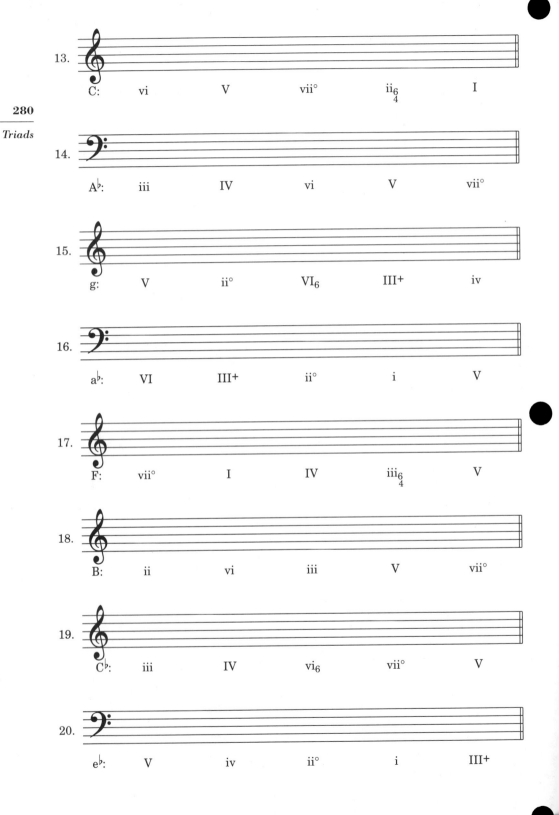

13. C: vi   V   vii°   ii$_4^6$ I

14. A♭:   iii   IV   vi   V   vii°

15. g: V   ii°   VI$_6$ III+   iv

16. a♭:   VI   III+   ii°   i   V

17. F: vii°   I   IV   iii$_4^6$ V

18. B: ii   vi   iii   V   vii°

19. C♭:   iii   IV   vi$_6$ vii°   V

20. e♭:   V   iv   ii°   i   III+

21. 𝄢

F#:   IV   ii₆   I   iii   vi

22. 𝄢

E: I   IV   V   vii°   vi

23. 𝄢

d: III+   VI   V   i₆₄   ii°

24. 𝄞

C#:   IV   vi   V   I   iii

25. 𝄞

B♭:   ii   vii°   iii   vi₆₄   V

26. 𝄢

a: ii°   VI   i   vii°   V

27. 𝄞

f#:   VI   iv₆   III+   ii°   vii°

28. 𝄢

e: i   VI   vii°   ii°   III+

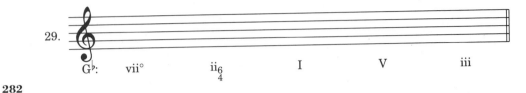

29.

G♭:   vii°   ii⁶₄   I   V   iii

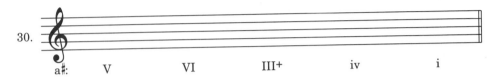

30.

a♯:   V   VI   III+   iv   i

Pitch Name Identification

In the system of pitch name identification, the letter name of the triad is substituted for the roman numeral. While this no longer indicates the relationship of the various triads to the key, it does convey triad information more directly and, therefore, is useful in a variety of performing situations.

This system of labeling supplies both the name of the triad and its quality. An uppercase letter indicates major triads (D, G, A); an uppercase letter plus a lowercase *m* indicates minor triads (E*m*, F♯*m*, B*m*); an uppercase letter with a + or with the abbreviation *aug.* indicates augmented triads (G+); and an uppercase letter with a ° or with *dim.* indicates diminished triads (C♯°, F♯°, D♯°).

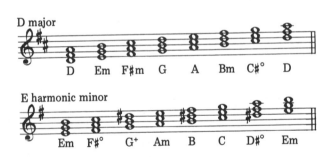

D major

D   Em   F♯m   G   A   Bm   C♯°   D

E harmonic minor

Em   F♯°   G+   Am   B   C   D♯°   Em

One current style of jazz notation indicates a minor chord with a minus sign (−) instead of a lowercase *m*. In this system, F♯−, B−, and A− are minor triads. The other chord symbols remain the same.

F♯−   B−   A−

EXERCISE 10·18

Label the following triads using pitch name identification.

12.

EXERCISE 10·19

Write the triads indicated below. All triads should be in root position.

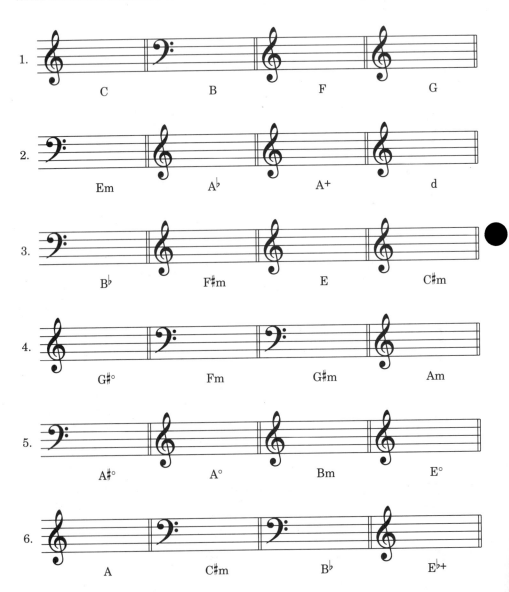

1.   C   B   F   G

2.   Em   A♭   A+   d

3.   B♭   F♯m   E   C♯m

4.   G♯°   Fm   G♯m   Am

5.   A♯°   A°   Bm   E°

6.   A   C♯m   B♭   E♭+

MUSICAL PROBLEM

The following composition has been analyzed by the pitch name identification system. As a class, discuss the kinds of information this analytical system conveys to the performer.

"St. James Infirmary"

The Dominant Seventh Chord

So far we have dealt only with the triad—a three-note chord. The triad is, after all, the fundamental structure of tonal harmony. But music is not made up exclusively of triads. Composers of the past and of the present sometimes add a fourth pitch, and occasionally even a fifth and sixth pitch, to the triad. And while some styles of music, such as folk music or early rock-n-roll, function primarily with triads, other styles, such as recent jazz or the Romantic compositions of Chopin and Liszt, utilize four-, five-, and six-note chords extensively. But no matter what the style, when extra pitches are added to the triad it is always for the purpose of increasing the harmonic tension.

Even though the study of chords more complex than the triad is beyond the scope of this book, we need to take a brief look at the most frequently used four-note chord—the **dominant seventh chord**. Because it is used so extensively, it is sometimes difficult to find an example of tonal music that *doesn't* contain at least one dominant seventh chord. In this chapter, you will learn how to write it and recognize it.

All seventh chords are so called because the fourth note creates the arithmetic distance of a seventh above the root of the chord.

interval of a seventh

Although seventh chords can be built on any degree of the scale, the one built on the dominant, that is, the dominant seventh chord, is used more frequently than any of the other possibilities. This is because the additional note enhances the harmonic tension already inherent in the dominant triad.

The dominant seventh chord is *always* a major triad with an added minor seventh above the root. This is true for both major and minor keys. This constant structure — a major triad with an added minor seventh — is what gives the dominant seventh chord its characteristic sound. Notice in the following example that when working in a minor key, the harmonic minor version of the scale is necessary in order to create the major triad.

Dominant Seventh Chord in B♭ Major

Dominant Seventh Chord in b♭ Minor

The dominant seventh chord is identified by the notation V_7, in which the roman numeral V indicates the triad built on the fifth, or dominant, note of the scale, and the subscript 7 indicates the interval of a seventh. In harmonic analysis, both symbols are necessary in order to identify correctly the dominant seventh chord. In pitch name identification, the symbol F_7 would be used for both of the previous examples.

Before beginning Exercise 10-20 and the Musical Problems that follow, play the following two patterns on the piano. Notice how the dominant seventh chord (V_7) produces an increase in harmonic tension. Listen to the difference between the V and the V_7 several times. The dominant seventh sound is an extremely common sound in all styles of tonal music and one that you should begin to listen for and recognize.

C: V   I   C: V_7 I

EXERCISE 10·20

Practice writing dominant seventh chords in root position in the keys indicated. When dealing with a minor key, remember to use the harmonic minor version. Remember also that the dominant seventh chord is always a major triad with an added minor seventh.

EXAMPLE:

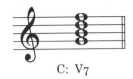

C: V_7

288

Triads

1. F: V_7 a: V_7 c: V_7 E: V_7

2. g: V_7 D: V_7 b: V_7 D♭: V_7

3. e: V_7 F♯: V_7 A: V_7 B♭: V_7

4. d: V_7 G: V_7 E♭: V_7 C♯: V_7

5. B: V_7 A♭: V_7 G♭: V_7 f: V_7

MUSICAL PROBLEM

You should learn to hear the difference between a seventh chord and a triad.
Your instructor will play various lines from the preceding exercise. Some chords
will be played as seventh chords, others as triads. In the following space, indicate
whether you hear a seventh chord or a triad.

1. _____ _____ _____ _____

2. _____ _____ _____ _____

3. _____ _____ _____ _____

4. _____ _____ _____ _____

5. _____ _____ _____ _____

MUSICAL PROBLEM

The following example illustrates roman numeral analysis of a piece of music.
Pitches that are nonharmonic to the chord are circled. Listen to the music several
times and study the analysis. Discuss in class what kinds of information this
type of chord identification does and does not provide.

Diabelli: Bagatelle

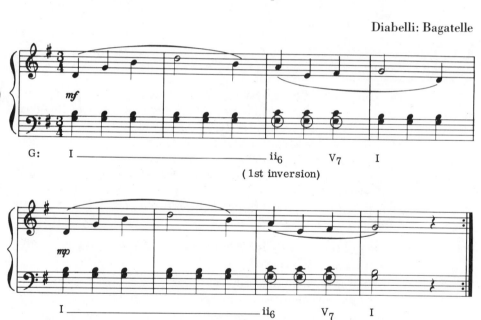

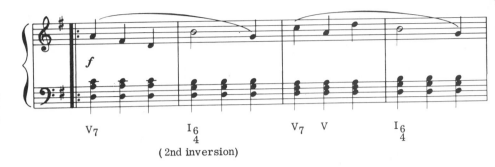

V_7 I_4^6 V_7 V I_4^6

(2nd inversion)

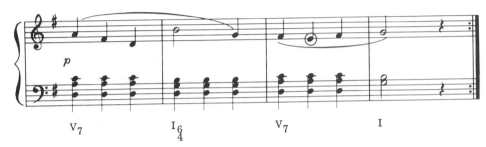

V_7 I_4^6 V_7 I

MUSICAL PROBLEM

The ability to identify chord progressions, or even individual chords, by ear is extremely useful. But for people with little background or practice at this it can be extremely frustrating, particularly at first. Unless your ear is unusually well developed, it is unreasonable to expect that you could begin by taking the chords off a recording of your favorite piece. This is an extremely sophisticated skill that only comes to most people with consistent practice. While this may be one of your goals, it is not where you begin.

If you are just beginning, keep in mind these three points as you practice this musical problem.

1. You must practice consistently in order to improve. Ear training is not unlike preparing for an athletic event.

2. Success seems to come in plateaus; don't be overly concerned if you don't appear to show improvement every day or even every week.

3. It is better, and easier, to build on success. Ideally, your success rate should be in the area of 80 to 85 percent. If it is much lower, you are probably attempting material that is too difficult for you. This can actually slow your progress.

With this in mind, try the following:

Your teacher or another student from the class will play a major or minor scale as a reference. Then he or she will play a triad that is either the tonic or the dominant triad of that key. In the spaces provided, indicate which triad is being played.

1. _____   5. _____

2. _____   6. _____

3. _____   7. _____

4. _____   8. _____

Now try this using three triads — the tonic, dominant, and submediant. It helps to remember which triads are major and which are minor.

1. _____   5. _____

2. _____   6. _____

3. _____   7. _____

4. _____   8. _____

Finally, see if you can correctly identify one of four different triads — tonic, dominant, submediant, and subdominant.

1. _____   5. _____

2. _____   6. _____

3. _____   7. _____

4. _____   8. _____

Focus

The triad is the foundation of tonal music. On one level, the triad is a simple musical structure; it is this basic characteristic that has been the main subject of this chapter. On another level, however, the triad is a subtle and complicated musical pattern, for triads in combination can express a wide range of musical emotions. From before the time of Bach and up to the present, composers — of jazz and popular music as well as concert music — have conceived of and expressed the majority of their musical ideas through the use of triads.

As an instructional tool, it is true, the triad is a simple musical structure that can be manipulated, as in this chapter's exercises, to produce simple right or wrong answers: You identify the triad correctly, or you don't; the triad is spelled correctly, or it isn't. This type of drill is absolutely essential for every musician, but don't mistake it for musical artistry.

On a musical level, there are no absolutely right or wrong answers. Most harmonic problems, for instance, have more than one correct solution. Composers faced with such ambiguous musical situations must often make choices that subtly affect the character of their work. Good composers seem to make the right choices consistently. Others write "theoretically correct" music that may seem good but is uninspired.

11

Tonality

The first ten chapters of this book have focused on the individual elements of music. Essentially, our work consisted of gaining and understanding musical facts. Now, we need to begin to unify this information—these facts about music—into an understanding of how, theoretically, real music works. Although, ultimately, this understanding of music is a lifetime goal, or at least several more semesters of work if you plan to continue in music, we can begin to apply this information and at the same time, we can draw our work in this book to a logical close.

The material covered in this chapter deals with tonality, that somewhat elusive term whose definition most Western musicians take for granted. In its simplest sense, tonality is tonal music, that is, music in which both the melody and the harmony are derived from major and minor scales. But in a more subjective, personal sense, tonality is also that unique ability of musical tones within a scale to appear to relate themselves to one another, to establish a hierarchy in which one tone becomes the point of rest, the tonic, around which the other scale degrees interact with varying degrees of tension and importance. This interrelationship of tonal degrees, as you will learn from future courses in music, regulates not only the details of music—consonance and dissonance, phrase structure, and cadences—but the overall form of each work as well. For our purposes, we will concentrate on four fundamental aspects of tonality: tendency tones, the dominant/tonic relationship, cadences, and simple chord progressions.

Of course, we can only begin to explore these topics. The material covered in this chapter generally needs quite a bit more time to work through and absorb than any of the previous chapters. But if this is your *only* class in music theory, then this chapter will show you some practical applications for the information you have gained. If you plan further study of theory, then this chapter will introduce many of the concepts you will encounter in your later studies. Either way, it is important to remember that this is only the beginning.

Tendency Tones

In our earlier study of scales, you probably noticed that not all pitches of the major scale sound equal. That is, some pitches, like the tonic, appear completely at rest, while others, like the dominant or the leading tone, sound active and full of tension. You can experience this feeling of tension for yourself by singing an ascending major scale and stopping on the seventh scale degree. The desire you probably feel to complete the scale is strong because the leading tone is an active scale degree requiring, to our ears, resolution to another tone, in this case the more restful tonic.

You can experience a similar sensation by singing the major scale again, this time descending, and stopping on the supertonic. The second scale degree is also active, but to a lesser extent. Although not as powerful, it too appears to want to resolve, in this case also to the tonic.

If you wish, you can repeat this experiment, stopping on other tones of the scale and deciding their degree of activity and the direction of their attraction, or pull, toward other notes. What you will discover if you do this is that not all tones seem attracted directly to the tonic. Some, such as the subdominant, seem to pull equally toward the dominant.

This apparent attraction of various scale degrees to one another is referred to as **tendency tones**; that is, certain pitches within a scale, or a melody, have a *tendency* to move toward other tones. This is an important concept because it explains, in part, how melodies appear to move from one point in time to another. The sense of melodic motion we experience comes partially from melodic lines moving through differing levels of activity and tension toward a final resolution on the tonic.

At one time, some theorists believed that these tendencies, or tendency tones as they are usually called, were so strong that a chart could be made of how each scale degree above the tonic should move and resolve. But actual music is always more complicated and subtle than the charts that try to explain it, and these charts of tendency tones could never really be applied with much success to the melodies composers had written. Nevertheless, the idea of tendency tones is still valid. What is important to remember is that there is a strong relationship between all the tones of the scale, both among themselves and with the tonic. Furthermore, this relationship allows the tonic to become the primary tone— the center of gravity—to which all the other tones seem to be related and to want, eventually, to resolve. Perhaps imagining an analogy with our solar system, with each planet at varying distances from the sun in the center, will be useful in understanding the unique part each scale degree plays in the idea of motion and tension/resolution in tonal music.

Sing through the following melodies several times. Some of these are melodies with which you have probably been familiar for some time. As a class, discuss both the active pitches and the points of rest within each melody. To do this, try stopping on various notes as you sing and discussing what that particular tone is contributing to the forward motion or the resolution of the melodic line. Remember that each degree of the scale contributes its own unique quality. Remember too that although this experience can be difficult to verbalize and discuss at times, our ears make these distinctions automatically.

1. "Frere Jacques"
2. "London Bridge"
3. "America"
4. "Joy to the World"

The Dominant/
Tonic Relationship

Beyond the tension and release inherent in the movement of all tonal melodies, a sense of forward motion and resolution also exists in tonal harmony. Nowhere is this more evident than in the simplest of chord progressions—the dominant to tonic relationship. This relationship—the dominant triad moving to the tonic triad—is, without doubt, the most frequently used progression in tonal music. The reason this is true is because of the strong gravitational attraction established between V and I. This relationship is so strong that these two triads, by themselves, can clearly establish the tonal center, or key, of a work.

To understand why this is true, it is important to consider the dominant triad for a moment. It includes not only the fifth degree of the scale, but also the leading tone and the supertonic. Remember from our discussion of tendency tones that these are all active scale degrees that, to our ears, appear to require resolution. Remember also from our discussion of triads that a fourth pitch—a minor seventh above the root—is often added to the dominant triad to make it sound even more active. The dominant triad, then, is an active sound, full of tension. And all of this tension is released, or resolved, when it moves to the tonic triad, the point of rest in tonal music. This movement between tension and resolution gives the harmony, as it does the melody, a sense of both forward motion and centering within the key.

In the following example, a French folk song, notice that the entire melody can be accompanied by only tonic and dominant harmonies.

"Sur le Pont d'Avignon"

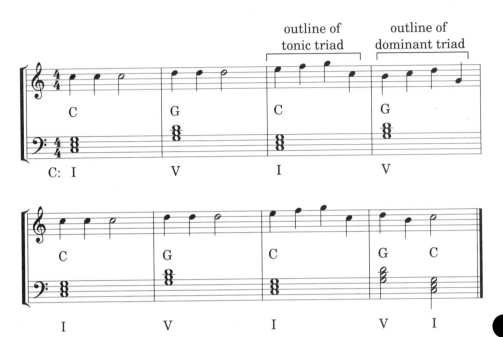

Notice also that both the melody and the harmony parallel each other. That is, when the triad changes, the melody also moves primarily to pitches that make up the triad (measures 3 and 4, for example). This movement between tonic and dominant in both the melody and the harmony, and the tension and resolution that are generated, are fundamental to the establishment of tonality and are the basis for all harmonic movement in tonal music, no matter how complicated.

MUSICAL PROBLEM

Ask someone in class to play or sing the melody of the previous example while you sing the root of each tonic or dominant triad. Can you feel the tension of the V chord resolve to the I?

Now try the opposite, with you singing the melody while someone else plays the I and V triads on the piano. Can you feel how the melody and harmony support each other?

Remember that this is a simple example with only one level of tension, the dominant triad. More complicated pieces of music will have many subtle levels of tension created by the availability of many other chords from which to choose.

Cadences

Another important point to keep in mind is that chords do not move randomly through a piece of music. Instead, they are generally arranged into phrases, following the outline of the melody, much in the same way that a paragraph of prose consists of several sentences, each made up of a complete thought. Further-more, each phrase of the melody and harmony appears to come to its own point of rest, in the same way that sentences end with a period. Unlike a sentence, however, these points of rest, or cadences as they are called, vary in their strength and feeling of completeness. Understanding the concept of the cadence, and the types of cadences that frequently occur, is the next step in understanding tonality.

A *cadence* is a momentary or permanent point of rest, either within a com-position or at its conclusion. Cadences occur in both the harmony and the rhythm of a composition. (We will not go into the rhythmic cadence.) The **harmonic cadence** consists of two chords. Four kinds of harmonic cadences occur most frequently in tonal music: the *authentic cadence*, the *plagal cadence*, the *half cadence*, and the *deceptive cadence*. Each cadence is a different formula of two chords.

The Authentic Cadence

The **authentic cadence** in a major key is the chord pattern V–I; in a minor key it is the chord pattern V–i.

Authentic cadence, major key

Authentic cadence, minor key

D: V   I

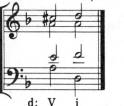
d: V   i

What makes a cadence work? A cadence gives the impression of stopping musically because of the interaction of the melody, the harmony, and the rhythm. While the chord pattern V–I can occur many times, as it does in the previous example, "Sur le Pont d'Avignon," not all occurrences create a cadence. Notice in the following examples how the melody, harmony, and rhythm work together to produce a strong feeling of conclusion. The authentic cadence gives the strongest sense of conclusion of all the cadential patterns.

Hymn: Dundee

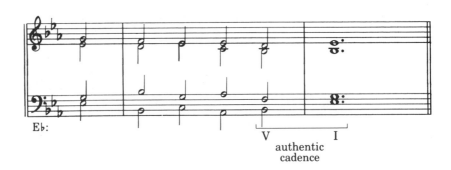

Kuhlau: Sonatina in C Major, Op. 55, No. 1, II

The authentic cadence is considered the strongest cadence because the sense of resolution — from the tension of the dominant triad to the restful nature of the tonic triad — feels most complete. This sense of resolution can be made to appear even stronger if the tension of the dominant triad is increased. As we learned in the previous chapter, this can be accomplished by the use of the dominant seventh chord. The additional note, located a minor seventh above the root, adds extra tension to the dominant sound which, in turn, is released with a stronger feeling of completeness when it moves to the tonic. Although dominant seventh chords can be used anywhere within a chord progression that seems appropriate, their most frequent use over the past three hundred years has been in the authentic cadence. Play and listen to the following two examples of authentic cadences that use the dominant seventh chords. Compare these examples to the two previous ones that used the dominant triad. Notice that the tension/release qualities of the cadence seem heightened when the dominant seventh chord is used.

Hymn: Winchester New

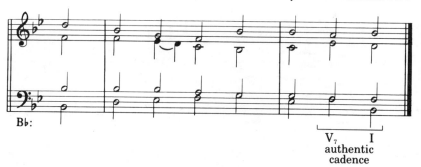

Bb:

V₇ I
authentic
cadence

Bach: Chorale, "Herr, ich denk' an jene Zeit"

Eb:

V₇ I
authentic
cadence

The Plagal Cadence

The **plagal cadence** is the chord progression IV–I in major or iv–i in minor.

Plagal cadence, major key

D: IV I

Plagal cadence, minor key

d: iv i

A plagal cadence is most likely to appear in the *Amen* ending of a hymn. This cadence, while capable of producing a feeling of permanent rest, is considered not as strong as the authentic cadence; consequently, it is used less frequently.

The Half Cadence

The **half cadence**, or **semi-cadence** as it is sometimes called, conveys a feeling of stopping that is only temporary. The half cadence never functions as a true conclusion to a section or to an entire piece because the half cadence formula ends on a dominant chord (V). The V in a half cadence can be preceded by any chord, but in practice it is most often preceded by the I or the IV in major and the i or the iv in minor.

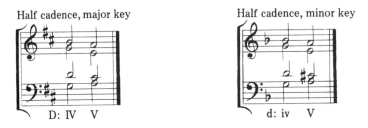

The half cadence gives the impression of a pause, but the pause is in the middle of a musical statement rather than at the end. In the following example, the first phrase ends on a half cadence, followed by a second phrase that ends on an authentic cadence. This is a common sequence in tonal music.

Mozart: Sonata in B♭ Major, K. 333, III

V   I
authentic cadence

The Deceptive Cadence

The **deceptive cadence**, in its most common form, sounds at first as if it is going to be an authentic cadence. That is, the first chord of both the authentic and the deceptive cadence is a V or V_7, and our ear expects the final triad to be the tonic. Although this is true for the authentic cadence, it is not what happens in the deceptive cadence. Instead, the V or V_7 goes to an unexpected triad, usually the vi. The result is that our ear has been momentarily deceived.

Deceptive cadence, major key   Deceptive cadence, minor key

D: V   vi   d: V   VI

     Ask someone to play the following example on the piano, first as written, and then a second time substituting the tonic triad for the submediant triad in the cadence.

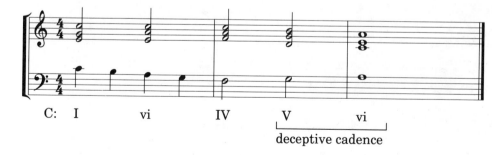

C: I   vi   IV   V   vi

deceptive cadence

Notice that the authentic cadence created by the substitution of the I chord for the vi chord works well in this situation. In fact, our ear is led to expect it. This momentary deception of our ear allows the deceptive cadence to function as an *unexpected* point of repose. It cannot, however, function as the final cadence of a piece of music.

MUSICAL PROBLEM

The following excerpts contain examples of the cadences we have studied in this chapter. Listen to each excerpt played several times, and identify by ear where the cadences occur. Then analyze each cadence as to type, both by ear and with the music.

Bach: Minuet from Suite No. 1 in G Major for Violoncello

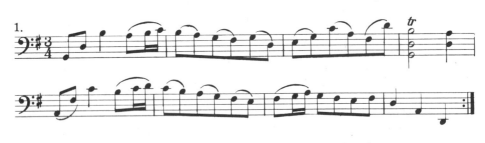

Clementi: Sonatina, Op. 36, No. 3, III

Schumann: "Soldiers' March" from *Album for the Young*

Bach: Chorale, "Ermuntre dich, mein schwacher Geist"

4.

Schumann: "The Poor Orphan Child" from *Album for the Young*

5. **Langsam**

Kuhlau: Sonatina in C Major, Op. 55, No. 1, I

6. **Allegro**

Simple Chord Progressions

Exactly how do chord progressions function? As musical phrases move through various levels of tension and release, the alternation between activity and restfulness gives a feeling of movement to the music. This musical motion is supported by the melody, harmony, and rhythm; the interrelation of these three elements is what allows the V–I progression, for instance, to function as a cadence at one time but not another. Harmony contributes to a feeling of motion through the variety of chords. Every triad is, to some extent, active and tension producing, or passive and restful.

The alternation between harmonic tension and release can be demonstrated in almost any tonal music example. Pieces that utilize the full range of harmonic possibilities, however, are generally rather complicated and difficult to talk about; they are more appropriate to advanced theoretical study. Our discussion will be limited to the concepts of tension and release and will deal with simple progressions only.

Two-Chord Progression

The simplest progression consists of only two chords — in almost every case, the tonic triad and the dominant triad. The tonic triad, which is actually the center of gravity of *every* tonal chord progression, is the most restful chord. The dominant triad, on the other hand, is considered the most active chord. Therefore, a chord progression that alternates between the tonic and the dominant possesses great potential for tension release.

Most folk songs, because they are intended to be sung and played by persons with little or no musical training, use relatively few chords. Take the following example, "Tom Dooley." It has only one chord progression for the entire song: I–V–I. Listen to someone from your class play this piece, and concentrate on the accompaniment rather than the melody. Can you feel the change in tension when the V chord appears in measure 4? Notice how this level of tension is maintained for four measures before it resolves back to the I chord. It is this difference in tension level, and the harmonic motion between them, that allows such a simple progression to work.

"Tom Dooley"

MUSICAL PROBLEM

The following well-known melodies can be harmonized with only tonic and dominant chords. As a class, sing each of these melodies several times and decide, by ear, which parts of the melody require tonic chords and which parts need dominant chords. If you play piano, you may wish to pick the melody out at the keyboard and to add tonic and dominant chords to accompany it.

1. "Down in the Valley"
2. "London Bridge"
3. "He's Got the Whole World in His Hands"
4. "Wayfaring Stranger"

Three-Chord Progression

When a third chord is introduced into a harmonic progression, it is often the subdominant chord. Remember that the plagal cadence (IV–I) is considered not as strong as the authentic cadence (V–I), because the tension created between IV and I is not as great as that between V and I. The subdominant chord is considered less tension producing than the dominant chord. Thus, in the three-chord progression I–IV–V, the IV chord stands intermediate in tension between the V chord and the restful I chord.

The subdominant chord usually appears in one of two ways: I–IV–V–I or I–IV–I–V–I. The following folk song has the I–IV–V–I progression.

"The Wabash Cannon Ball"

When used in this way, the subdominant chord contributes a first-level tension, which the dominant chord further increases to a second level. The harmonic tension is then resolved by the return to the tonic chord.

The next example of a three-chord progression uses the chord pattern I–IV–I–V–I.

"Michael, Row the Boat Ashore"

Here the subdominant chord establishes a first level of tension, which is resolved by the return of the tonic chord. Then, a second level of tension is introduced by the dominant chord, also resolved by the return of the tonic. Sing this example in class, with half the class singing the melody and the other half singing the root of each chord. Do you notice the different kinds of tension produced between I–IV–I at the beginning of the progression and I–V–I in the second half of the progression?

MUSICAL PROBLEM

The chord progressions for "The Wabash Cannon Ball" and "Michael, Row the Boat Ashore" are written in the previous examples as block chords in the treble clef in order to make them easier to see. In performance, however, they would never be played exactly this way. Ask someone in the class who plays piano and someone who plays guitar to perform one or both of these pieces, providing their own suitable accompaniment. As a class, discuss each accompaniment. What are the musical contributions of an accompaniment? Why do the block chords written in the examples not make a suitable accompaniment?

MUSICAL PROBLEM

The following folk melodies involve only I, IV, and V chords. Play or sing each song several times. Then, indicate with roman numerals below each line of music the appropriate chord progression. Put the chord symbol directly below the spot in the music where the chord changes. Begin by deciding what key each piece is in, and indicating that in the appropriate place.

"This Old Man"

"Skip to My Lou"

"New River Train"

"Red River Valley"

"Wildwood Flower"

Harmonizing a Melody

You are probably already aware that the previous musical problem asked you to harmonize a melody. The musical decisions you made for that problem are exactly the kinds of decisions you must make whenever you are determining the most appropriate chords for a melody. Such decisions, however, will become more difficult as your vocabulary of chord possibilities grows to include all the diatonic chords as well as some of the chromatic possibilities. Other difficulties arise when you deal with unfamiliar melodies. We leave the exploration of additional chords and unfamiliar melodies to independent study; however, here are a few final suggestions.

The first step in harmonizing an unfamiliar melody is obvious — become familiar with the melody. Play it. Sing it. This will help you locate the areas of tension and restfulness.

Once you feel you know the melody, next decide where the cadences should occur. If you don't do this early, chances are good that the harmony will wander aimlessly, contributing little to the buildup of tension and the subsequent cadential release. Plan your cadences well, and the chord progression will not seem haphazard. Remember — different kinds of cadences produce different levels of finality. The authentic cadence, as the most final sounding of all cadences, should not be overused. When two phrases sound related, try ending the first phrase on a half cadence and the second phrase on an authentic or plagal cadence; this device will make the first phrase sound somewhat incomplete and allow the second phrase to finish the musical idea.

Once you have planned the cadences, you are ready to fill in the rest of the chords. Although a great number of melodies can be harmonized with only the I, IV, and V chords (and an even larger number if the vi chord is also included), many melodies seem to require additional chords. If you are working with a melody of this type, keep in mind that any pitch can be harmonized in three different chords; for example, in the key of C, G can be the root of the V chord, the third of the iii chord, or the fifth of the I chord. If you have difficulty harmonizing a particular pitch in a new melody, begin by exploring these three diatonic possibilities.

Also, be certain you correctly understand the **harmonic rhythm** of the melody, that is, its rate of chord change. Some pieces have a rapid, steady harmonic rhythm, with chord changes almost every beat. In the case of a piece with a slow, irregular harmonic rhythm, it is easy to make the chords change too rapidly, which is frustrating because it feels as if *no* chord is appropriate. In such a situation don't try to force a chord change where none is needed.

Finally, don't grow discouraged. Harmonizing a melody, like everything else, improves with practice.

Focus

The study of tonal music and how it works can be fascinating. This chapter has given you a good beginning, but it is only that, a foundation. If you are to become proficient in this understanding, you must continue to build on what you have learned here.

Do you fully understand the material this chapter contains? One continuing problem many beginning musicians experience is the misunderstanding of the significance of cadences in harmonic structure. A related problem is not fully understanding simple chord progressions. Only if you do will you be able to handle more complicated progressions later on. If you understand the levels of tension and release created by various simple chord patterns, then the chromatic patterns will not seem so complicated or ambiguous.

This book began by drawing a distinction between musical talent and musical knowledge. Let me now remind you that the task of balancing your talent and your knowledge of music will be with you for the remainder of your musical life. This is both a challenge and an opportunity; all good musicians find their own ways of maintaining the balance. Good luck.

The following questions cover material presented in Chapter 10. If you have difficulty with any of these questions, review the relevant sections.

1. Identify the root of each of the following triads, and label each as major (M), minor (m), augmented (A), or diminished (d) in quality.

a.

root _____   _____   _____   _____

quality _____   _____   _____   _____

b.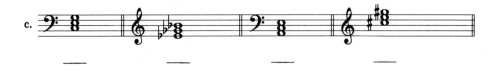

_____   _____   _____   _____

c.

_____   _____   _____   _____

d.

_____   _____   _____   _____

e.

Focus on Skills

2. The following triads are in either first or second inversion. Identify the inversion, the root of the triad, and the quality.

a.

inversion ____   ____   ____   ____

root ____   ____   ____   ____

quality ____   ____   ____   ____

b.

____   ____   ____   ____

____   ____   ____   ____

____   ____   ____   ____

c.

____   ____   ____   ____

____   ____   ____   ____

____   ____   ____   ____

d.

____   ____   ____   ____

____   ____   ____   ____

____   ____   ____   ____

3. Write the following triads in close position.

a.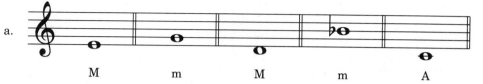

M m M m A

b.

d m m m A

c.

M A d M d

4. Write the following triads in open position.

a.

M d A M m

b.

m M m d A

5. Complete the following triads and dominant seventh chords in close position.

a.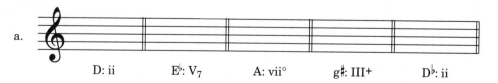

D: ii   E♭: V₇   A: vii°   g♯: III+   D♭: ii

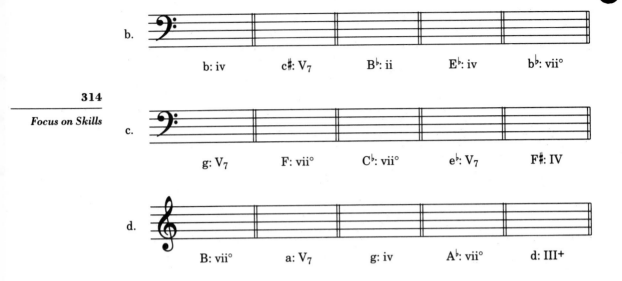

b.

b: iv   c♯: V_7 B♭: ii   E♭: iv   b♭: vii°

c.

g: V_7 F: vii°   C♭: vii°   e♭: V_7 F♯: IV

d.

B: vii°   a: V_7 g: iv   A♭: vii°   d: III+

Appendix A

Rhythms for Counting and Performing

315

8. 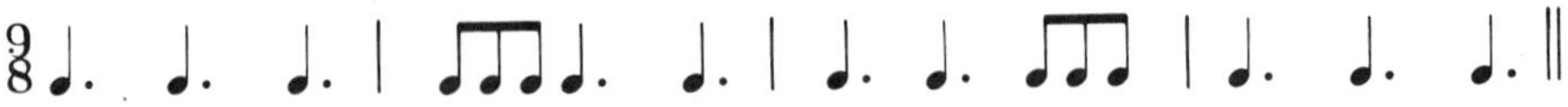

9. 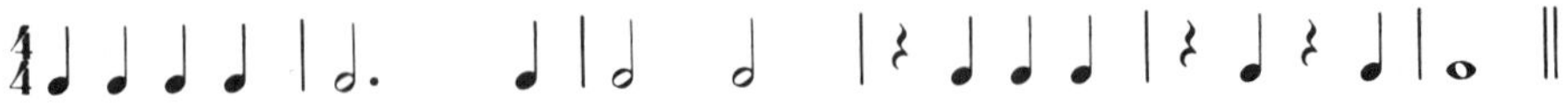

10. 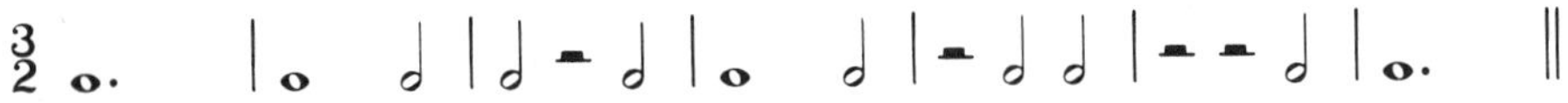

11. 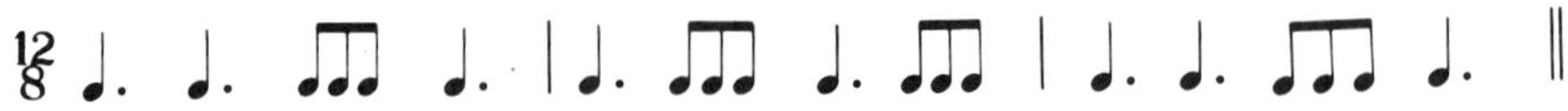

12. 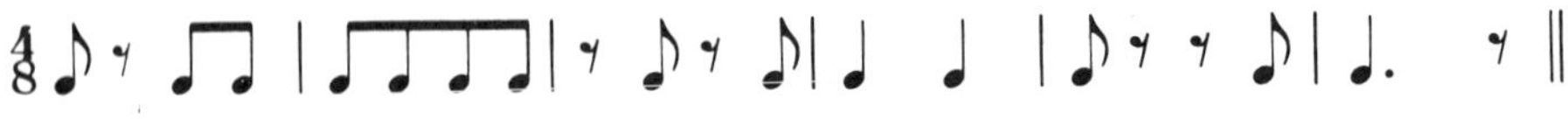

13. 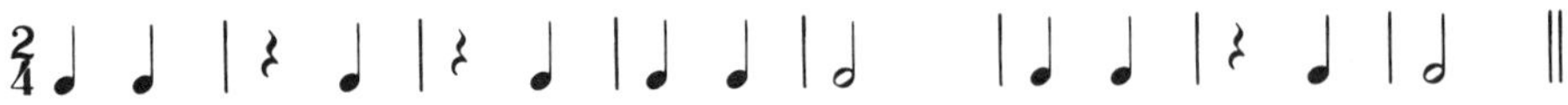

14. 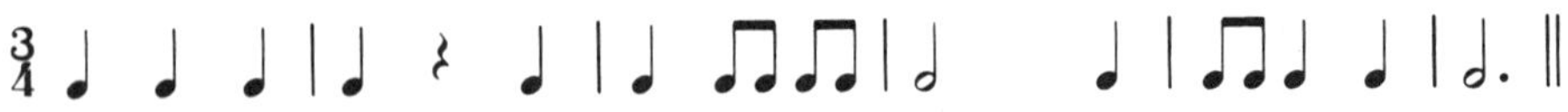

15. 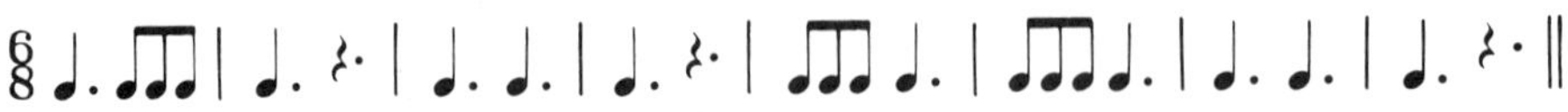

16. 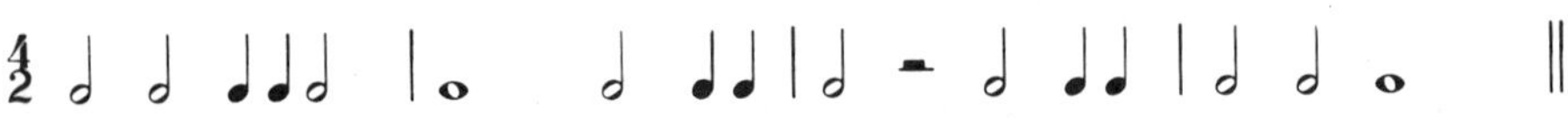

17. 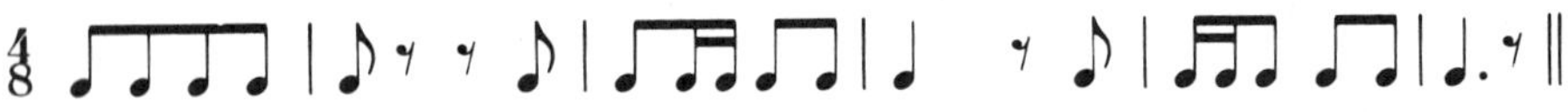

18. 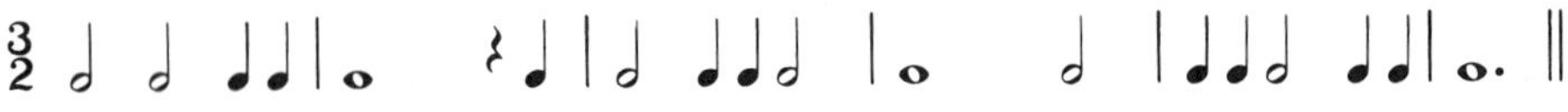

19. 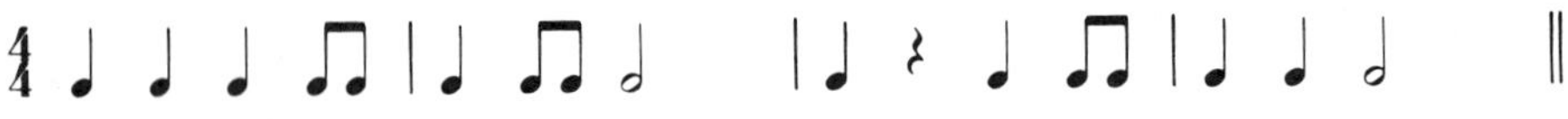

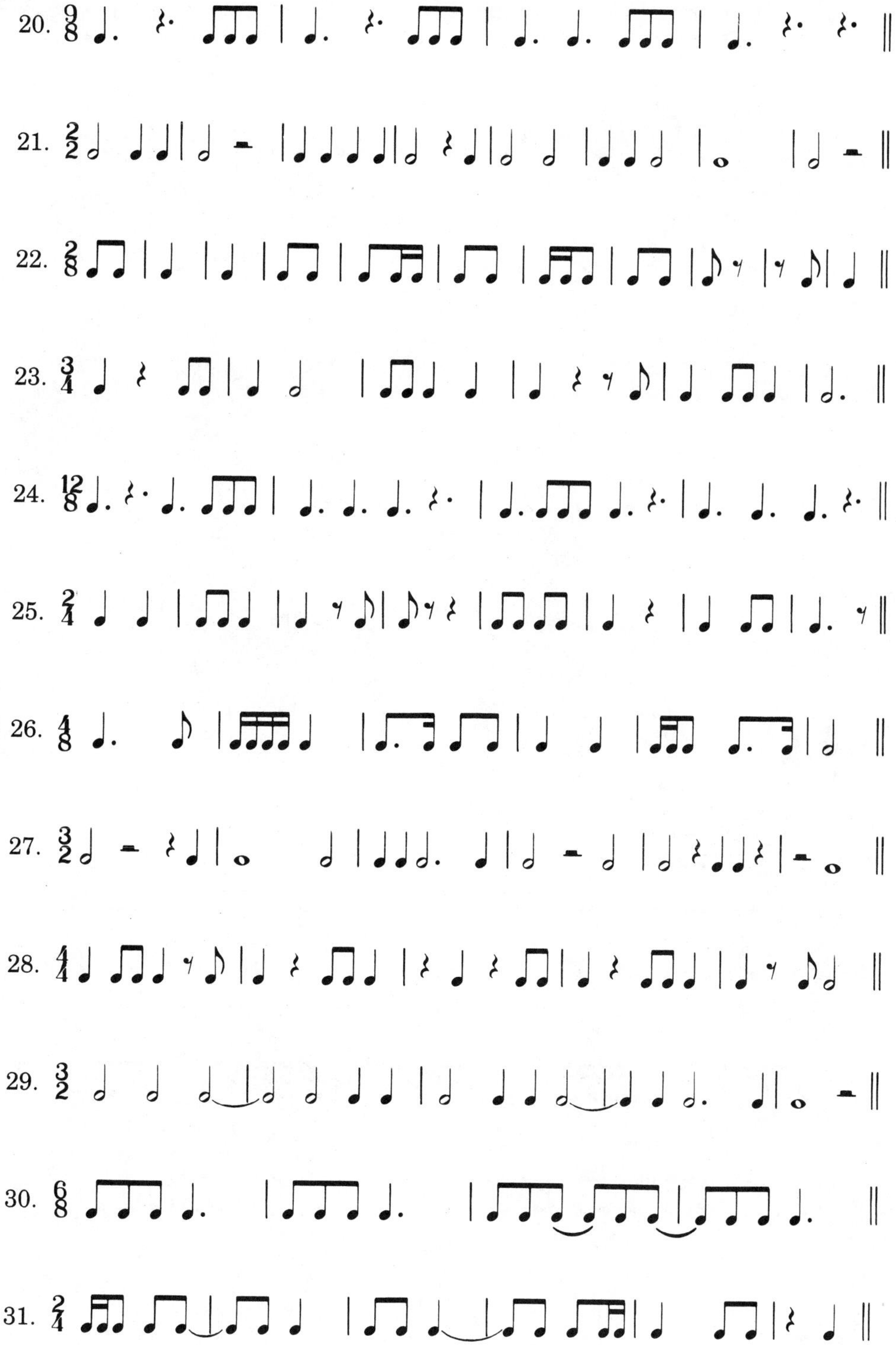
20.
21.
22.
23.
24.
25.
26.
27.
28.
29.
30.
31.

32. 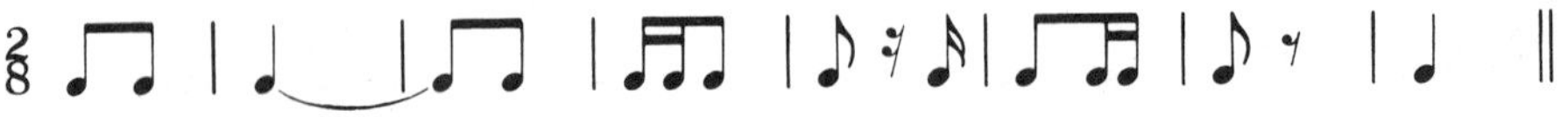

33. 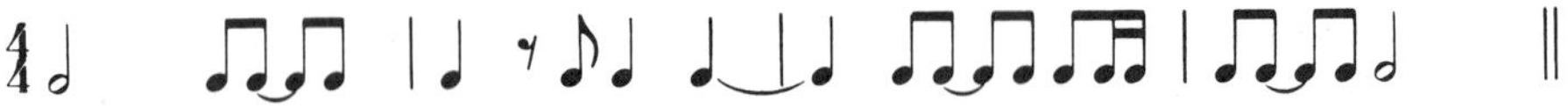

34. 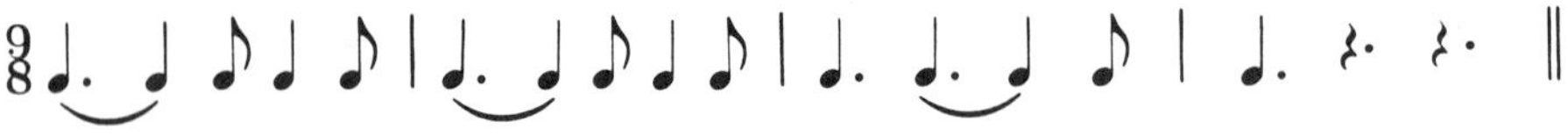

35. 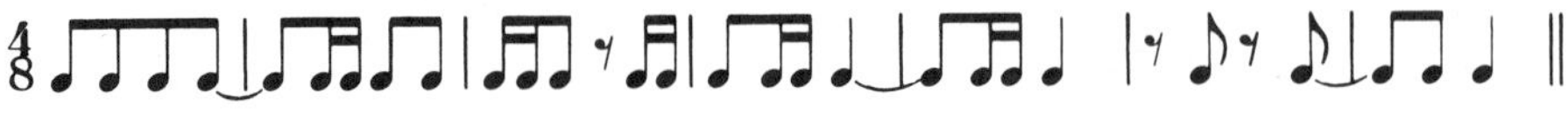

36. 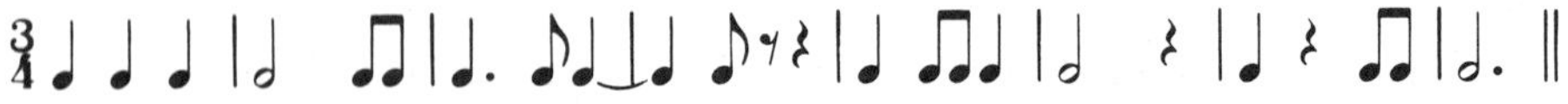

37. 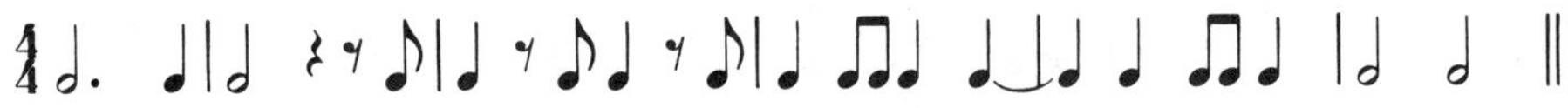

38. 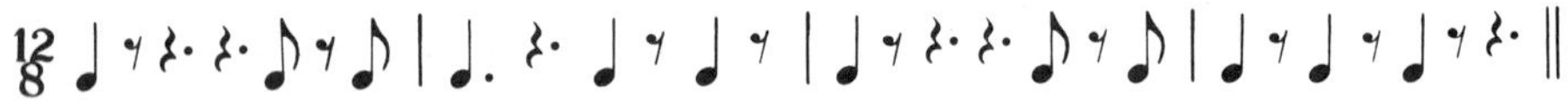

39. 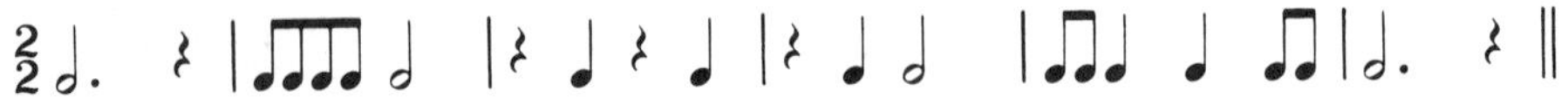

40. 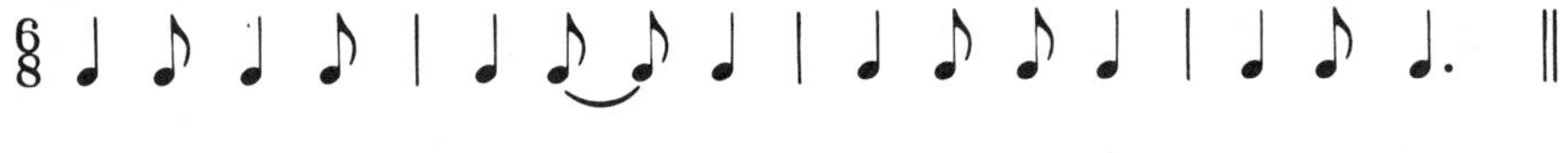

41. 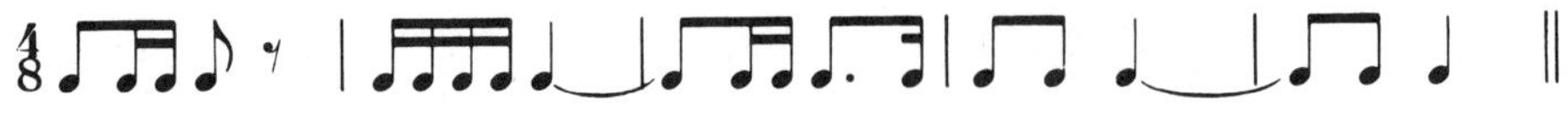

42. 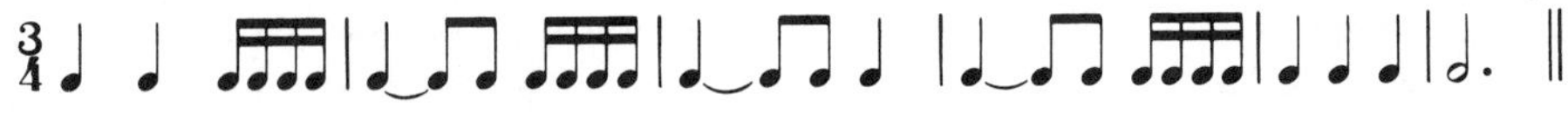

43. 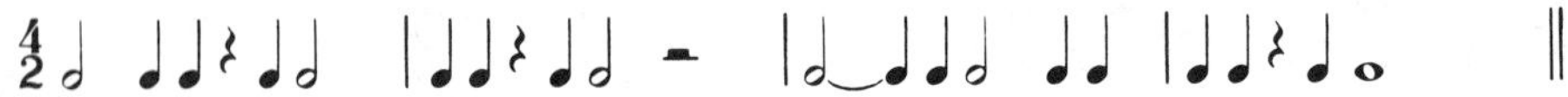

44. 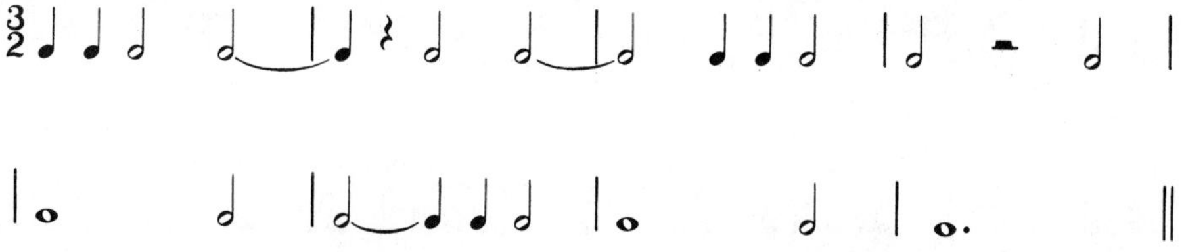

45. 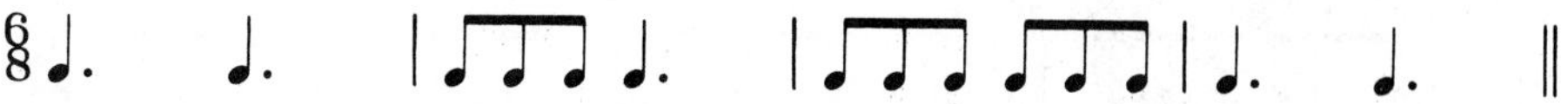

46. 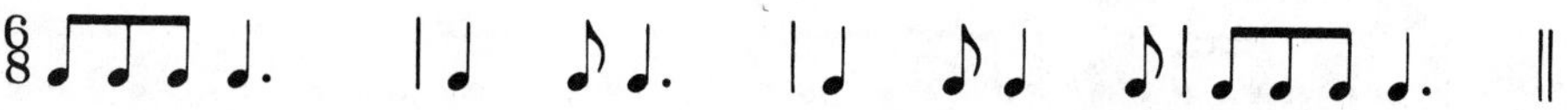

47. 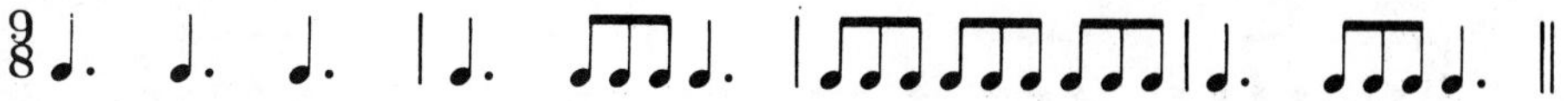

48. 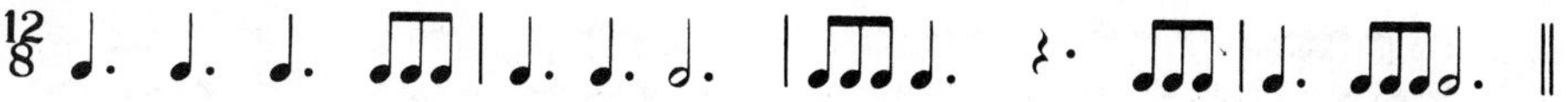

49. 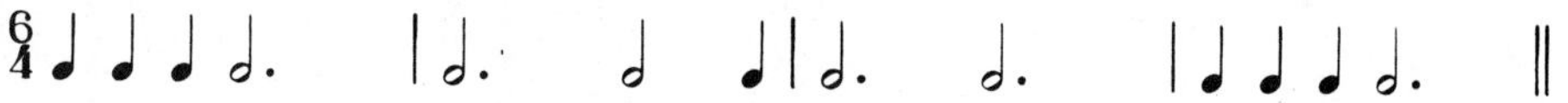

50. 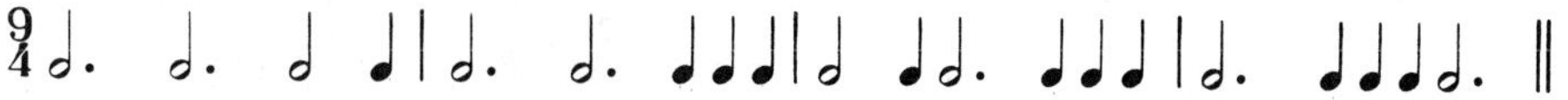

51. 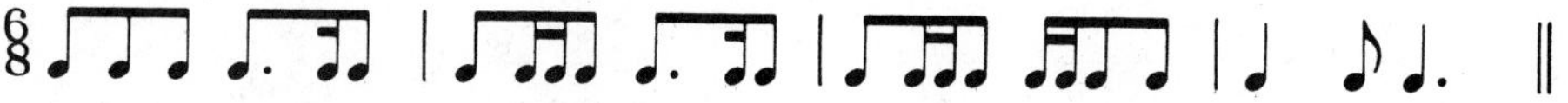

52. 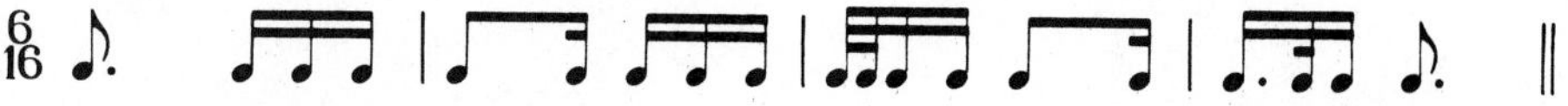

53. 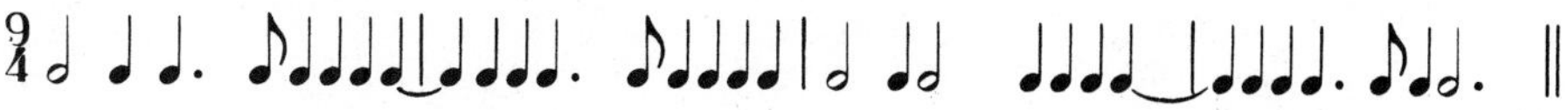

54. 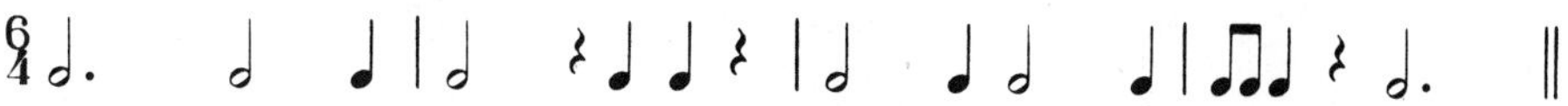

55. ...

56. ...

320

Appendix A

57. ...

58. ...

59. ...

60. ...

World Rhythms
in Two and
Three Parts

The following two- and three-part rhythmic excerpts are adapted from a variety of musical styles and traditions from throughout the world. They can be practiced with hand clapping or performed with "found" percussion instruments that students bring to class. Notice that many of the three-part patterns can be repeated a number of times. In these cases, adding or subtracting a voice on each repetition will increase the musical interest.

323

Appendix B

Fast   **African**

11.
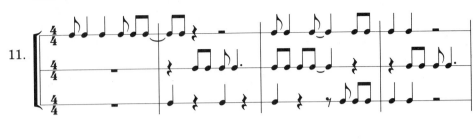

Slowly   **Western Europe**

12.

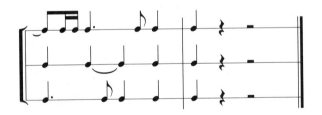

Moderate   **South America**

13.
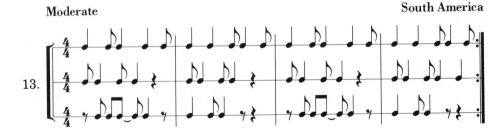

Moderate

Africa

14.

Appendix B

Syllables for Sight-Singing Scales and Modes

1. Chromatic scale — ascending:
   do, di, re, ri, mi, fa, fi, sol, si, la, li, ti, do
   Chromatic scale — descending:
   do, ti, te, la, le, sol, se, fa, mi, me, re, ra, do

2. Major scale:
   do, re, mi, fa, sol, la, ti, do

3. Natural minor scale:
   do, re, me, fa, sol, le, te, do

4. Harmonic minor scale:
   do, re, me, fa, sol, le, ti, do

5. Melodic minor scale —
   ascending:
   do, re, me, fa, sol, la, ti, do
   Melodic minor scale —
   descending:
   do, te, le, sol, fa, me, re, do

6. Dorian mode:
   do, re, me, fa, sol, la, te, do

7. Phrygian mode:
   do, ra, me, fa, sol, le, te, do

8. Lydian mode:
   do, re, mi, fi, sol, la, ti, do

9. Mixolydian mode:
   do, re, mi, fa, sol, la, te, do

10. Pentatonic scale — version one:
    do, re, mi, sol, la, do
    Pentatonic scale — version two:
    do, re, fa, sol, la, do

11. Whole-tone scale:
    do, re, mi, fi, si, li, do

Melodies for
Sight-Singing
and Playing

14.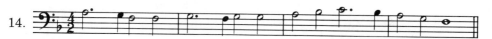

15.

16.

17.

18.

19.

20.

21.

39.

40.

Major-Scale Fingerings for Keyboard Instruments

In the following staves, the top line of numbers gives the fingering for the right hand, and the bottom line for the left hand. The numeral 1 always indicates the thumb.

C major

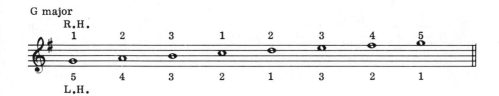

G major

D major

Appendix E

A major
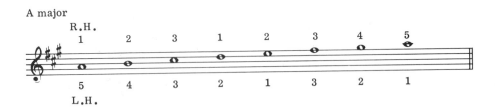

E major
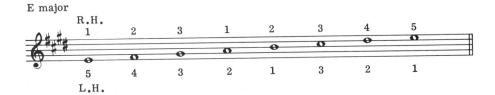

B major

C♭ major
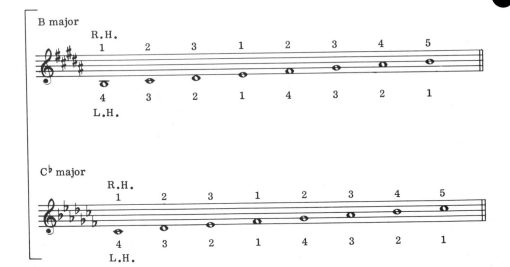

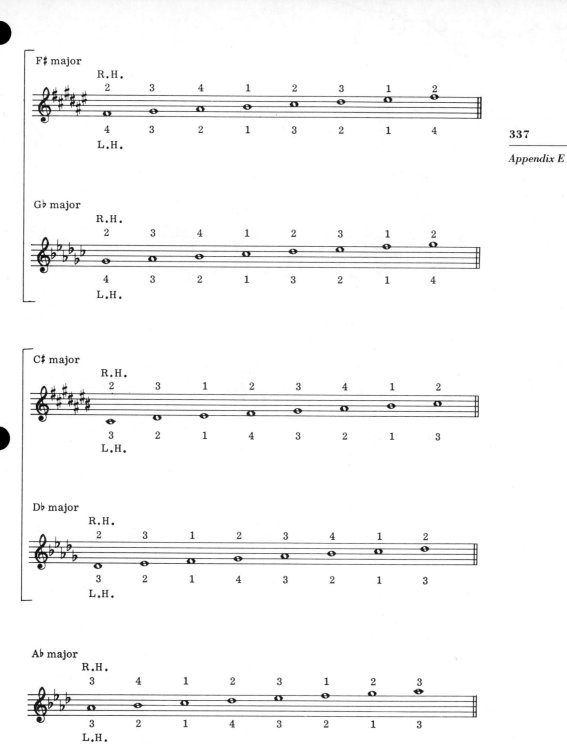

Eb major

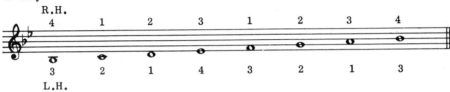

Bb major

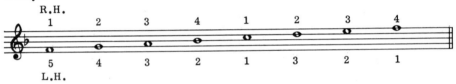

F major

The C Clef

The C Clef

Although the treble clef and the bass clef are widely used, they are not the only clefs that appear in music. Several hundred years ago most music, both vocal and instrumental, was written in the **C clef**. Today, such instruments of the modern orchestra as the viola, cello, bassoon, and trombone either use the C clef exclusively or employ it frequently. It is also vital for the study of counterpoint. If you expect to study and perform early music, to work with orchestral instruments, or to continue your study of music theory, you will need to be able to read the C clef.

Unlike the treble or bass clef, the C clef does not always appear in the same location on the staff. It is movable and may be used on any line of the staff.

C clef positions

| soprano | mezzo-soprano | alto | tenor | baritone |

Today, however, it is most commonly found in one of two positions. When located on the third line of the staff, it is referred to as the **alto clef**; when located on the fourth line, it is known as the **tenor clef**.

alto clef   tenor clef

In all cases, whether in the alto or tenor or some other position, the C clef identifies the location of the note C. Furthermore, this C is always middle C — that is, the C in the middle of the great staff. In the following example, this same C is indicated in four different clefs:

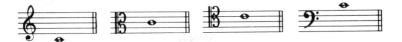

Practice drawing the C clef in the alto and tenor clef positions. The C clef is made by (1) drawing two parallel vertical lines as long as the depth of the staff and (2) drawing two curved lines to the right of the vertical lines that meet the right-hand vertical lines above and below the third or fourth line of the staff, depending on which of the positions is being drawn.

1. Draw two vertical lines first.

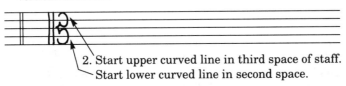

2. Start upper curved line in third space of staff.
Start lower curved line in second space.

Now identify by letter names the following pitches in the alto and tenor clefs. Remember that both alto and tenor clefs identify middle C.

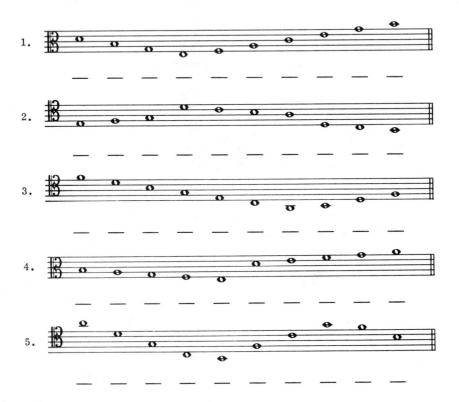

6.

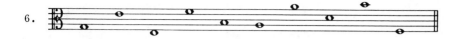

— — — — — — — — — — —

Now try the following. First identify the given pitch. Then rewrite the same pitch, but in the other clef.

1.

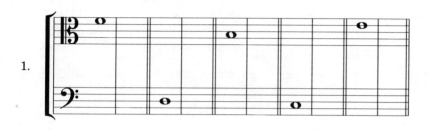

— — — — — — —

2.

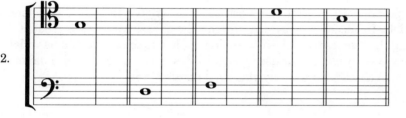

— — — — —

3.

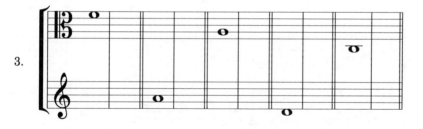

— — — — — —

The following musical example is the opening of the chorale "Ein' Feste Burg" from Cantata No. 80 by Bach. Notice that in this excerpt the soprano, alto, and tenor voices all employ various positions of the C clef. The soprano voice uses a position of the C clef known as the *soprano clef*, while the alto and tenor voices use the two positions you have been working with. The variety of positions in which the C clef appears here is the result of the composer's interest in keeping all the voice parts on or near the staff.

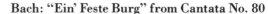

342

Appendix F

Here is a phrase from another Bach chorale, written in treble, alto, tenor, and bass clefs. In the space provided, rewrite the phrase in a single great staff, transferring the pitches from the alto and tenor clefs to the treble and bass clefs, as indicated. Be careful in your use of ledger lines. Your instructor or a member of the class can check your work by playing it on the piano.

Bach: "Heut' Triumphieret Gottes Sohn"

Appendix G

A Brief
Discussion of
Dynamics

Composers indicate degrees of loudness and softness (called **dynamics**) by annotating their music with specific words and abbreviations, most often Italian, occasionally French or German.

Volume in music is usually either maintained at steady levels or gradually changed. The standard words and symbols for a *steady volume* are:

English	*Italian*	*Abbreviation*
very soft	**pianissimo**	*pp*
soft	**piano**	*p*
moderately soft	**mezzo piano**	*mp*
moderately loud	**mezzo forte**	*mf*
loud	**forte**	*f*
very loud	**fortissimo**	*ff*

Occasionally, extremes in volume are desired, particularly in contemporary music. In such cases, the symbols *ppp*, *pppp*, *fff*, and *ffff* are used.

Gradual changes in volume are indicated by the following words and symbols:

English	*Italian*	*Abbreviation*	*Symbol*
become softer	**diminuendo**	*dim.*	>
	decrescendo	*decresc.*	
become louder	**crescendo**	*cresc.*	<

343

Where the symbols for *diminuendo* or *crescendo* are used, the length of the symbol indicates the relative length of time in which the volume change is to occur. For example, *p*————————*f* indicates a gradual change from *piano* to *forte* and taking approximately twice as long as *p*————*f*. Furthermore, the change in the latter example will sound more obvious to the listener, because it will move through *mezzo piano* and *mezzo forte* more quickly than the first example.

Whereas the symbols that dictate gradual volume changes suggest the time in which the change is to occur, the Italian terms or abbreviations are less specific unless the Italian terms **subito** (suddenly) or **poco a poco** (little by little) are added to the volume indicator. *Subito f*, for example, means suddenly loud, while *dim. poco a poco* means gradually softer.

A Brief
Introduction
to Timbre

Timbre refers to the unique sound quality of an instrument or voice that allows us to distinguish it from other instruments playing the same pitch. Timbre is determined, in part, by the way in which the sound is produced, the size of the instrument, and the design of the instrument.

When an instrument or a voice produces a tone, we hear it as a single pitch. In actuality, the tone is a composite of a fundamental frequency and a series of **overtones**. We hear a single pitch because the overtones are not as loud as the fundamental. This phenomenon is known as the **harmonic series**, and it consists of a fundamental pitch plus its first fifteen overtones.

The term **partials** refers to all the pitches within a harmonic series, including the fundamental. When the reference is to *overtones*, however, the fundamental is considered a separate element. Thus, the following example, showing the harmonic series for the pitch C, is said to have either a fundamental and fifteen overtones or sixteen partials.

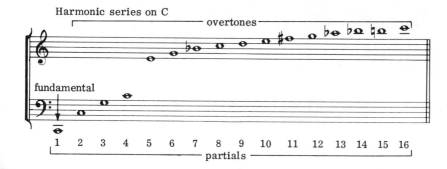

For instance, when a violin string is played, it begins to vibrate. Not only does the entire string vibrate, but shorter vibrations occur simultaneously over various lengths of the string. The vibration of the entire string produces the fundamental pitch we hear, while the shorter vibrations (the overtones) color the sound.

One instrument differs from another in timbre because each instrument is designed to amplify certain overtones and suppress others. It is, therefore, the design of an instrument that accounts, in large part, for its characteristic timbre.

Two other factors influence instrumental timbre: the size of the instrument and the way in which the sound is produced. In general, the larger the instrument the lower the pitch range. Mentally compare the pitch ranges of a violin and a string bass, or a trumpet and a tuba. Both sets of instruments produce pitches in the same way. In each case, it is the size of the instrument that gives one a soprano range and the other a bass range.

Orchestral instruments are grouped into families according to how the sound is produced (strings, woodwinds, brass, and percussion). Members of each family of instruments sound related because their similar way of producing sound helps create a similarity in timbre.

Strings: Violin, Viola, Cello, String Bass

A string instrument produces sound when a string is set in motion by a bow or is plucked by a finger. The vibration of the string is amplified by the body of the instrument. Pitch is determined, in part, by the length of the string — the longer the string, the lower the pitch. The diameter and the tension of the string also affect pitch.

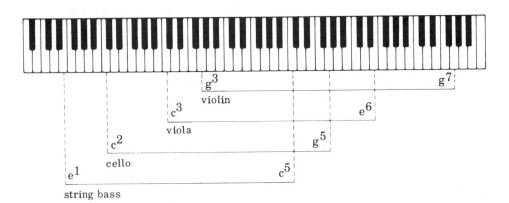

This illustration and those that follow show the approximate pitch range for each family of instruments.

Woodwinds: Piccolo, Flute, Oboe, English Horn, Clarinet, Bass Clarinet, Bassoon, Contra Bassoon

A woodwind instrument produces sound when the column of air inside the instrument is set in motion. Since this is done in a variety of ways, the sound of the woodwind family is less homogeneous than that of other families of instruments. The air column in a flute or a piccolo is set in motion by blowing across an air hole; in a clarinet or a bass clarinet by blowing against a single cane reed; and in an oboe, an English horn, a bassoon, or a contra bassoon by blowing against a double cane reed. The pitch on all woodwind instruments is controlled by finger holes on the instrument, which allow the performer to control the length of the air column — the longer the air column, the lower the pitch.

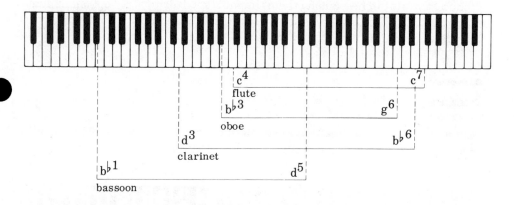

Brass: Trumpet, French Horn, Trombone, Tuba

The air column inside a brass instrument is set in motion when the performer buzzes his or her lips into a cup-shaped mouthpiece. Pitch on the trumpet, French horn, and tuba is controlled by three valves that open and close various lengths of tubing, thereby making the air column longer or shorter. Pitch on the trombone is controlled by the slide, which varies the length of the air column.

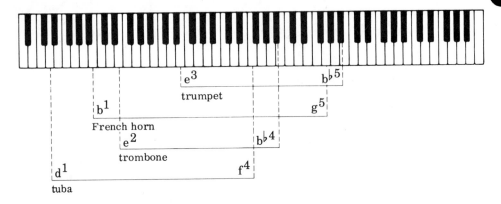

Percussion

Sound is produced on percussion instruments by striking them, usually with a wooden stick or a felt- or yarn-covered mallet. Some percussion instruments produce definite pitches, among them timpani (kettledrums), xylophone, chimes, and orchestra bells. The percussion instruments that produce an indefinite pitch include snare drum, bass drum, cymbals, and gong.

Voices

Human voices are classified into four main categories, by range: soprano, alto, tenor, and bass. The average range for each classification is as follows:

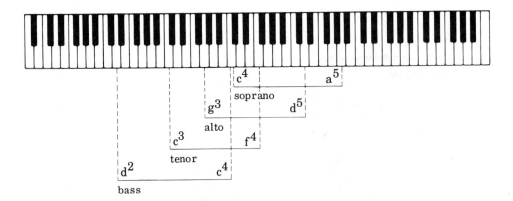

A further subdivision of voice types, shown here, is often made, particularly in opera, in order to indicate which vocal technique and which portion of the range are stressed.

   I. Soprano
- A. coloratura — emphasizes agility and range
- B. lyric — emphasizes a more gentle voice quality
- C. dramatic — emphasizes dynamic range

  II. Mezzo-Soprano — a high alto/low soprano

 III. Alto — the term *contralto* refers to a very low female voice

 IV. Tenor
- A. lyric
- B. dramatic (*Heldentenor* in German)

  V. Baritone

 VI. Bass-Baritone — has some of the baritone's high tonal qualities and some of the bass' low tonal qualities

VII. Bass

A Brief
Discussion
of Acoustics

Acoustics may at first appear an unlikely topic for a book concerned with music fundamentals. But acoustics is becoming more relevant every year. The dramatic increase in the number of synthesizers and in the use of home computers to make music has brought the study of acoustics to the forefront.

Every musical sound has four characteristics: pitch, volume, duration, and timbre. On a mechanical level, these are the components manipulated when we play an instrument or sing. The same is true on an electronic level for synthesizers and the music programs of computers. Sounds are created on these instruments by altering and adjusting the four basic characteristics of sound. If you plan to become involved with programming synthesizers, or in composing with computers, you will need a solid understanding of acoustics.

Frequency

Musical sounds, in fact all sounds, are made up of physical vibrations of air molecules. The air molecules themselves do not move forward. Instead, they vibrate back and forth in repeated patterns called oscillations. These patterns in the air are similar to the ripples in a pond created by throwing in a stone.

Air molecules are set into motion in a number of ways. Saxophone players do it by causing their reed to vibrate; string bass players pluck a string; trombone players buzz their lips inside the mouthpiece. Once the sound is begun, air molecules near the vibrating source are set into motion, and they, in turn, transfer this pattern of motion to adjacent molecules. This is how sound travels through the air.

It may be difficult at first to think of a musical pitch as a vibrational pattern of air molecules, but that is what it is. Furthermore, the faster the vibrating pattern, the higher the pitch; the slower the pattern, the lower the pitch. When thought of this way, the more accurate term for pitch is frequency.

Frequency is the number of times a vibrational pattern repeats itself. This repetition is generally measured in vibrations per second, and the term for this is Hertz (normally abbreviated Hz). When musicians talk about the pitch the orchestra tunes to as A-440 (the A above middle C), they are actually referring to a frequency of 440 Hz, that is, an air displacement of 440 vibrations per second.

Another interesting characteristic of pitch is that when the frequency is reduced by one-half, the pitch we hear descends by one octave. While the A above middle C vibrates at 440 Hz, the A directly below middle C vibrates at only 220 Hz, and the A below that at 110 Hz. The vibrating frequencies for all the As on the piano follow.

3,520 Hz
1,760 Hz
880 Hz
440 Hz
(middle C)
220 Hz
110 Hz
55 Hz
27.5 Hz

Amplitude

The pitch or frequency of a sound is determined by the speed of the vibrational patterns. But the speed of the vibration does not determine how loud a sound is. In other words, the dynamics can change without affecting the pitch. Loudness, known as amplitude, is controlled by how far each air molecule is displaced. That is, the more air movement in the initial displacement, the farther the displacement will carry through the air, and the louder the sound will appear. Scientists measure amplitude in decibels; musicians use less precise terms like *mezzo piano* and *forte*.

An important point to remember is that excessive volume, particularly when listening on headphones, can cause permanent hearing loss. This has been thoroughly documented. Although many people enjoy loud music, it is important to use caution when listening at high volume, since a loss of hearing can never be corrected.

Duration

Musical sounds have three distinct parts — attack, sustain, and decay. The initial attack describes how the sound begins. It can be quite sudden and forceful, as when a trumpet player moves his or her tongue and releases air into the instrument. Or it can be more gentle, as when a pianist lightly touches the keys. Most instruments are capable of a variety of attacks.

Once a sound is begun, the second stage is the sustain stage. Some instruments, such as the organ, can sustain a sound indefinitely. Others, such as a clarinet, can sustain only as long as the breath of the performer holds out. And other instruments, such as the xylophone, have a sharp attack but almost no sustain time at all.

Once a sound begins to fade it is considered to be in the decay stage. Musical sounds normally come to an end in one of two ways: There is a gradual loss of amplitude until the sound is no longer audible, or the sound is cut off abruptly by stopping the air or muting the string.

Synthesizers and the music programs of computers work by controlling the attack–sustain–decay characteristics of a sound. By manipulating one or all of these elements, well-known sounds, such as the sound of a flute, can be created electronically, or new sounds can even be invented.

Timbre

You will remember from Appendix H that every instrumental sound is really a composite consisting of the fundamental pitch plus the overtones of the harmonic series. Each instrument, including the human voice, emphasizes certain overtones and suppresses others. This creates a unique vibrational pattern for each instrument, but it does not alter the frequency. Therefore, two instruments, such as the flute and the oboe, can play the same pitch (frequency) but still maintain their own characteristic and distinct tone color (timbre).

Terms appearing here are **boldfaced** in text.

Accelerando A tempo marking indicating a gradual change to a faster tempo.

Accent mark (>) A sign that indicates that the note above or below it receives more stress than the surrounding notes.

Accidentals A set of signs that, when placed in front of a notehead, alter the pitch of that note chromatically. See also **Sharp sign**, **Flat sign**, **Double sharp sign**, **Double flat sign**, **Natural sign**.

Adagio A tempo marking indicating a slow tempo.

Allegro A tempo marking indicating a fast tempo.

Alto clef See **C clef**.

Andante A tempo marking indicating a moderate tempo, about walking speed.

Arithmetic distance The letter-name distance between two pitches. The arithmetic distance identifies the interval (third, fourth, and so on), but not the interval quality (major, minor, and so on).

Augmented interval The increasing of a perfect interval or a major interval by one half step.

Authentic cadence A momentary or permanent point of rest in a harmonic progression created by the two-chord progression V–I in major or iv–i in minor.

Bar lines Vertical lines, placed immediately before the accented pulse, that divide written music into measures. The meter is more easily read when music is divided into measures. Compare with **Double bar lines**.

Bass clef (F clef) (𝄢) A sign that locates the note f on the fourth line of the staff. This f is then used as a reference point for locating other pitches.

C clef (𝄡) A sign that locates the note c¹ on the staff. This sign is movable and may appear on any of the staff's five lines. Today it is commonly found on the third line (alto clef) or the fourth line (tenor clef). In either position the c¹ becomes a reference point for locating other pitches.

Chord The major component of tonal harmony; three or more pitches sounding simultaneously. See **Triad**.

Chromatic half step A half step that involves two pitches of the same letter name and staff location, such as G to G♯, A to A♭, or E to E♯. See also **Diatonic half step**.

Chromatic scale A scale formed by the division of the octave into twelve equal half steps.

Clef A sign that locates a particular pitch on the staff. This pitch is then used as a reference point for other pitches on the staff. The commonly used clefs are treble clef, bass clef, and C clef.

Compound interval Any interval greater than an octave in arithmetic distance.

Compound meter Any meter in which the basic pulse is normally subdivided into three equal parts.

Crescendo (*cresc.* or ⟨) A dynamics marking indicating that the musical passage is to grow louder.

Deceptive cadence A temporary point of rest in a chord progression, in which an unexpected chord, usually vi, follows a V or V_7 instead of the tonic triad that is expected.

Decrescendo (*decresc.* or ⟩) A dynamics marking indicating that the musical passage is to grow softer.

Diatonic half step A half step that involves two pitches with adjacent letter names and staff locations, such as A to B♭, G♯ to F, or B to C. See also **Chromatic half step**.

Diminished interval The decreasing of a perfect interval or a minor interval by one half step.

Diminuendo (*dim.* or ⟩) A dynamics marking indicating that the musical passage is to grow softer.

Dominant The fifth tone or triad of a major or minor scale.

Dominant seventh chord (V_7) The chord formed by adding a fourth note, a minor seventh above the root, to the dominant triad.

Dotted note A dot placed beside a note increases the value of the original note by one half. Thus, a dotted half note is equal to three quarter notes. Any note can be increased by half its value by adding a dot.

Double bar lines Two vertical lines used in written music, most commonly to indicate the beginning of a new section in a large work or to mark the end of a work.

Double flat sign (♭♭) An accidental that, when placed in front of a note, lowers the pitch of that note by two half steps (one whole step).

Double sharp sign (×) An accidental that, when placed in front of a note, raises the pitch of that note by two half steps (one whole step).

Downbeat The strongest beat of any meter, always written as the *first* beat of the measure.

Duple meter A division of the musical pulse into a recurring pattern of one strong and one weak beat.

Duplet A borrowed division in compound meter, in which a note normally subdivided into three equal parts is subdivided into two equal parts.

Dynamics A characteristic of musical sound involving degrees of loudness and softness. In written music, volume is indicated by specific words and abbreviations.

Enharmonic pitches The use of two different letter names for the same pitch. C♯ and D♭, F♯ and G♭, and E♯ and F are examples of enharmonic pitches.

F clef See **Bass clef**.

Flat sign (♭) An accidental that, when placed in front of a note, lowers the pitch of that note by a half step.

Forte (*f*) A dynamics marking indicating *loud*.

Fortissimo (*ff*) A dynamics marking indicating *very loud*.

G clef See **Treble clef**.

Great staff A treble clef staff and a bass clef staff joined together by a vertical line and a brace. It is employed in music that requires a range of pitches too wide for a single staff, such as piano music.

Half cadence A temporary point of rest in the harmony of a piece of music created by a momentary pause on the dominant chord. The half cadence itself is a two-chord progression, the most common being IV–V or I–V in major, and iv–V or i–V in minor.

Half step The smallest interval in tonal music. On the piano, it is the distance between any key and the key immediately above or below it.

Harmonic cadence A momentary or permanent point of rest in the harmony of a piece. There are several types, each a different formula of two chords. See also **Authentic cadence, Plagal cadence,** and **Half cadence**.

Harmonic interval The musical distance between two pitches sounded simultaneously. See also **Interval**.

Harmonic minor scale An altered version of the natural minor scale. The seventh degree is raised a half step to create a leading tone. This, in turn, creates the interval of an augmented second between the sixth and seventh degrees of the scale.

Harmonic rhythm The rate of change—fast or slow, steady or irregular—of the chords in a piece of music.

Harmonic series A fundamental frequency plus a series of overtones, heard as a single pitch. All musical pitches contain the harmonic series, or parts of the series.

Interval The musical distance between two pitches. Intervals may be harmonic (sounding simultaneously) or melodic (sounding successively). Interval quality may be perfect, major, minor, augmented, or diminished.

Key signature A grouping, at the beginning of a composition, of all the accidentals found in the major or natural minor scale on which the piece is based.

Largo A tempo marking indicating a broad, very slow tempo.

Leading tone The seventh tone or triad of a major, melodic minor, or harmonic minor scale; a half step below the tonic.

Ledger lines Short lines above or below the staff that function to extend the pitch range of the staff.

Lento A tempo marking indicating a slow tempo.

Major scale A seven-note scale based on an interval pattern of five whole steps and two half steps, the half steps occurring between the third and fourth, and the seventh and first tones.

Measure A division in written music that allows the meter to be seen more clearly. Measures are created by bar lines placed immediately before the accented pulse.

Mediant The third tone or triad of a major or minor scale.

Melodic interval The musical distance between two pitches sounded in succession. See also **Interval**.

Melodic minor scale A scale developed to avoid the augmented second of the harmonic minor scale. In the ascending form, the sixth and seventh degrees of the natural minor scale are raised; in the descending form, they are lowered to their position in natural minor.

Meter The division of the musical pulse into a recurring pattern of strong and weak pulses. The most common patterns or meters are duple meter, triple meter, and quadruple meter.

Meter signature Two numbers, one above the other, that appear at the beginning of a piece of music. The top number indicates the meter of the music; the bottom number tells which note value represents one beat.

Metronome An instrument invented in the early 1800s that produces a certain number of clicks per minute. Since each click can represent one beat, it is a more precise way of indicating tempo than the Italian terms also commonly used to mark tempo.

The metronome marking in written music is given by the symbol M.M., which stands for *Maelzel's metronome*.

Mezzo forte (*mf*) A dynamics marking indicating *moderately loud*.

Mezzo piano (*mp*) A dynamics marking indicating *moderately soft*.

Minor scale A seven-note scale, of which there are three versions. See also **Harmonic minor scale; Melodic minor scale; Natural minor scale.**

Moderato A tempo marking indicating a moderate tempo.

Modes A group of seven-note scales consisting of five whole steps and two half steps. By changing the placement of the two half steps, seven modes were created (Ionian, Dorian, Phrygian, Lydian, Mixolydian, Aeolian, and Locrian). These scales, from which the present-day major and natural minor scales were drawn, were the basis of Western music until the early 1600s.

Modulation The act of moving from one key center to another within a composition. Sometimes this is done by using a double bar and a change of key signature. Other times, the key signature remains the same, but accidentals are introduced into the music that actually change the key.

Movable *do* A system of sight-singing in which the tonic of any scale is always *do*, and the subsequent syllables are assigned to each succeeding pitch of the scale.

Natural minor scale A seven-note scale consisting of five whole steps and two half steps. The half steps occur between the second and third tones and the fifth and sixth tones.

Natural sign ( ) An accidental that, when placed in front of a note, cancels (for that note) any existing sharp, flat, double sharp, or double flat.

Noteheads The small oval shapes drawn on the staff to represent particular pitches.

Octave sign (*8va*) A sign indicating that the notes below it are to be performed one octave higher than written (*8va - - - ⌐*), or that the notes above it are to be performed one octave lower than written (*8va - - ⌐*).

Overtones The pitches above the fundamental pitch in the harmonic series.

Parallel keys A major key and a minor key with the same tonic but different key signatures.

Partials All the pitches of the harmonic series, including the fundamental.

Pentatonic scale A scale with five pitches per octave. A variety of pentatonic scales exists; the most well-known version contains no half steps.

Perfect pitch The ability to always recognize by ear any pitch when it is sounded. See also **Relative pitch.**

Pianissimo (*pp*) A dynamics marking indicating *very soft*.

Piano (*p*) A dynamics marking indicating *soft*.

Pitch The frequency at which a given sound vibrates.

Plagal cadence A momentary or permanent point of rest in the harmony of a piece of music created by the two-chord progression IV–I in major or iv–i in minor.

Poco a poco A dynamics marking meaning *little by little*, as in *dim. poco a poco* (gradually softer).

Presto A tempo marking indicating a very fast tempo.

Pulse The constant, regular beat in music. It can be represented visually by a line of quarter notes, half notes, eighth notes, and so on; it is felt as the beat to which you tap your foot.

Quadruple meter A division of the musical pulse into a recurring pattern of one strong and three weak pulses.

Related keys A major key and a minor key with the same key signature but different tonics.

Relative pitch The ability to identify a second pitch or pitches once a reference-point pitch is known. See also **Perfect pitch.**

Repeat sign (‖: :‖) A sign consisting of double bar lines plus two large dots either before or after the bar. This sign occurs in written music at the beginning and the end of measures that are to be immediately repeated.

Rest   A musical sign used to indicate duration of silence. Every note value has a corresponding rest sign.

Ritardando   A tempo marking indicating a gradual change to a slower tempo.

Scale   A group of pitches, generally in patterns of whole steps and half steps, that form the basic pitch material for a composition. See **Major scale, Minor scale, Modes, Pentatonic scale,** and **Whole-tone scale.**

Semi-cadence   See **Half cadence.**

Sharp sign (♯)   An accidental that, when placed in front of a note, raises the pitch of that note by a half step.

Simple interval   Any interval that is one octave or smaller.

Simple meter   Any meter in which the basic pulse can be normally subdivided into two equal parts.

Slur   A curved line, extended over two or more notes of different pitch, used to indicate a smooth, connected style of playing or singing.

Staff (pl.: staves)   A set of five parallel lines on which music is notated. The five lines, the four spaces between the lines, and the spaces above and below the staff are used to indicate pitch. Normally, the higher on the staff a symbol is located, the higher the pitch.

Subdominant   The fourth tone or triad of a major or minor scale.

Subito   A dynamics marking meaning *suddenly*, as in *subito p* (suddenly soft).

Submediant   The sixth tone or triad of a major or minor scale.

Subtonic   The seventh tone or triad of a natural minor or descending melodic minor scale; a whole step below the tonic.

Supertonic   The second tone or triad of a major or minor scale.

Syncopation   Occurs when an accent is placed on what would otherwise be a weak beat.

Tempo   The speed at which a piece of music moves; the speed of the pulse. In written music, Italian terms or a metronome marking are used to indicate the tempo.

Tendency tones   The apparent attraction of various scale degrees to one another. In general, the need for active tones, that is, the fifth, seventh, and second, to resolve to less active tones, that is, the tonic.

Tenor clef   See **C clef.**

Tie   A curved line connecting two notes of the same pitch, and used for creating notes of long duration.

Timbre   The unique sound or tone color of an instrument or voice. The timbre is determined, in part, by the size and design of the instrument, and by the way in which its sound is produced.

Time signature   See **Meter signature.**

Tonal music   Music in which both the melody and the harmony are derived from major or minor scales.

Tonic   The first note or triad of a major or minor scale; the pitch to which the other tones of the scale seem to be related.

Transposition   The act of moving a piece, or a section of a piece, from one key level to another. Often, singers will transpose a piece to another key in order for it to be in a range better suited to their voice.

Treble clef (G clef) (𝄞)   A sign that locates the note g¹ on the second line of the staff. This g¹ is then used as a reference point for locating other pitches on the staff.

Triad   The basic chord of tonal music. A three-note chord constructed of two superimposed thirds. Four qualities of triads are possible — major, minor, augmented, and diminished.

Triple meter   A division of the musical pulse into a recurring pattern of one strong and two weak beats.

Triplet   A borrowed division in simple meter, in which a note normally subdivided into two equal parts is subdivided into three equal parts.

Upbeat   The beat before the downbeat, that is, the final beat of a measure.

Vivace   A tempo marking indicating a quick and lively tempo.

Whole step   An interval consisting of two half steps.

Whole-tone scale   A scale consisting of six pitches per octave, each a whole step apart.

Subject Index

This index includes topics discussed in the text. See also *Glossary* for specific terms, and *Index to Musical Examples* for names of composers and titles.

Index to Musical Examples